Out East of Aline

Out East of Aline

An Adoption Memoir

by
Rex L. Wilson

The Uncommon Buffalo Press
Rapid City, South Dakota

ISBN 0-9641688-4-7

Library of Congress Cataloging-in-Publication Data

Wilson, Rex L.
    Out east of Aline : an adoption memoir / by Rex L. Wilson
        p.   cm.
    ISBN 0-9641688-4-7
        1. Wilson, Rex L.   2. Adoptees—United States—Biography.
        3. Depressions—1919—Oklahoma. I. Title

HV874.82.W55 A3 2000
362.73'4'092--dc21
[B]   00-029882

Table of Contents

Acknowledgments

From the very first talk of writing this book, my wife Susan has been completely supportive and has devoted countless hours to reading the manuscript, offering insights, and making suggestions. She helped with the organization of the story line and encouraged the use of my native Oklahoma idiom. Thank you, love.

And to my dear friend Emma Keels Price for her technical skills and constant encouragement, my sincere appreciation and thanks.

Not a word of this book was committed to paper before Susan and I drove back to Oklahoma to visit with old Round Grove School friends. We had a great time sitting around kitchens and talking about old times. And these friends confirmed my recollections of experiences we shared so long ago. My grateful thanks to Claude and Glenda Bocock Ryel, Kenneth Rexroat, Garrell Green, Perry Watkins, and Norma Jean Elliott Wharton. I deeply regret that Claude, Garrell, Perry, and Norma Jean departed this life before the book went to press.

My sincere thanks, also, to all those who read the manuscript or over the years asked "How's the book coming?" or otherwise encouraged me, especially Sue Cecil, Frances Reiher, Martha Edmonds, Tam Ford Mitchell, and Betty Scott.

My respect for skillful editing grew considerably during the writing and publication of *Out East of Aline*. My thanks to Connie Buchanan, who gave helpful suggestions early on, and, most of all, my thanks to Shirley McDermott, the Editor-Publisher who agreed to take on this book.

Introduction

Most people in Cedar Creek, Oklahoma, including my birth parents, suffered grievously during the early 1930s from the effects of the Great Depression. My father was much older than my mother when they married in 1917; he died at age seventy-one, widowing her in the spring of 1931. Without income, supportive family, or property, my mother had no choice but to surrender her children to the nearest state orphanage. It was a terrifying experience that I remember clearly although I was only four years old. At five and a half I was adopted by an honest, hardworking farmer and his wife who were unable to have children, who lived out east of Aline.

For most of my life I have avoided dealing with this, the most traumatic and horrifying episode of my life. I had been taken by car from the only home and family I had ever known and deposited in what seemed like a cold and scary prison. From my little boy's point of view, my mother, whom I loved and who I knew loved me, had abandoned me to total strangers without ever explaining why.

Using the words of that little boy, telling the story from a child's perspective, I have returned to that agonizing feeling of betrayal and cleared it from my psyche by writing this book. It is probably one of the most difficult things I have ever done.

You will not find Cedar Creek on any map of Oklahoma; to protect privacy I use fictitious names for the town and for my birth parents. Although I use my teachers' real names, other characters have fictional names and are composites. Real names are used for members of my adoptive immediate family and fictional names for most of my extended family.

Aline, surrounded by sandy loam or red clay wheat and alfalfa fields, is located beside a rusting Santa Fe Railroad track in Oklahoma's northwest quadrant, around fifty miles east of the 1930s "dust bowl." Halfway between Cleo Springs and Carmen, the little town lazes in the sun, unnoticed by travelers going by on the blacktop highway, State Route 8, a mile to the east. The wind almost never stops blowing. All during spring, summer, fall, and winter one is aware of a strong wind coming from the south and blowing straight north. There are no mountains or hills to stop it and what trees there are, are stunted and scraggly.

As the crow flies, Aline is thirty miles west-northwest of Enid, the largest city in northwest Oklahoma. Cherokee, the Alfalfa County Seat, is eighteen miles to the north and Helena, about eight miles to the east and once known as the site of the West Oklahoma State Home for White Children, is in rapid decline, no longer an active trading center. Indeed, Aline, Carmen, Helena, Cherokee, and Cleo Springs today are just remnants of the bustling towns I knew as a boy.

People out where I grew up did not talk much about where their families came from or which side they supported during the Civil War. Most had English surnames. They seldom spoke of how their forbears took part in the land run that opened the Cherokee Strip for white settlement in the fall of 1893. An estimated one hundred thousand people from far and wide took part in the run, the largest in recorded history.

For miles and miles around Aline almost everyone I knew in the 1930s lived on what was called a "quarter section," which was a 160-acre farm. Whether owners or sharecroppers, they all raised—or tried to raise—wheat and row crops. They sold the harvested wheat at the elevator in Aline or McWillie and fed the cowpeas and other row crops to their milk cows. Some oats were grown by farmers who kept work and riding horses. Most farmers raised Jersey or Guernsey cows because their milk produced more cream.

Some beef cattle were raised for eating or for sale at Carmen's Saturday afternoon livestock auction. On our farm, milk was separated from the rich cream twice a day and mixed with slop to feed the hogs. Poured into ten-gallon cream cans and kept cool in the milkhouse, the cream was taken to Aline every Saturday and sold to the creamery.

That is all changed now. Few families live on the farms and all the unpainted and overcrowded little farm homes have disappeared. Lands once planted to wheat have become grazing for beef cattle. Round Grove School, which I attended for seven years, is gone along with all the other little one-room country grade schools like McWillie, Oak Grove, and Square Cedar. No trace remains of the playgrounds and outbuildings. Any children living outside of the towns are bussed now to consolidated schools. Electric fences have replaced barbed wire fences. The only prominent feature of the landscape that has not changed is the loose white sand in the roads that define section lines. Much of that fine sand moves with the constant wind the way it always has, north during most of the year, south during the coldest weeks of winter.

Hundreds of blackjack oak trees grew on the farms where I lived out east of Aline. They were wild and scrubby, always green in the spring and summer, a uniform brown in the fall, and naked black in the winter. Fall wasn't pretty and it was the season I liked least. Yellow sunflowers, lavender thistles, ragweeds, and sandburs grew profusely, along with a great variety of other weeds, everywhere we didn't want them. For much of the year cattle grazed on short grass that farmers never allowed to grow to maturity.

During June, July, and August, heat and humidity were difficult to live with in my part of Oklahoma. Evenings were almost unbearable, a situation not relieved until after World War II when the Rural Electrification Association (REA) strung electricity on tall poles along the dirt roads. Without even the crudest form of air conditioning in the house during summer nights, I was always happy when my folks allowed me to sleep outside between our big frame house and the hog pen. Sometimes in the winter east-west roads were blocked with snow drifts caused by the brisk north wind that seemed never to stop blowing. Seldom did we have snow that lay uniformly on the ground. It was sometimes bitterly cold, and made colder by the constant wind. Stock tanks and ponds would freeze over.

Blackjack wood burned in stoves for heat because no one who lived in the country had central heating. Bedrooms were usually uncomfortably cold while potbelly stoves heated the dining-living rooms. Of course, wood-burning cookstoves in the kitchen kept those rooms warm and cozy.

Most people I used to know out east of Aline were honest, hard-working, dawn-to-dark farmers, like my adoptive parents. They had to be in order to feed, clothe, and house their families. Wives and mothers, some with many children, worked just as hard as their husbands; long hours of endless chores included housecleaning, raising chickens, growing and harvesting large gardens, canning fruit and vegetables, cooking three large meals every day, washing clothes, tending the sick, ironing. All that and more every day, year-round. Everything was primitive by today's standards: there was no electricity to power a washer and dryer, a range in the kitchen, an iron, a vacuum cleaner, lamps, radios, refrigerators. There were no television sets to watch during brief rests in the day. Few had telephones.

My adoptive parents' friends all seemed to have narrow Puritan views about what was proper morality and behavior. Sundays were considered days of rest. Most families we knew attended Sunday school and preaching somewhere. We went to the Church of the Brethren, as did a few of our closest neighbors. Most families I knew well attended the Nazarene Church just around the corner from Round Grove School. From hearsay I learned something about holy rollers and pentecostals in the neighborhood who, for religious reasons, had nothing to do with doctors or using medicines. A few people drove all the way into Aline to attend the Methodist or Christian churches. Others didn't attend church at all.

My adoptive mother believed strongly in education and had two years of college, but my adoptive dad had finished only the eighth grade at Round Grove School. To most people I knew, education could easily be overdone. One didn't need a lot of book learning to be a farmer, so why spend the time and money to go further than grade school?

There were two holidays each year, Christmas and the Fourth of July, when, except for daily chores, we didn't work or go to school. And chores meant feeding and milking cows and slopping hogs morning and night. Chickens had to be fed at

least once a day and eggs had to be gathered late every afternoon. Add to that separating the cream from the milk and keeping the cream sweet until Saturday. There wasn't much time to
visit, travel, or stay any length of time away from home. Work,
taking care of business, always came first out east of Aline.

Looking back, I realize we were better off than most of our
neighbors. First, there were only three of us: Mother, Dad, and
me. Some families had as many as nine children. Dad had a
blacksmith shop and a small hammermill that ground grain. He
raised cane crops for cattle feed. Wheat was his main money
crop. Because my Dad had all kinds of farming equipment, he
was often hired to harvest wheat crops for farmers who didn't.
And because he farmed one of my Grandpa Williams' farms
north of McWillie, my Grandpa Wilson's place, and our home
place, he kept busy all the time. It was not unusual to have one
or more hired men to help my dad, and a hired girl helped
Mother during wheat harvest time.

As an adult, and after the deaths of my adoptive parents, I
felt free to seek my biological roots. With the help of historians,
old records, and newly found relatives, I learned that my earliest American ancestors arrived in Virginia from Great Britain
about 1738 and settled on a King's Grant near the James River
in Virginia nine generations ago. It was a sweet coincidence that
my wife and I chose to live in beautiful, wooded Virginia when
I retired and it is here, in Richmond, that I have written the
stories you are about to read.

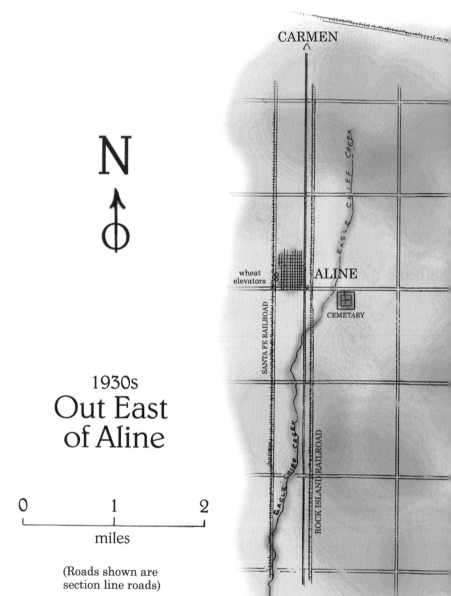

N

1930s
Out East
of Aline

0   1   2

miles

(Roads shown are
section line roads)

CARMEN

EAGLE CHIEF CREEK

wheat
elevators

ALINE

CEMETARY

SANTA FE RAILROAD

EAGLE CHIEF CREEK

ROCK ISLAND RAILROAD

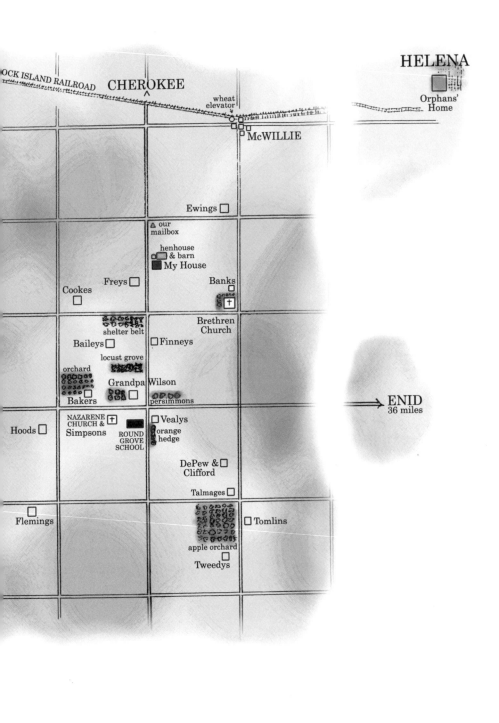

OCK ISLAND RAILROAD CHEROKEE

wheat elevator

McWILLIE

HELENA

Orphans' Home

Ewings

△ our mailbox

henhouse & barn
My House

Freys
Cookes

Banks

Brethren Church

shelter belt

Baileys   Finneys

locust grove

orchard

Grandpa Wilson
Bakers   persimmons

NAZARENE CHURCH &
Simpsons   ROUND GROVE SCHOOL

Hoods

Vealys
orange hedge

DePew & Clifford

Talmages

Flemings

Tomlins

apple orchard
Tweedys

ENID
36 miles

Whatever happened to Billy Joe?

Chapter 1 ————————————————————— «

Ma'am woke Jefferson and me the same as always, by yanking back the bedcovers and announcing firmly, "All right, boys, time to get up."

I noticed right away that the house was strangely quiet. There was no coughing coming from the other bedroom.

Jefferson and I slept in a big bed and were warm under the heavy quilt, which had been homemade of squares of cloth cut from somebody's winter clothes. Two nice ladies from the Methodist Church down the street had given it to us for Christmas. We didn't mind the smell of mothballs on the cloth because the quilt was lots better than the thin blanket we had been using, the one Bonnie, our little sister, now had in her crib. There wasn't much heat in our room so we were shivering before we got our clothes on that morning.

We lived on the south side of Cedar Creek, Oklahoma, in an unpainted little frame house with a tin roof and a brick chimney. It looked like most other houses in our neighborhood. When I went outside and looked straight down the red dirt street, I could see houses off to the west that were two or three times as big as ours, some with shingled roofs, some painted white. Bonnie and Jefferson and I played on the linoleum-covered kitchen floor on days when Ma'am wouldn't let us go outside. Sometimes Ma'am would sit down on the floor to play with us. We liked that a lot, but most of the time she was busy with Pap. After Jefferson left for school, Bonnie and I played by ourselves. We didn't have many toys but we had fun playing with some big pasteboard boxes and pieces of wood that somebody had given us. We pretended they were cars and trucks and wagons. On special occasions Ma'am would tell us stories about when she was a little girl on a farm over east of Pawnee near the Arkansas River. She said her family had lived there for a long, long time. She never seemed to run out of stories about growing up on what was once an Indian reservation and how she had met Pap at church and married him when she was still very young. She once told us that she was proud to be part-Indian, that she got her black hair and eyes from her mother, who was a half-blood Pawnee.

It was late January of 1931 and I was four and a half years old. Jefferson was seven, maybe eight, a second grader, and he didn't seem surprised when Ma'am told us at breakfast that Pap had died during the night. Maybe I shouldn't have been surprised either. Ever since Christmas, Pap had been lying sick in bed in the room next to Jefferson's and mine, the room he and Ma'am and Bonnie slept in. I could hear Pap choking and coughing and I wondered how he could stand to do that.

"He's gonna die and he knows it," Jefferson had warned me. "I don't reckon he's gonna live much longer. He's real old an folks die when they git old. To tell you the truth, I never even seen anybody as old as Pap is."

Ma'am looked real tired and old and almost sick herself that morning, like she hadn't had enough sleep during the night. Plumb worn-out. I looked closely at her face as she fixed breakfast for Jefferson and me. I had often seen her cry, but she wasn't crying this morning.

"Maybe she's all dried up, plumb outta tears," Jefferson

whispered in my ear. "Maybe she's better off now that Pap's outta his misery."

Pap's sickness and dying would have been hard for me to understand if it hadn't been for Jefferson. Especially Jefferson. I talked a lot more with him than I did with Ma'am. I guess that was because he was a boy, too, and older. He could understand better than I could what was going on. And I think Ma'am told him more than she told me. Of course, she probably talked a lot with Pap before he was sick in bed, but she never mentioned it to Jefferson and me. I thought Jefferson was real smart and real grown-up for his age, and when he talked, I listened; when he told me something, I believed him. He was my brother and I loved him more than anybody. He was the only person in all the world whom I could tell secrets to and who would answer all my questions. He taught me all kinds of things, like the four directions, how to tell time, how to count, and how to predict the weather. Except for Jefferson, I wouldn't have known much of anything.

Bonnie was still sleeping as Jefferson, Ma'am, and I ate breakfast. We sat on each side of Ma'am at the end of the kitchen table and I could study her face and her eyes—especially her sad eyes—in the light of the coal oil lamp. She just sort of sat there, all limp in her chair, now and then taking a bit of her oatmeal, a sip of her coffee. After Jefferson had finished his oatmeal and drunk his glass of milk, he put on his coat and cap, kissed Ma'am on the cheek, and left for school.

Ma'am seemed to sense my great bewilderment over what was happening to us that morning. I missed hearing the coughing from Pap's bedroom.

"Is Pap really dead?" I was almost afraid to ask her that, but I had to know.

"Yes, Billy Joe, he died in his sleep. And I'm very sad. You know that he was awful sick an the doctor told me a long time ago that he probably wouldn't live through the winter. I'm thankful that he could spend one more Christmas with us. You're too little to remember, but he always loved Christmas." She paused and gave me a long, sad look. Then she sighed. "He was sufferin an he coughed a lot of the time but I think he died peacefully. The last thing he said to me was that he loved all of us an that he was ready for the Lord to take him up to heaven."

I wanted to ask her about the Lord and heaven but from the sad look on her face I decided against it.

"Now," she said, "I'm gonna run over to Mrs. Tidwell's an use her phone to call the funeral home an ask them to come for Pap's body. What I want you to do is stay right here so that if Bonnie wakes up while I'm gone she won't be afraid. I won't be gone very long but while I'm out of the house, you can take a look at Pap if you wanta see him one last time."

After Ma'am was gone, I tiptoed over to her and Pap's bedroom, opened the door a crack, and peeked in. Even though the window shade was down, I could see Pap lying on the bed, face up, his eyes open as though he was counting the cracks in the plaster ceiling. He needed a shave pretty bad and his hair was all mussed up. I reckon he hadn't been out of that bed in quite a spell. I wasn't able to see Bonnie, whose crib was pushed over into the corner of the room, but since I didn't hear any noise from her I figured she was still asleep. Closing the door as quietly as I could, I tiptoed back to the kitchen. I looked at my cold oatmeal but couldn't eat it.

I wondered what life would be like without Pap, without the tobacco smoke that filled the house before he got sick. He would always light up after supper and smoke until he was ready to go to bed. It seemed like he would no more than finish one cigarette than he would take out his can of Prince Albert and package of papers and roll another smoke. Jefferson said Pap smoked so much because he worked so hard on the railroad, day in and day out.

Pap never had much to say but he was kind and gentle to

Ma'am and us kids. And I don't think he would have picked
me up and hugged me and bounced me around on his knees
and patted me on the head if he hadn't loved me. I never had
a chance to ask Pap why he was so much older than Ma'am
and I didn't think I ought to ask Ma'am a question like that.
It was something I could talk to Jefferson about, some time
when we were alone.

Before long Ma'am was back from the Tidwells'. She got
Bonnie out of bed, helped her dress, and gave her some oatmeal. Then, as we had been doing for such a long time, Bonnie
and I put on our caps and coats and walked over to Mrs.
Tidwell's house. To get there we walked down a little dirt path
that led to our toilet, past the oil drum that we put the trash
in, by the Tidwells' little chicken house where pigeons roosted
on the rusty tin roof, and around to the front of their house
where the door was. Their house was just like ours and
Bonnie and I knew exactly where we were going. Mrs. Tidwell
must have been watching for us because, before I could knock,
she opened the door, gave us a big smile of welcome, and we
stepped into her sweet-smelling kitchen. The big gas lamp on
her kitchen table made it all bright inside and I liked being
there. Mrs. Tidwell didn't need to remind us to take off our
shoes and leave them on a braided rug beside the door; we
always did that so as not to track mud on her clean and shiny
linoleum floor. She let us go anywhere in the house so long as
we weren't wearing our shoes.

Like Pap, Mr. Tidwell worked for the railroad, and I
almost never saw him. His name was "Lester." I think Mrs.
Tidwell liked having Bonnie and me at her house. Mrs.
Tidwell laughed much more than Ma'am or Pap did, and she
almost never spoke crossly to me. Even when she did, she had
a good reason, like when I did things that I knew I wasn't
supposed to do. This morning she was especially kind.

"I'm sorry your papa died; he was a good man an a good
friend to Mr. Tidwell an we'll miss him. An I know you kids

will miss him, too. But everything's gonna be all right, you'll see. You an your mama an Jefferson will always have us here to help look after you."

Mrs. Tidwell had been taking care of Bonnie and me all day every day since Pap took sick and couldn't go back to work. "Around Thanksgiving time," Mrs. Tidwell said.

It was late afternoon when Ma'am came for us. Her eyes were all swollen and red and I guessed she had been crying all day. She sat down at the table with Mrs. Tidwell. As they drank black coffee, Ma'am told her the undertaker had come during the morning and had taken the body away. Listening closely, I shivered when Ma'am said "the body" as though it was something disgusting. I wondered why she didn't just say that the undertaker had taken Pap away to the funeral home. It seemed to me, too, that it pained Ma'am to talk about it and I felt so sorry for her that I could hardly keep from crying. She told Mrs. Tidwell there would be a service at the Methodist Church on Saturday morning, the day after tomorrow—the sooner to get it over and done with—and hoped she and Lester would be able to come. She said the Methodist preacher, Mr. Dickenson, who had married her and Pap back in 1917, was going to preach the funeral sermon even though he had been retired from the ministry for several years.

"He told me this morning that he had never forgotten the time he had married a fifty-seven-year-old man to a seventeen-year-old woman," Ma'am said.

We had just finished breakfast on Friday morning when Mr. Dickenson came calling. Ma'am asked him to come inside where it was warm, to sit down, and to join her in a cup of coffee while they talked about Pap's funeral arrangements. She told him she hoped he wouldn't mind that the children stayed around to listen to what was said.

"There are some things you can say to them about what's happened better than I can," she said. "An I kept Jefferson home from school today just so he could meet you."

Jefferson, Bonnie, and I found a warm corner of the kitchen and sat quietly on the linoleum floor so we wouldn't be too much in the way. I listened as hard as I could. Mr. Dickenson seemed comfortable with all of us in the room together and seemed to be enjoying his coffee. Every now and then he would turn away from Ma'am and look straight at us, as if he were talking to us and was making sure we knew it. Sometimes he smiled and I couldn't understand what there was to smile about. At the same time, I knew he was really serious about what he wanted to say.

I liked the preacher. Maybe it was because he looked a little like Pap did before he took sick and died, kind of old and wrinkled, grey-haired and partly bald-headed in the front and back. And from where I was sitting I could clearly see that his gold-framed glasses were smudged. But even though he looked something like Pap, he wasn't wearing the same kind of clothes. Instead of striped overalls, like all railroad men wore, he was dressed in a heavy black suit, white shirt, and bow tie. And he didn't smoke, like Pap did. He didn't smell of tobacco, and I was glad.

As soon as he had finished his coffee, Mr. Dickenson got down to business, asking that we bow our heads and close our eyes while he said a prayer. Then, ever so gently, he turned toward Ma'am and asked so softly that I could barely hear, "Now, Mrs. Tolliver, did you say there won't be any relatives comin to the funeral? No one at all?"

"Not a one!" Ma'am was quick to answer, like she was a little angry. "No, Frank's family—and there's a bunch of em— are all back in eastern Tennessee an I can't expect them to come all the way out here. There's one cousin who lives in Enid, I think, but I don't know him and don't know how to reach him in time. No, I'm pretty sure there won't be anybody here from his side of the family."

"And what about your family?"

"My family!" Ma'am's voice had turned louder and she

sounded almost mean. "Nobody in my family wanted me to marry Frank in the first place; none of them came to the wedding and none ever came to see us or even wrote us letters. It was like they never thought much of Frank an the children. An they seemed to be mad at me for marryin someone who wasn't Pawnee. I remember how you helped me talk my mother into signin the paper so I could marry him in your church. No, sir, I don't expect anyone in my family to show up for the funeral!" By now her eyes were overflowing. She put her head in her hands and began to shake all over.

I couldn't understand what Ma'am meant when she said those things about her family; maybe that was because I couldn't remember ever having met them, not even my grandma and grandpa. The only family I had ever known was Ma'am and Pap and Jefferson and Bonnie. And I had never heard any mention of Pap's family back in Tennessee.

Mr. Dickenson said Pap's funeral service would be held in the small chapel down at the Methodist Church where he and Ma'am were married almost fifteen years ago. He hoped she wouldn't mind, he said, but it was the only Methodist church in town. He said that ordinarily the service would be held in the sanctuary but because there were so few people expected to show up, the weather being cold and windy and all, he thought it best to have it in the smaller room that wouldn't cost so much to heat. It would be a short service followed by the removing of the body to the cemetery just outside of town. He said the plot had been donated by the Oddfellows Lodge and that the Lodge had also arranged to have somebody dig the grave. By now Ma'am had wiped the tears from her cheeks and eyes, she had relaxed, and she seemed glad to know that the funeral arrangements were all made.

She seemed glad, too, to hear that some of the Methodist ladies would be bringing food over to our house while the rest of us were at the funeral and cemetery, so that folks could drop by after the funeral to pay their respects and get a cup of coffee and a bite to eat before going back to where they came from. "If that's all right with you, Mrs. Tolliver," the preacher said.

Ma'am said that yes, that would be just fine, that she appreciated what he and the Methodist ladies were doing, and that anybody who came would surely be welcome.

Mr. Dickenson stayed with us for quite a while that morning. Turning toward us, he asked Jefferson about his school and what he was learning. He asked me if I could count and if I knew my ABCs. All the while Bonnie played on the floor over by the stove where it was warm. She had her little doll and she didn't pay much attention to the preacher. Then Mr. Dickenson explained that what had happened to Pap eventually happened to everybody.

"God called your father to his reward in heaven," he said. He said that God didn't take Pap's body, but instead, and more important, he took his soul to be with him up above, to a better place, a happier place, a beautiful place where all the streets were paved with gold and where angels spent their time doing good things and playing their harps and singing pretty songs all day long. I was glad to know that Pap would never again be sick or in pain or have to cough. He told us to remember Pap as a good father and a good man who was respected by everyone who knew him. Mr. Dickenson seemed to understand how sad we all were and I wished he could have stayed longer with us.

Saturday morning we all put on our good clothes and our coats and walked down to the Methodist Church. I had seen it on the way to the grocery store with Ma'am and it was familiar to Jefferson because he walked by it every day on his way to and from school. The church was a red brick building with a tall pointed roof. I had never been inside. Lots of green stickery bushes grew up next to the building, even right by the big, brown, wooden front door that had little square colored-windows near the top. We walked around the north side

of the church on a little brick walk close to the stickery bushes, until we reached a white door that opened into the chapel.
It seemed pretty big to me, a lot bigger than I had expected.
There were rows and rows of seats and a large wooden cross
right in the middle of the wall opposite the door we had come
through. Ma'am said the windows on the north side of the
chapel were stained-glass windows. They were like the ones
in the big wooden door at the front of the church, only much
bigger. The windows were like none I had ever seen, like
great big pictures made of colored glass. They were beautiful
with the outside light shining through them.

Several people I didn't know were already waiting in the
long seats. A thin woman in a black dress and felt hat told us
we were to sit up in the front row. I could feel the eyes of the
people following every move we made. As I held tight to
Ma'am's hand, I wished I could have stayed at home. People
stared at us as we walked by, as though we didn't belong in
their church. Off to one side, another woman in a black dress
was playing soft church music on a piano.

Because I was looking around I almost stumbled into a
long and shiny black box that sat on something like a little
wagon right up in the front of the room. We had to walk by it
to reach our seats. After what seemed a long time, Mr.
Dickenson came into the chapel, climbed up a little stairway,
and stood behind the shiny black box. For the first time I
noticed there was a lid on one end. Whispering to Jefferson,
I asked what it was.

"That there's a casket an Pap's inside of it," Jefferson
whispered back. I think the preacher heard us whispering
because he looked straight at us, smiled like he did when he
visited the day before, then turned to face the other people.

"Let us pray," he said in a loud voice.

After he finally said "amen," the preacher read from the
Bible, then started to talk about dying, about what kind of a
man Pap was, and about God and heaven and what you had

to do to get there. He even said some nice things about Ma'am. I kept looking at the casket and thinking of Pap lying inside in the dark. I wondered if his eyes were still open and tried to guess what he was wearing, and I reasoned that he was dressed in the black suit he sometimes wore to Lodge meetings. I was hot and uncomfortable in the chapel. I couldn't stop wiggling, maybe because I still had my coat on. And I couldn't understand all the things the preacher was saying. Ma'am and Bonnie cried. Jefferson and I didn't.

After Mr. Dickenson finished preaching and said another prayer, we left the chapel through the same door into the cold. And there we stood in the dead-grass churchyard, shivering in the blustery wind. I guess most of the people who had been inside came over one by one to shake Ma'am's hand and mumble something about how much they thought of Pap and how sorry they were that he died. I figured some of the men were Oddfellows. One really old man and woman told Ma'am that Pap's death was a blessing and I didn't think that made much sense. But it made Ma'am cry even harder. Although there were tears running down both her cheeks, she didn't make a sound except to say "thank you for coming" to those who shook her hand. They all sort of moved away to one side to make room for somebody else to speak to her. Most of the people at the funeral were old and I figured they didn't have anything else to say to Ma'am. Before long some men carried Pap's casket outside through the same door of the chapel we had used. Nobody in the little crowd moved or said anything; we all just watched as the casket was shoved into the rear of a long black car that had black curtains at the windows.

After the car drove slowly away, people seemed to relax. Some of the men lit cigarettes. Mrs. Tidwell came over, picked up Bonnie in her arms, took my hand, and said, "All right, kids, let's go back to the house."

As we walked away, I turned around to see Jefferson and

Ma'am climb into Mr. Dickenson's car. Other people were also getting into cars and leaving.

"Where are Ma'am and Jefferson going?" I asked Mrs. Tidwell.

"To the cemetery," she answered.

"Oh," was all I could say.

A couple of days after Pap's funeral, Ma'am told us she would be going to the hospital over on the east side of town. But not to worry, she told us, it wasn't because she was sick or anything like that, but because Mrs. Tidwell knew somebody there who might give her a job. She said she would be home around four o'clock, before Jefferson came home from school, and that Bonnie and I would be spending the day with Mrs. Tidwell. She said that if she got the job, Bonnie and I would probably be spending the days over there, just like we had when Pap was sick during the winter.

So Ma'am began working at the hospital. This meant we all had to get up earlier and eat our breakfast earlier, and that Jefferson had to leave for school earlier. Ma'am said he was to stay in the schoolyard and not play anywhere else before school started. And, of course, Bonnie and I went over to Mrs. Tidwell's house earlier than we had before.

Ma'am never played with us again. She said that mopping floors all day at the hospital and emptying bedpans was hard work, that she could hardly stand the smells, and that everyone bossed her around. Ma'am had very little to say to me. I sure missed the fun we had before Pap died. But I had trouble remembering Pap. Funny, I couldn't even remember what he had looked like except that he was old, tall, and slim and didn't usually let his whiskers grow and wore a long, heavy army overcoat when it was cold.

So I didn't really miss Pap but I would have been lost without Ma'am, even this changed Ma'am, and Jefferson and my little sister Bonnie.

I couldn't wait for spring to come so Bonnie and I could

play in Mrs. Tidwell's nice yard. There wasn't much to do in the house, and we had heard over and over again the stories of Little Red Riding Hood and the Three Bears. It was hard to keep track of the days of the week because they were all the same. One long day it got later and later and it was already evening before Ma'am came to get us.

"I didn't mean to be this late getting back," she told Mrs. Tidwell, "but the whole business took longer than I had expected. I hope you weren't worried."

"No, I figured everything was all right, an that you'd be back as soon as you could," replied Mrs. Tidwell. "But I could tell Billy Joe was getting concerned about you. Lately, I've noticed that he gets uneasy when he's away from you for any length of time."

"Well, we'll be getting on home now. An again, I can't tell you how much I appreciate your tendin the younguns for me. These last few weeks have been awfully hard on me."

"I know," Mrs. Tidwell said, "an I'm always glad to help out when I can. You can always count on me."

It was already dark by the time we left Mrs. Tidwell's and I was surprised to see no light at our house.

"Ain't Jefferson back from school yet?" I asked Ma'am.

"No, he won't be back this evenin."

"Why not, where is he?"

"Well, Billy Joe, there's somethin I've gotta tell you. You're a big boy now an I want you to know about some things that have been happenin since Pap died." She led me into her bedroom—Bonnie followed close behind—and we sat down together on the edge of her bed while Bonnie played on the floor. Ma'am put her arm around me and for the longest time held me tight.

"Jefferson has gone to live for a while at a special place way out west of here. It's a nice place that's especially for children whose folks have died or who have nobody to take care of them. Jefferson will stay there until I get a good job and make enough money so's I can take care of all of you. Do you understand what I'm sayin?"

"Yes, ma'am. I think so. When did he go?"

"Well, a man came this mornin and took him away. Jefferson was glad to be goin somewhere in a car an the man let him sit in the front so he could see out better. He was happy to be goin because one of his schoolmates was goin too. It's a long trip but they should be there by now."

"When will he come home?"

"I can't say for sure but I don't think he will mind being out there because there are lots of kids to play with an things to do. There are nice people to take care of him, he'll have a warm bed all his own, an he'll have good things to eat."

"I hope he comes home soon."

"So do I, Billy Joe," Ma'am said, hugging me again.

That night I was so lonesome without Jefferson beside me under the heavy quilt that I could hardly stand it. I missed him an awful lot. And I thought, if I could only talk to him he would explain why these terrible things kept happening to our family. I couldn't help crying, lying there alone, trying to keep warm, thinking of my big brother. ✦

Chapter 2

After Jefferson went away the days seemed to drag past. Ma'am no longer smiled the way she used to. She stared out the window a lot and always had a troubled look on her face. When she spoke to Bonnie and me it was usually to ask us to play quietly and to try to keep from getting dirty. When Ma'am was home we weren't allowed to leave the yard, even to go over and visit Mrs. Tidwell. In the middle of February it snowed and the north wind blew the snow into drifts that froze into dirty lumps.

Bonnie turned three and Ma'am gave her a new coat. That was all. Then Ma'am lost her job at the hospital and Bonnie and I stopped spending every day at Mrs. Tidwell's. We had to stay inside. Bonnie and I made a playhouse near the stove where it was warm.

Finally, February turned into March. In Oklahoma that meant wind, constant wind, blowing dust, shredded waste paper, tumbleweeds, leaves, chicken feathers—anything that would come loose. It seemed never to stop, often blowing all day and all night, strong enough to make the windows rattle. Within a few hours, neat little ridges of red dust formed on the windowsills and under the doors, anywhere it could get in, no matter how snugly the windows and doors fit their frames. Dust on everything, in everything. You could even taste it. And it was cold in March, especially around the first of the month, so cold I couldn't play outside in the long wooden banana crate that Jefferson had brought home last summer.

And then one day everything changed again. Once more Ma'am sent Bonnie and me over to Mrs. Tidwell's. She was happy to see us and said she had missed us and I told her how lonesome I was for Jefferson. Bonnie stayed busy on the floor close to the stove with her doll and a tiny cup and saucer that Mrs. Tidwell would let her play with while we were at her house. She gave me a lead pencil and a piece of paper to draw on, and carefully folded back part of her tablecloth so I could use the bare table to lay my paper on. It was warm and cozy in Mrs. Tidwell's kitchen.

When Ma'am came to get us she seemed different. Her black hair was pinned back and her head was no longer drooping. There were bright spots of color in her cheeks. And she was breathing in a funny way. Her breathing seemed hard and fast, like she had been running

But it was her eyes that bothered me most. And I was even a little scared. They had lost their steady look and they kept darting all around the house, as if she couldn't find anything to look at. Her eyes seemed to slide right over Bonnie and me, move to Mrs. Tidwell's clock, then shift to the stove or the door. For some reason she didn't seem to want to look directly into our faces.

Ma'am said, "no thank you" to Mrs. Tidwell's offer of a cup of hot coffee. I could hear her funny breathing clear across the room. Mrs. Tidwell's face turned stiff. She wasn't smiling as she carefully helped Bonnie and me with our coats and caps. Ma'am shooed us out the door before we could properly say "thank you" or "we had a nice time" to Mrs. Tidwell.

That evening Ma'am gave me and Bonnie baths. She stood us on a folded towel, one at a time, and she scrubbed us using a bucket of warm soapy water and a new white wash-cloth. Then we put on clean underwear before we got into our pajamas. We had hot soup and crackers for supper. After she put Bonnie in her crib, Ma'am tucked me into bed. Then, for the first time ever, she lay down on Jefferson's side of the bed. She told me that tomorrow a man was going to come for us and take us for a long ride in his car.

"Who is he?" I asked.

"He's a nice man, you'll like him," she said. "His name is 'Mr. Collins.'"

"Where's he gonna take us?"

"Well, he's takin us over to Helena, way out west, to see Jefferson. Do you remember my tellin you a while back where Jefferson was?"

"I remember. When will we see him?"

"We'll see him tomorrow, I hope. Now go right to sleep. Tomorrow's gonna be a big day for you an Bonnie, an morning will be here before you know it."

Ma'am was doing something in the kitchen the next morning when I jumped out of bed before she had to wake me. I landed on the cold wooden floor in my bare feet. I was always glad that I didn't get splinters in my feet when I did that. As quickly as I could I pulled on the brown woolen socks that I had left lying beside my bed the night before. Ma'am had set up her ironing board on one end of the kitchen table and was pressing my best overalls with an old iron she would have to set on the stove until it got hot enough to use. She used the iron for a little while until it cooled off, then she sat it on the stove again. There were still some clothes she had-n't got to, some of mine and some of Bonnie's, lying in a damp pile on the table.

For breakfast Ma'am had already fixed the little pot of oat-meal we had every morning. She carried a white bowl of it over and set it down at my place. I picked up the spoon she had set out for me and waited until she put a little sugar and Pet milk in the oatmeal and mixed it up for me. Bonnie was still asleep.

"Is this the day Mr. Collins comes?" I asked.

"Yes, he's comin today." She kept ironing.

"When's he gonna get here?"

"I got a letter from him the other day an it said he's comin around three or four o'clock this afternoon. I reckon he'll want us to be ready to go when he gets here."

"Are we goin in his car?"

"Yes, Billy Joe, he said he'd be drivin his own car, even if it is a little crowded. He didn't figure we'd mind too much."

"We're gonna ride in a real car?"

"Yes, Billy Joe. Now eat your breakfast before it gets cold."

After finishing ironing something, Ma'am folded it carefully and laid it inside a pasteboard box sitting on the floor near the end of the kitchen table. As I ate my sticky, barely-warm oatmeal I enjoyed the sweet smell coming from our neatly-ironed clean clothes.

Bonnie and I spent the morning playing on the kitchen floor, the only place in the house where there was enough room and where the old cook stove kept the room cozy and warm, except for a place over near the door where it could be pretty uncomfortable when it was cold and the wind was blowing like it was that morning. The wind blew all the time. Cold air and dust were coming in around the door even where Ma'am had stuffed rags into the cracks. Whenever she forgot to do that, I could see daylight coming in all around the door.

Right after Ma'am woke Bonnie and me from our afternoon naps, I heard a car grinding up close to our house. It stopped in the street right out front. Looking through the window, I saw that it was a dark blue coupe with a man behind the steering wheel. There was no one with him and I reckoned it was probably Mr. Collins, the man we were expecting. He opened the car door and stepped out. The car door went "clunk" and the man headed for our house. Even though I had not been outside, I knew it was cold out there because the man was wearing a felt hat and an overcoat that came down below his knees.

"Ma'am, there's a man comin to the door!" I shouted.

"It's probably Mr. Collins," she said. "He wrote in his letter that he'd probably be showing up about this time." She pushed back a long strand of hair that had fallen into her eyes, then wiped her hands on her apron and walked quickly to the door. Bonnie and I crept back into a dim corner of the kitchen to be out of the way; a stranger was coming and we were not sure what to expect. The man had knocked only once before Ma'am turned the knob and pulled open the door.

"Howdy, Mrs. Tolliver," he said in a deep and clear voice, steam coming from his mouth like he was smoking a cigarette. He wasn't smoking, I knew, it was just very cold outside. "I'm Ed Collins. I wrote to say I'd be here today."

"It's good to see you, Mr. Collins. I hope you had a good trip. Come on in before you catch your death of cold out there! I declare, I didn't realize it was so cold today." As she spoke, she released the little hook on the sagging screen door. The wind was blowing so hard that it jerked the door right out of her hand and blew it back against the house where it slammed with a loud, familiar bang.

"I hope that ole door didn't hit you," Ma'am said. "The wind just jerked it right outta my hand."

"No harm done," he replied with a wide grin. "It came pretty close but it missed me."

"Thank goodness, that's a relief! It coulda hurt if it'd hit you on the knee. Come on in."

Mr. Collins removed his hat as he stepped quickly into the kitchen and set his small leather briefcase on the end of the table. From the shadows where I stood with Bonnie, I watched as he pulled off his wool gloves, nicer than any I had ever seen, and shoved them into his overcoat pockets. I wondered if maybe his wife had made them for him. They looked a whole lot warmer than the brown cotton gloves I had that

Mrs. Tidwell had given me for Christmas. He reached out to
Ma'am to shake her hand before taking off his overcoat.

Mr. Collins was good-sized, but not much taller than
Ma'am. And he seemed very friendly. Looking around the
kitchen, he finally noticed Bonnie and me standing in the
corner watching him. He smiled at us, then spoke to Ma'am.

"I brought along the papers you'll need to sign before we
can leave," he said, opening his briefcase and taking them
out. "Please take your time an read them carefully before
you sign. The one on top is a new form that you'll need to fill
out as best you can. The state just started using that one."

"Of course," Ma'am said. "Just have a chair and make
yourself comfortable. I won't take long. Would you like a
cuppa coffee? I've got some hot on the back of the stove."

"Well, ma'am, don't mind if I do. Yes, ma'am, I'd like very
much to have some coffee. I haven't had a cup since early this
morning. But please don't go to any trouble on my account."

"There's sugar an Pet milk if you'd like some," Ma'am
offered.

"No, ma'am, just black for me, thanks." Steam was rising
from the big white mug as Mr. Collins held it in both hands,
sipping carefully. Ma'am sat down opposite him at the table,
her back to Bonnie and me, and picked up the several printed
pages that Mr. Collins had laid on the oilcloth where the light
was best for reading. Resting her chin in her hand, she began
to read.

As Mr. Collins sipped his coffee, he looked straight at me
over the rim of the thick mug. His eyes were clear and
bright, blue as the sky in summer. "Your name's 'Billy Joe,'
isn't it?" His gentle voice seemed to invite me to come closer
and get acquainted. His broad smile showed the wide space
between his upper front teeth. I began to like him and
moved closer. He stretched out his right hand the way he
had with Ma'am. "Isn't that your name, son?"

"My name's 'Billy Joe Tolliver,'" I answered, pleased that

he seemed interested in me. We shook hands the way I had seen grownups do. He was the friendliest man I had ever met.

"How old are you, Billy Joe?" His voice was warm and kindly.

"I'm four years old," I said proudly, "but I'll be five next summer."

"Do you remember your brother, Jefferson?"

"I sure do. I've really missed him!"

"You don't need to shout, Billy Joe," Ma'am said.

"Are we really gonna get to see him today?" I asked Mr. Collins. "How far do we have to go?"

"It's quite a ways. But yes, you're gonna see him." Mr. Collins took another swallow of coffee. "Is this your little sister?" he asked, looking over to where Bonnie, in her shyness, had not moved out of our corner.

"Yes, sir, her name's 'Bonnie' an she's three."

What a nice man, I thought.

"Do you remember your papa, Billy Joe?" Mr. Collins asked, smiling but looking right into my eyes.

"I remember him a little," I answered honestly. "I think he was pretty old. All of a sudden one night he died. There was a funeral at the Methodist Church an they buried him in the ground."

"I'm sure sorry he died, son," Mr. Collins said softly, as though he meant what he was saying. He was no longer smiling and his eyes had turned a little sad. From the way he looked and acted I figured he was really sorry Pap had died, that he wasn't just saying he was sorry to make me feel better. His eyes began to shine and were becoming watery.

"Well," he said at last, smiling again, "we're gonna have a nice trip this afternoon out west to a town called 'Helena' and we're gonna see your big brother. I know he'll be just as glad to see you as you will be to see him."

"Do you have any kids at your house?"

"Why yes, as a matter of fact I do."

I could tell he was proud. The happy look returned to his broad face, little wrinkles appearing at the corners of his eyes. "I've got two little girls. One's about Bonnie's age an her name's Mary Lou; the other's a little older than you. Her name's Cynthia. She'll be in the first grade next fall."

"Where do you live?"

"Well, I live down in Oklahoma City. You know where that is? It's quite a ways from here. An it's a real big city. Lots of people live there an there's lots of buildings an lots of cars. I've lived there all my life."

Mr. Collins could see that my eyes had strayed to the gold watch fob hanging from one of his vest pockets. "What's that thing hangin outta your pocket?" I pointed to the watch fob. I had never seen anything like it before.

"You mean this thing? Well, son, that's what's called a 'watch fob.' It's fastened to a watch that I keep in that pocket." He pulled on the fob and, sure enough, out came a thin gold watch that was fastened to the fob by a black leather strap with a little gold buckle on it.

"You see this thing here?" He pointed at the other end of the watch fob. "That's the official symbol of the Masonic Order I belong to down in Oklahoma City. It's kind of a club, a bunch of men like me who get together once in a while to talk an study things an generally enjoy ourselves. Maybe when you grow up you'll be a Mason like me."

About that time Ma'am interrupted.

"I'm ready to sign now, Mr. Collins."

She spoke very softly, so softly I could barely understand what she was saying. I wondered if she was telling Mr. Collins something I wasn't supposed to hear. "You'll probably wanta witness my signature."

"You can use my pen, Mrs. Tolliver. Everything needs to be signed in ink." Mr. Collins took a huge black fountain pen from inside his suit coat. He unscrewed the cap and handed the pen to her. The pen was pointed at both ends, with two bands and a clip on it that looked like pure gold.

As Ma'am signed each page Mr. Collins finished his coffee. When Ma'am handed him the signed papers and his pen, he wrote something on each page and slipped them all inside his briefcase.

"Now, Mrs. Tolliver, I've got one little piece of business to attend to down at the courthouse before we can get started for Helena. What I'd like to do is to come back at four o'clock if that's convenient for you and the children. That'll probably give you enough time to get the kids ready for the trip. Be sure to dress them warmly. It's real cold out there an the heater in my car only wants to work part of the time. I've got a quilt you can wrap around your legs if it gets too cold."

Ma'am followed Mr. Collins to the door, let him out, and watched him drive away. From the window, I also watched his car until it was out of sight, seeing steam coming out of the back and the little cloud of red dust it made as it sped down the street.

"We haven't much time before Mr. Collins comes back so let's all get cleaned up before we get our good clothes on," Ma'am said to Bonnie and me.

"Billy Joe, go an wash your face an hands. An help your little sister wash an dry hers. Don't forget to use some soap."

Just before we expected Mr. Collins to get back, Ma'am took Bonnie outside to the toilet, then told me to go. "Even if you don't really need to," she said.

"It'll be better to peepee here than have to stop somewhere along the road."

Before I left the rickety old toilet and went back inside our warm kitchen, I carefully pushed the door closed and wired it to the rusty nail on the outside so the wind wouldn't blow it open.

We bumped along in Mr. Collins' car for what seemed like a long time down the rough dirt streets in our part of town before we finally turned onto a paved road. I didn't know

where Helena was but I was pretty sure we were headed
west because the bright sun was shining through the window
and windshield right into Mr. Collins' eyes and Jefferson had
taught me about the sun and the four directions. Mr. Collins
had put a black cloth cushion with orange and red flowers on
it in the seat of his car so I could sit in the middle between
him and Ma'am, who was holding Bonnie on her lap. From
low down in the seat I couldn't see much outside the car. All
I could see were the bare tops of tall trees, telephone and
electric poles and the wires they held up, and the roofs and
chimneys of houses we passed. After we were out of town and
into the country, I could see the top of a windmill now and
then.

Ma'am used Mr. Collins' quilt to protect her legs and
Bonnie from the cold draft coming through the cracks in the
floor of the car. Mr. Collins was right about the heater in his
car; it wasn't working a lot of the time and he would hit it
with his hand again and again but couldn't keep it working.
Ma'am hardly spoke. Even Mr. Collins, who had seemed to
enjoy talking before, had almost nothing to say in the car. I
couldn't help wondering if one of them had maybe hurt the
other's feelings or something. I didn't talk much, either.

Before long Bonnie was asleep, her little head cradled in
the crook of Ma'am's arm. Her eyes were closed tightly, her
face was relaxed, and I could see that she was comfortable,
no longer cold in the unheated car. I sat as quietly as I could.

Mr. Collins kept raising his right hand for no apparent
reason as we drove along, and I became curious.

"Why do you do that, Mr. Collins?"

"Why do I do what?"

"Why do you keep liftin your hand up like that?"

"Why, I'm just being neighborly. I'm wavin to people along
the road an to people in the cars meetin us on the highway.
Everybody does that an all it means is everybody's tryin to be
friendly. Didn't you know that?"

I didn't know. I had never ridden in a car before.

Seeing that I was getting fidgety, Mr. Collins pointed to the speedometer and told me what it was for. He said we were going a little more than forty miles an hour. He told me to watch some little numbered wheels that were turning slowly and those that were turning faster. He said they were counting the miles we drove.

All the while I could feel and hear the "clunk-clunk, clunk-clunk" of the bumps in the concrete highway. The car jumped twice every time we drove over one of the bumps. I counted them but only until I got to fifty, because Jefferson hadn't taught me to go any higher than that. Mr. Collins guessed what I was doing and explained that the road was bumpy because it was an old highway that had been fixed lots of times.

By this time I was tired of riding along with nothing to do and nothing to see.

"Do you always wiggle like that?" Mr. Collins asked me. "Do you need to go to the toilet?"

I didn't have an answer but I wasn't wiggling because I needed to go to the toilet. I was excited because this was the first time I had gone on a long trip. But mostly I was excited because soon I would be meeting my brother, Jefferson, and I hoped I hadn't forgotten what he looked like.

"I know what let's do," Mr. Collins said after we had been driving for an hour or so. "Let's stop at the next nice filling station. We can use their rest rooms an get a drink of water. There's a Texaco in the next town where they keep their rest rooms nice and clean."

Before we left the Texaco station, Mr. Collins took a red tin box with blue and white printing on it out of the back of his car, pulled off the lid, and offered big oatmeal cookies all round, even to Bonnie, who had awakened when we stopped.

"My wife made these," he said with a grin. "She's real good about that. Whenever I have to go out of town on business she'll bake up a bunch of cookies and send them with me in this old marshmallow can. They're my favorite kind of cookies; try another one."

"Take a couple," he said to me. "Maybe these'll help you not to wiggle so much," he smiled teasingly.

After what seemed like a very long time we drove into Helena. I knew it was late because the sun that had been shining in my eyes had turned to an orangey-red color. Most of the buildings in Helena looked old. I didn't like Helena and figured Jefferson probably didn't either.

We drove slowly through the little town, probably because the streets were even bumpier than they were back in Cedar Creek. The cold wind was still blowing, and the tree tops were moving back and forth. There was pink dust in the air and a film of it had settled all over the inside of Mr. Collins' car and probably all over us, too, even though the car windows had been tightly closed ever since we had left Cedar Creek.

From the middle of town we turned west again into the setting sun. I hoped we were almost to where Mr. Collins was taking us. I was tired and hungry but I hadn't said anything since we had left the paved highway and begun driving on dirt roads. Neither had Ma'am and neither had Mr. Collins. There was just the rumbling, squeaks, and rattles of Mr. Collins' very cold coupe. Because there was still daylight, I could see large brick buildings not far in the distance. And we were headed right for them. No doubt I would have been alarmed if I had had a clear view through the car's windshield but the large cushion I had been sitting on all afternoon didn't allow me to see where we were going. The street leading to the big buildings was dirt and it was rough, like the one in front of our house, but as we came close we drove onto smooth pavement where Mr. Collins stopped the car before a huge iron gate. It was about as high as the roof on our house back in Cedar Creek and I could see a chain and big padlock in the middle of it. It looked like the gate was part of a high fence that kept people and animals away from the buildings.

Mr. Collins rolled down his window as a policeman stepped out of a little house on one side that had a window in it where the light was shining through. The man came over to the car and asked Mr. Collins, "What can I do for you?"

Mr. Collins took a paper from his pocket and handed it to the man.

"My name's 'Collins.' I'm with the state and I'm here on official business," he said.

The policeman looked at the piece of paper, then handed it back to Mr. Collins through the open window.

"Yes sir, gimmie a minute to open the gate an you can drive on through."

It was almost dark and lights were shining through the windows of the big buildings. Mr. Collins stopped the car in front of one of them and turned off the engine. Scrambling out on his side, I bumped my knee pretty hard on the steering wheel. But it didn't hurt enough to make me cry; besides, it was my fault for being in such a hurry to get out of the car. Cookie crumbs fell from my lap onto Mr. Collins' seat as I climbed across, and I hoped he wouldn't be mad at me. It wouldn't be any trouble to brush them off onto the ground before we drove back to Cedar Creek; I'd remember to tell him.

"Where's Jefferson?" I asked, expecting him to meet us.

"You'll be seein him soon," Ma'am said. "I'm sure somebody who works here will go get him when they find out we've come to visit."

We walked toward a brick building with an electric light above some concrete steps that led us to a white door. There was a sign on it but I had no idea what it meant. Mr. Collins opened the door and motioned us inside.

Stretching out before us was a long, wide hall. It was completely empty but the gray concrete floor was partly covered with a strip of black rubber down its middle. Ma'am said the rubber was to keep people from slipping when their shoes were wet. Except for the high, white ceiling, everything was painted gray: the floors, the walls, the doors. Electric lights on long wires hung from the ceiling. In a way the building reminded me of the courthouse in Cedar Creek where I had gone with Ma'am right after Pap died. It had the same unpleasant smell of disinfectant.

"Is this place a courthouse?" I asked Ma'am.

"No, Billy Joe, it ain't a courthouse but it smells a little like one."

Mr. Collins opened one of the hall doors and held it so Ma'am, Bonnie, and I could go through, and then we walked into a large gray room that looked very much like the one I had seen in the courthouse. There were big gray wooden chairs lined up in rows in the room. We sat down to wait for Mr. Collins who talked with the old, gray-haired woman sitting at a desk with a little blue lamp on it. She wore a white dress with a small tag pinned to the front of it. Her glasses were round and gold-trimmed, and the piece in the middle looked like it had bitten deep into the bridge of her nose. She spoke to Mr. Collins and he handed her some papers. After a brief glance at them, the old woman pushed her chair back, stood straight up, and stepped around to the front of her desk. She walked over to us and looked directly at me.

"Young man," she growled through clenched teeth, "come with me."

She reached out and grabbed me in a firm, warm grip, pulled me out of my chair, and yanked me after her through the door into the long gray hallway.

Scared and confused, I tripped and nearly fell when I turned to look back through the open door at Ma'am and Bonnie. By now Mr. Collins had turned his back on what was taking place. But Ma'am hadn't turned away and I could tell she was crying. Her tears shone in the ceiling light and were streaming down her cheeks. Bonnie was standing in her chair now, clutching Ma'am with all her might, looking up into her face. She, too, had begun to cry.

I never saw nor heard from any of them again: not Ma'am, not Bonnie, not Mr. Collins. Ma'am never wrote a letter or sent presents or pictures. For me the only world I had ever known ended before supper that evening. A new life in the West Oklahoma State Home for White Children had been arranged without my knowledge and nobody ever told me why. ✦

Chapter 3 ————————————————————

The old woman held my hand tightly in her fat, freckled one, dragging me down the hallway toward a closed door. She walked so fast I had trouble keeping up with her. Pulling the door open with her free hand, she shoved me ahead of her into a huge room. I was startled to see so many beds all in one place. They were unlike any beds I had ever seen. Each was painted white. Each was made for one person to sleep in, had a number, and looked exactly like the others, with a brown blanket folded on one end and a small pillow on the other. As I looked around, I wondered why on earth the old woman had brought me here. She pointed to a bed near the middle of the room. It was number fourteen.

"This'll be where you sleep from now on," she said. "An you'll be responsible for keeping your bed neat. Don't even touch any of the other beds, them's for other boys who live here. Do you understand what I'm tellin you?"

I nodded my head. I couldn't talk or even look at her.

"You'll be expected to make up your bed every morning before breakfast and if you don't know how, one of the other boys will show you. But you'll have to do it for yourself around here after you've learned how, and if you don't, you'll be punished. An don't forget it! Now come with me!"

She grabbed my hand firmly once again and roughly pulled me from the bedroom and dragged me on down the hall. If the old woman knew how frightened I was, she never showed it. We turned a corner, and a few steps down this hall was a door with a big sign on it. For the first time in my life I was looking at a door that didn't have a knob. There was a flat piece of metal where the handle should have been. I watched the old woman as she pushed the door open with her free hand; then she pulled me inside. The place reminded me of the toilet in the courthouse in Cedar Creek, where Ma'am had taken me one time. This one had more white toilets and wash basins, but it smelled the same. Glancing about, I noticed a small room off to one side. I thought it might be the place where people took baths.

"Here's where you'll wash your face and hands and brush your teeth every day and do your number one and two an take baths," she growled, then pulled me back around the corner to the big bedroom.

From somewhere she found new clothes for me; a blue shirt and a pair of blue overalls that looked like they would fit Jefferson but were much too big for me.

"You're already late for supper, so get out of your old clothes and into these new ones. You'll wear these every day, just like all the other boys do. Put these on and be quick about it. I'll send one of my helpers to find you and show you where to go for supper. The other boys are already there. Now get busy."

Without another word she turned, stomped to the door, and disappeared. I was terrified of the old woman. I was bewildered by everything I had seen and heard. I had expected to see Jefferson, visit with him for a while, and then go home with Ma'am and Bonnie. No one had said anything about staying here. The old woman was the complete opposite of Ma'am and Mrs. Tidwell, the only other women I knew, who had always been nice to me. Not once had the old woman smiled. Why was she so mean to me? I wondered. I felt sick to my stomach. I wasn't sure what "punished" meant but it sounded bad when she said it. I wanted to cry but I couldn't. Why didn't Ma'am come and get me? And where was Jefferson? He hadn't met us when we had arrived in Helena and I was sure he would have been here. Hadn't Ma'am told me so before Mr. Collins came to our house in Cedar Creek? Why would she tell me I would see Jefferson if she didn't mean it?

After supper everybody put on his pajamas and we climbed into our beds. A tall woman dressed in gray, the same one who took me to supper, stood near the door. She looked around the room, seeming satisfied, and smiled when she saw that I was watching her closely.

"Goodnight boys, go right to sleep," she said, and turned off the lights.

Moonlight shone through the windows. I saw her step into a small room next to our big room. Through a large indoor window she could keep an eye on all of us. I was still too scared even to cry. I just lay there in my pajamas that smelled new, in a strange bed in a strange place, trying not to wiggle and mess up the bed, remembering that I would have to make it up the next morning.

The next morning we all lined up to go to breakfast early. I had tried to make my bed like the other boys were doing but it wasn't as neat as it had been when I had first seen it. I hoped the old woman wouldn't be mad at me. After we had eaten breakfast and marched back to our room, my spirits rose when I saw that my bed, like the others in the straight rows, had been made up as neat as it had been before I had slept in it. A boy named Charlie explained that every morning while we were at breakfast two big girls who worked at the orphans' home remade the beds for all the boys who hadn't turned six yet.

"But after you get to be six," he warned, "you gotta make it perfect by yourself." I had not forgotten the old woman's comment the evening before and wondered why she had threatened me with punishment if somebody was going to make my bed for me.

From the look on his face and the tone of his voice, I was sure Charlie wanted to be my friend and I felt better after he had explained about making my bed. I wanted to trust him, but everything was still too new. Having watched to see what the other boys did, I, too, put on my coat and cap and went outside to play.

The second night I slept a little better, though my mind was still busy. I had counted the beds in the big room; there were sixteen of them and most of them were being used. But all the time I was thinking. Where are Ma'am and Bonnie? Did they go home without me without saying goodbye? Is Jefferson really here in this great big place? I've been here a whole day and I haven't seen or heard from him. Maybe he doesn't know I'm here. How will I find him? Were Ma'am and Mr. Collins storying to me when they said I would see him here?

Charlie and I had talked on the playground my first day at the orphans' home. That's the name Charlie used—"orphans' home." He said he had been at the home since before Christmas, and had been taken from his family just like I had been.

"I know how you're feelin," he said, "but I'm kinda gettin used to it."

Charlie was almost six and talked to me pretty much the way Jefferson used to. Charlie also told me that six-year-old boys and older boys went to school all day long and that we wouldn't see any of them during the day except maybe for a little while in the morning and evening.

After a couple of days I was sure Charlie was someone I could tell my troubles to. He knew I was disappointed that I hadn't found Jefferson. "Heck," he said, "he probably ain't got any way of knowin you're here. Maybe you can ask one of them women who wear uniforms, you know, the ones we see in the halls all the time."

I asked the first one of these women who smiled when I looked into her face. She was about Ma'am's age and size but with her curly red hair, blue eyes, and light skin she didn't look anything like her. I said, "Can I ask you somethin?"

"Why, yes," she said, seeming eager to be helpful, "you're the new boy around here, aren't you? What can I do for you?"

"I'm lookin for my big brother."

"What's your name, son?"

"'Billy Joe Tolliver.' My brother's name is 'Jefferson' and he's either seven or eight, I can't remember fer sure."

"All right, I'll see what I can find out. Maybe by this time tomorrow I'll have an answer for you. Would you please ask me again, about this time tomorrow night?"

When I saw my new friend in the hall the next evening after supper she had nothing more to tell me about Jefferson. But she said she had not given up, that she would keep trying. She seemed happy to talk to me.

"How long have you been here, Billy Joe?"

"Two or three days but it seems longer."

"Did anybody tell you about this place?"

"Ma'am told me it was a real nice place."

"Is that all she told you?"

"Yeah, an she said that Jefferson was here."

"Well, this place is a special home for a lot of orphan children like you. It's a home for children who don't have mothers an fathers or other kinfolk who can look after them anymore or who don't have a house to live in. Who brought you here, Billy Joe?"

"Ma'am an Mr. Collins did."

"Is Ma'am your mother?"

"Yes."

"Did Ma'am tell you why she was leavin you at the

orphans' home?"

"No. She never told me. I just thought we were comin here to see my big brother. Bonnie's my little sister; she came, too." "I imagine your mother left you here because she an your father weren't able to take care of you. Is your father living?"

"No, he died right after Christmas."

"Do you think your mother left Bonnie here, too?"

"I don't know."

"Well, I'll first try to find out if your brother is here. He might be in this very building; it's pretty big. But if he isn't here, he might be in the big boys' building next to this one. There are lots of children in the orphans' home an there are several buildings for them to stay in. It may take me a while to find out about Jefferson but I'm gonna try."

She smiled and walked away, leaving me with more questions than I had before we talked. Did Ma'am really mean to leave me here? Was Jefferson here, too?

The few sickly-looking trees growing just inside the high fence over to the east and behind our buildings began to show tiny green leaves and the days weren't as cold as when I had first come to the orphans' home. One day I asked Charlie about the high fence and he told me that it was there to keep us in and to keep other people out. He asked me if I remembered the big iron gate I had come through the evening I had arrived in Helena. He said his brother told him that you had to have special permission from a policeman to go through the gate. We agreed that we didn't like to live inside a cage.

The youngest boys in my part of the big brick building went outside to play only if it was a nice day. If it was rainy or cold, we were marched into a gymnasium where several women in gray dresses supervised us while we played with the big balls, learned games where we sat on the hardwood floor, and did somersaults on some big, thick floor mats.

However, every day, morning and afternoon and if it wasn't raining, we were allowed to go outside. I especially liked to play in the huge sandbox that had been put right next to the south wall of our building where it was warm in the bright sunlight and out of the cold wind. And every day the woman who lived in the little room next to ours would be on the playground to lead us in games and to scold anyone who didn't behave himself. She said I could call her "Mrs. Clark." She would unlock the door of a tin shed and take out rubber balls and other things to play with.

There was another playground for older boys and it was right next to ours, but Mrs. Clark said we were never to go over there because we might get hurt while the big boys were playing baseball or basketball. Charlie said we couldn't go over there even when the big kids weren't there. He said that one of his friends went over there once and got a whipping.

I was beginning to give up hope that Ma'am would come to take me home and I had almost forgotten what Bonnie looked like. But I couldn't get Jefferson out of my mind and couldn't overcome the feeling I had begun having in the night that maybe Ma'am had put Jefferson and me in the orphans' home because she didn't want us anymore. I remembered clearly how she had stood there that night with Mr. Collins, holding Bonnie and doing nothing to stop the old woman from taking me away down the hall.

Charlie had become my best friend, even though I was only four. He said he and his brother Roy Lee, who was nine, had been brought to the orphans' home at the same time. Their mother, he said, was sick all the time and wasn't ever going to get well and his daddy had been killed while working in a gravel pit over by Alva.

"Do you ever get to see Roy Lee?" I asked.

"Yes, I see him most every day out on the playground. I plumb forgot you tellin me you had a brother here, too. What's his name?"

"His name's 'Jefferson Tolliver' an he's older than I am. I think he's seven, maybe eight. One of the hall matrons tried to find him but gave up."

"He probably lives in the same building with my big brother. I know how to find out. Follow me."

He led me over to the edge of the playground and we looked over to where a crowd of big boys were playing softball and Charlie called out "Hey Buddy!" to a tall kid who seemed to be watching us. Then, with a little help from Buddy, Jefferson appeared out of the crowd and came running over, a big grin lighting up his face.

"Hey, Buster, how long have you been here?"

Never in my life had I been so happy about anything. Jefferson really was here and I had found my big brother. I could feel a smile crossing my face from ear to ear. We wrapped our arms around each other, squeezing hard, and he lifted me off the ground. We were yelling and laughing together. Some of the other boys had stopped playing and just stood there and watched with smiles on their faces.

Jefferson and I stood there and talked until we were called inside to get ready for supper. From then on, every time I went outside, I looked across to the big boys' playground hoping to see Jefferson, but he was almost never there. Then one day he was waiting for me. Jefferson had received a letter from Ma'am. The news was bad.

"She ain't never comin fer us," Jefferson said. "She figures we're gonna get adopted by somebody an when that happens we'll be lots better off."

"Whatta ya mean, 'adopted'?"

"Well, that's when folks take a kid outta the orphans' home an after a while they begin treatin him like he's theirs. But it don't always work out like that. I heard of one kid who went to live with some folks but later had to come back here cause they decided they didn't want him after all."

"Why doesn't Ma'am want us anymore? Ain't she still our mother?" I asked.

"You gotta understand, Buster, what I'm tryin to tell you.

We ain't got a mother anymore."

"Whatta you mean? She didn't die, did she?"

"Well, it's like this. Ma'am gave us up for adoption an what that means is that she ain't our mother no more. An if we ain't ever adopted, we'll stay here til we get big an they let us out."

"You mean forever?"

"Probably not that long. But hell, if we ain't adopted by somebody, we're not leavin this place any time soon."

"But what happens if we're adopted?"

"Well, it's like this here. When you get adopted you're taken into another family just like you had been born into it. This happens at the courthouse, all legal like. They change yer name to theirs an there usually ain't no way they can ever bring you back to this damn place."

The bottom dropped out of my world. This couldn't be happening. How could Ma'am, who loved us, do this? I started to cry; great sobs shook my whole body as tears streamed down my face. Jefferson put an arm around my shoulder.

"I know it hurts, Buster. It hurts me too. But we're both gonna be here for a while and we'll find ways of gettin together. And one of these days we may get adopted by some nice folks who will treat us like Ma'am and Pap did. We may even be adopted into the same family. So let's try to get used to bein here and try to stay outta trouble with the folks who run this place."

He stopped speaking and looked at me for a moment.

"And there's somethin else you ought to know. Buster, Ma'am had to put us in even though she hated to do it. She said in the letter that she's never gonna come an get us because there's no other place we can go now that Pap's dead. She said her Pawnee kinfolks don't want nothin to do with any of us because we're more white than Indian and Pap's whole family is still back in Tennessee and got problems of their own. She asked me to do my best to take care of you until you git adopted."

I stood there and cried because my heart was breaking.

The next Saturday Jefferson had a present for me when we met outside my building after dinner. It was a tin horn with a round wooden piece that you put into your mouth when you wanted to blow it. He told me the horn had been given to him by a boy in his building who had been adopted and had been promised a new horn and a whole lot of other good things.

"He didn't need it no more, not where he was goin," Jefferson said, "an I figured you'd like to have it. You just blow hard to make it work."

He was right, I liked the horn. It was painted red, white, and blue and made a honking sound when I blew it just right. It wasn't new, but it worked. I kept it under my bed at night and never took it outside the dormitory. I blew it only while marching in the halls of my building. The long halls were perfect for marching up and down and blowing my horn and the best part was that nobody ever asked me to stop.

After supper one night I was tooting along and started to turn the corner to the bathroom when another boy came running around the same corner right into me, knocked me down, and jammed the horn down my throat. It was a shock and it hurt. When I pulled out the horn there was blood in my mouth and all over the horn and on the floor where I fell. I started to scream, thinking that I was probably going to die. The next thing I knew, the old gray-haired woman had picked me up in her arms and carried me away, up the stairs to her apartment on the second floor.

The next morning I awoke in a strange bed, shorter than my cot downstairs. It reminded me of the bed Bonnie had slept in, with a side that went up and down so that she wouldn't roll out onto the floor.

"Good morning, Billy Joe, how're you feelin this morning?"

A strange woman in a white uniform was speaking to me. Although I had never seen her before, she smiled and seemed friendly. She had red hair, wore glasses, and smelled like soap. She lowered the side of the bed.

"I'm a nurse, Billy Joe. You know what that is, don't you? An I'm here to take care of you. That was an awful thing that happened to you last night, but you're gonna be all right in a few days. I'll see to that. So until you are all well again, you'll be staying here with me. You can call me 'Miss Wilson.'"

She pointed. "That woman over there in the kitchen is my mother. You can call her 'Mrs. Wilson.' Right now she's fixin something for your breakfast, somethin I think you'll like, somethin that won't hurt when it goes down. Now sit up straight and hold real still while I take a look at that sore throat."

I looked closely at Miss Wilson's face while she was talking and examining my throat. I wanted to say something, to ask questions, but even the thought of talking made me hurt. When she had finished the examination, she handed me a small glass with something in it that looked like syrup.

"Here, swallow this right down. It won't hurt and doesn't taste bad either." Obediently I swallowed the medicine and Miss Wilson smiled at me.

"Now, Billy Joe, if you need to use the toilet, it's right over there down the hall. You'll see that the door is open. Be sure to wash your hands when you're through, then come back in here so you can have some breakfast."

Taking my hand in hers, she helped me get out of the bed, then went over to where the old woman she had called Mrs. Wilson was working in the kitchen. Mrs. Wilson was the old woman who had taken me away from Ma'am. I didn't want to look at her and kept my eyes on the floor until I found the bathroom door.

Both women were sitting at a round table, waiting for me, when I came out of the bathroom.

"You can sit right here, Billy Joe," Miss Wilson said as she patted a wooden chair just like the one she was sitting on.

Mrs. Wilson sat in a chair across the table and now, for the first time, I managed to look straight at her. I was surprised to see that she was smiling. Her eyes, behind her little round glasses, sparkled as she looked directly back at me. She was, I was certain, the same mean old gray-haired woman who had taken me away from my mother, but now, as she smiled, she seemed like a different person.

"I've made you somethin that I think you'll like, Billy Joe. You don't have to chew it, it'll go down easy, and it's gonna make you feel better. Now you don't need to say anything. I know your throat hurts so it's all right if you just shake your head yes or no."

What she had made for me was Cream of Wheat. I knew that because we sometimes had it for breakfast back in Cedar Creek. This was soupier than Ma'am used to make and it was easy to swallow. The old woman watched me while I ate.

"You can call me 'Miss Edith' if you'd like to," Miss Wilson said. "Maybe it'll be easier to remember than 'Miss Wilson.'"

"An you can call me 'Mrs. Wilson,'" the old woman said, "because I'm her mother and I'm a lot older. Miss Edith and I live here in this apartment."

Every day my throat felt better, and I felt more and more at home with Miss Edith and Mrs. Wilson. They gave me a set of blocks with letters and numbers on them, and lots of paper and a new set of crayons, and they took turns telling me stories at bedtime and before my afternoon nap. Best of all, they read wonderful stories out of books.

Sometimes when Miss Edith talked with me, she referred to herself as 'Aunt Edith.' And even though Mrs. Wilson still growled and muttered words that I couldn't understand, especially when she was working in the kitchen, she never again spoke harshly to me. And sometimes, for no particular reason, she would hug me tight, smile, and kiss me on the cheek. Especially when she said goodnight. She felt soft and warm and comforting, and soon I had forgotten how afraid of her I used to be.

In a few days, my throat had healed, and I dreaded the idea of having to go back to the big room on the first floor. But no one said anything about my leaving. Mrs. Wilson and Miss Edith seemed happy to have me live with them and I felt safe and secure for the first time since I had come to the orphans' home.

One Saturday morning a man came to visit the two women. He called the older woman "Mom" and the younger woman "Sis" or "Edith." Both women called him "Frank" and I finally figured out that he was Mrs. Wilson's son and that I should call him "Mr. Wilson."

Mr. Wilson had come to cut the boys' hair, something he did on Saturdays when the boys were not in school.

"You can be the first one to get a haircut today," he said.

Mr. Wilson made me climb up onto the tall kitchen stool and then wrapped a big white dishtowel around my shoulders. I didn't like having my hair cut. Instead of cutting my hair with scissors like Ma'am used to do, Mr. Wilson used clippers that he worked with his hand. As he roughly turned my head up and down, this way and that, side to side with his big, calloused hand. I hated having my head shoved around so I started to cry, more angry than hurt.

Removing the hair-covered dishtowel and helping me off the stool, Mr. Wilson said, "Now that wasn't so bad, was it? You don't hafta cry." I looked at him and said nothing.

A few days later Mr. Wilson came again, and this time he brought his wife, who came right over to me and leaned down smiling at me.

"My name is 'Mrs. Wilson,'" she said, looking me straight in the eye. I'm very glad to meet you, Billy Joe."

"Why don't you folks sit down?" Old Mrs. Wilson called from the kitchen. "I'll be with you in just a minute."

Mr. and Mrs. Wilson sat side by side on the sofa, both

smiling at me. Mrs. Wilson looked sort of like Ma'am. Her hair was very dark, her eyes were almost black, and her skin was the color of mine. I wondered if she was part Indian. Mr. Wilson had bright blue eyes and wavy brown hair that he combed straight back. His arms and the lower part of his face were red, but his forehead was white. He didn't say much, just smiled at me, and his wife did most of the talking. I could tell she liked me.

"We live on a farm not far from here an we have a dog an cat an cows an horses. There are lots of trees with birds living in them. Would you like to see our farm some day?"

I nodded my head, yes, and from that time on, Mr. and Mrs. Wilson visited us every day or so, in the evening just before I had to go to bed, and almost all day on Saturday and Sunday afternoons. They would ask me what I had been doing and we joked and laughed and sometimes Miss Edith and Mr. Wilson's mother left me alone with them.

Then came a surprising visit. After we had talked a while, Mrs. Wilson leaned toward me, took my hand in hers, looked me in the eyes, and said, "We're thinkin how nice it would be if you came to stay with us for a while."

Mr. Wilson didn't say anything but he was smiling, watching the two of us.

"Would you like to do that?"

"Yes," I answered, wondering what their house would look like, wondering what a farm would be like.

It all happened very suddenly. Mr. Wilson said he was ready to go home. Mrs. Wilson carried my clothes—as well as everything else I owned, including my new blocks and crayons and papers—in a brown paper sack with handles at the top. I said goodbye and thank you to Miss Edith and her mother and the three of us went down the stairs together. ✦

Chapter 4 ──────────────────────────── ❧

Compared to the only other car ride I ever had, it was a short drive to the Wilson's farm. All the way to their house Mr. and Mrs. Wilson asked me questions, mainly about my family. They were silent when I told them that some day soon Ma'am might come to get me and take me back home to Cedar Creek. Sure, Jefferson had sworn up and down that she never would, but I was not ready to give up hope that some day Ma'am would come back for me.

Mrs. Wilson asked me what I liked and didn't like to eat. Then she asked how I was treated in the orphans' home. I wasn't sure what she meant; was she talking about when I was downstairs with the others or after I had been taken upstairs?

"All right, I guess," was the only answer I could think of.

The sun was going down when we arrived at the farm. Mr. Wilson said he would see if the hired man had done the chores and he headed off to the big barn and corral a little ways downhill from the house. Mrs. Wilson took me by the hand and led me from the car over to the house, which sat under the spreading branches of a big tree that had dropped leaves on and around the stoop.

Inside the house it was dark. I looked for a light in the

ceiling and for a switch by the door to turn it on but there were no lights and no switches. Mrs. Wilson watched me and said, "We don't have electricity out here, Billy Joe. We use coal oil lamps. Would you like to watch me light them?" I nodded my head. I didn't tell her that we had coal oil lamps in our house in Cedar Creek.

Sitting in the middle of a big wooden table was a lamp made of plain glass. The bottom part was round and even though it was nearly dark, I could see that it was almost full of coal oil. "That's the fuel for the lamp," she said. Mrs. Wilson lifted the chimney, struck a match, and lit what she called the "wick," then put the chimney back on. A soft yellow glow spread through the room, leaving dark shadows everywhere that weren't close to the lamp now sitting in the center of the round table.

Lighting a smaller lamp, Mrs. Wilson asked, "Would you like to see where you'll be sleeping?"

What I really wanted was to go to the bathroom, and she must have noticed that I couldn't stand still because she asked, "Do you need to pee pee?" I nodded my head.

"We have an outdoor toilet," she said, "but just for tonight, step out the front door and get around on the other side of that mulberry tree. It's all right for you to pee pee there."

She was right about the tree. It was very big and private. I got around it where she couldn't see me and peed on the rough bark of the trunk. I had never done anything like that before and I thought it was sort of fun and I felt much better.

That night I slept in a bed with sides that went up and down, exactly like the one I had been sleeping in while I was in old Mrs. Wilson's apartment. And instead of being off in a room by myself, I was in the small bedroom where Mr. and Mrs. Wilson slept. It reminded me of how Bonnie had slept in her little bed in the same room with Ma'am and Pap.

Mr. Wilson was already working outside when I awoke from a deep night's sleep. Mrs. Wilson helped me get dressed.

She was so nice to me that I decided not to tell her I knew how to dress myself.

"I've fixed some hotcakes for your breakfast," she said. I had never eaten hotcakes before. On the plate with the hotcakes was a fried egg and a long piece of crisp bacon. A glass of milk sat next to the plate. I had been forced to drink milk at the orphans' home and had hated the taste because it didn't have the sweetness of the Pet milk, mixed with a little water, that Ma'am had always given me.

"I don't like milk," I said.

"Why, it's fresh milk. From our cows. Mr. Wilson milked them this morning before you got out of bed. You'll like this milk better than what you had at the home."

She sat across the table, watching me closely. I felt trapped. I took a small sip from the large glass. The milk was almost warm and tasted even worse than what I remembered from the orphans' home.

"It doesn't look or taste like the milk I got at my house," I argued. "How does Mr. Wilson get milk from cows?"

"Maybe you can see for yourself when Mr. Wilson does the milkin. Would you like to see where the milk comes from?"

I struggled to eat the breakfast she had fixed for me. She seemed especially interested in the way I managed to drink the warm milk. What I did to get it down was to fill my mouth almost full of hotcake, take a gulp of milk, chew fast to rid myself of the milk taste, then swallow the whole thing at once. It seemed to work but I was glad when breakfast was over and she allowed me to leave the table.

She offered me a glass of water but it tasted even worse than the warm milk.

"This water tastes funny," I said.

"Our well water isn't fit for people to drink, so we use cistern water instead. I'll show you where it comes from."

She led me out the back door onto a porch made of concrete and bricks. Right in the middle of the porch was a tin thing sticking up with a handle on one side and a spout on the other. She showed me how it worked by taking the handle in her hand and turning it around and around. There was a clinking and a rattle and before long a stream of water came flowing out of the spout into a bucket she had placed underneath it.

"The cistern is down under this thing," she explained. "It's a great big tank that holds lots of rain water. When it rains the water that falls on the roof of our house comes down through a pipe, into a charcoal filter over there." She pointed. "An then it flows right into the cistern. So when we want some water, we come out with a bucket an turn this crank an up comes water. It tastes a little funny but it's all right to drink."

"Oh," I said.

"Would you like to go out an play? Or would you like me to sort of get you acquainted with our place?"

"I guess so. Are there any kids to play with?"

"No, Billy Joe, we don't have any children of our own."

"You don't have any kids? How come?"

"Well, the Lord never blessed us with children. But both my husband an I like children an wish we could have had some boys an girls."

"Is there anybody I can play with?"

"No, you're the only child here. But there are lots of things to do. Let's take a walk outside."

The Wilson's farm was nothing like the orphans' home. The house was big, a two-story building with doors on three of its four sides. There were no high chain-link fence and iron gate to keep me from running away. The only fences I saw at the farm were to keep the cows, horses, pigs, and chickens where they belonged. The house also smelled better and there was none of the funny smell I associated with both the courthouse in Cedar Creek and the big brick buildings at the orphans' home.

Our first stop was the cellar, then the clothesline, the

chicken pen, the corral, and the one-hole toilet that sat about halfway up a small hill just southeast of the back porch of the house. It looked pretty much like the toilet we had in Cedar Creek, it worked the same way, and it even had old catalogs in it like we used at home. But it was cleaner.

By the time Mr. Wilson came in from the field at noon for dinner, I had seen most of the farm, had gotten the mail out of the mailbox down beside the sandy road in front of the house, and had helped Mrs. Wilson pull weeds out of the garden over next to the corral, and I was nearly worn out from seeing and doing so many new things.

Mrs. Wilson had a big meal ready for her husband. He washed his face and hands in a washpan that sat on a little table beside the back door, the one that led to the back porch where the cistern was. When he was finished he opened the porch door and threw the dirty water into the back yard. Then he used a big brown towel to dry himself. I watched his every move and I could smell his sweat and other smells when I followed him into the dining room.

There were lots of good things to eat, including sweet pickles, fresh bread, butter, and jelly. After we had finished eating, Mr. Wilson got up from the table, went into the living room, and lay down on a thick rug. He lay there for a half hour or so. I figured he was sleeping so I went outside to watch the pigs and didn't see him go back out to the fields.

I didn't see him until late in the day, and Mrs. Wilson explained that he always returned from the fields while it was still light and before the sun went down he put the cows in the barn and fed and milked them, fed the hogs, and did the other chores. She said it was usually after dark before he was ready for supper.

Mrs. Wilson didn't fix a big supper for Mr. Wilson, explaining to me that he didn't like to eat a big meal just before bedtime because he didn't sleep well with a full stomach.

"What he usually likes for supper is bread and milk or

crackers and milk. But you and I will have leftovers from dinner. I think you will like that better than bread and milk."

I was relieved to hear that.

We had only just begun to eat when Mr. Wilson looked across the table at me and said, "Well, Billy Joe, what have you been up to all day?"

I had to think a minute before I answered and I didn't know where to start.

"Mrs. Wilson showed me lots of things."

"Did you like what you saw?

"Those pigs looked just like ones I saw in a book at the orphans' home. Why did they grunt and run away when I got close to them?"

Mr. Wilson grinned. "Well, Billy Joe, those old hogs have never seen a little boy and you probably scared them."

Before long it seemed they forgot all about me and talked about the day's happenings to each other as if I wasn't there. I sat quietly and ate my food because I had nothing to add to the conversation. But I watched them carefully and I listened carefully. I didn't interrupt. I figured that by listening I could learn about them, their families, the neighbors, the crops, the weather, and the livestock. Most of what they were talking about was probably not meant for me to understand, but it didn't take me long to follow everything they said.

That night when I was put to bed I lay awake for a long time, thinking hard, pretending I was asleep. I went over in my mind all the things Jefferson had told me about adoption. Have the Wilsons brought me here because they want to adopt me? Should I ask them questions? Should I expect them to answer? What if they want me around only part of the time and plan to take me back to the orphans' home when they're tired of me? What can I do to keep that from happening? Mr. Wilson still scares me. He's big and loud and strong. I really like Mrs. Wilson. She talks a lot to me and tells me things. I like it here. Am I supposed to treat them the way I did Ma'am and Pap? How can I keep from doing something wrong? Are they trying me out for a son? Who can I ask?

I really didn't know what I should do, but before I went to sleep I decided that I would do my best to be a good boy, to make it as easy as I could for them to want me.

The next day started out better because I was feeling more comfortable with the Wilsons, and they seemed more comfortable with me. Even my glass of milk at breakfast went down easier than it had the day before.

Mr. Wilson spent most of his time outside working in the field, doing something with the livestock, working in his blacksmith shop, or on farm machinery. Mrs. Wilson spent most of her time inside taking care of the house, doing the wash, baking bread, and fixing meals, the way that Ma'am used to do.

Mr. Wilson was younger than any other man I knew, a whole lot younger than Pap. There were almost no wrinkles in his wide face except for some deep lines across his forehead. He had narrow lips and a mouth filled with straight white teeth. Huge teeth. And he didn't smoke or chew tobacco. Maybe, I thought, that is one of the reasons it always smells so good inside their house.

Mrs. Wilson's face was smaller; she smiled a lot and often sang while she worked. Her mouth had a lot of expressions and she moved it around a lot. She was shorter and wider than Ma'am was, and she was more pleasant than Mr. Wilson.

When Mr. and Mrs. Wilson were together they talked constantly, it seemed, about everything. I seldom saw them touch, but they sure liked to talk to each other. I figured that was because when Mr. Wilson was working outside he had no one to talk to. And since Mrs. Wilson spent all day in or around the house, she had no one to talk to except me.

Mr. Wilson said he would show me how he milked the cows. But they were scared of me and when I came near they snorted and ran away, so Mr. Wilson said it would be better if I stayed in the house at milking time. But when he had finished with the cows and had turned them into the pasture, I went back outside and followed him around. I followed him a lot those first few days, fascinated with everything he did.

I watched closely to see what he was doing out in the yard or in his blacksmith shop. There was always something that he needed to fix—that needed a hole drilled into it, that needed to be pounded into the right shape to fit something—so he wouldn't have to drive into town to buy a new machine part. It seemed to me that with his forge, his hammers and anvil, and his drill and all kinds of tools he could fix almost anything made of iron.

Mr. Wilson's blue overalls looked like they were several sizes too big for him. He said they were more comfortable than overalls that fit too tight. His shirts were blue, too, but lighter in weight than his overalls and they had long sleeves.

I never saw Mr. Wilson go outside without a hat on. Mrs. Wilson said he always wore a hat outside because he had a light complexion and sunburned easily. She said that was also the reason he always wore long-sleeved shirts. Mr. Wilson combed his hair straight back. If it was wet, it would be sort of plastered to his head; but when it dried, it was puffed up a little so that he looked like most other men.

I could tell Mrs. Wilson was trying to make me feel at home with them. When Mr. Wilson said we might be going over to the orphans' home one Saturday morning, she must have seen in my face how scared I was because she reached over, took my hand in hers, and said, "Don't worry, Billy Joe, we're not gonna leave you there. Remember, Mr. Wilson cuts the boys' hair one Saturday every month."

The first Sunday after I came to live with them, Mrs. Wilson took me to church a mile and a half from the house. She took care that I had clean clothes to wear, my shoes were shined, my face and hands were clean, and my hair was carefully combed. Mr. Wilson didn't go with us to church.

For my fifth birthday in late June, Mrs. Wilson baked the biggest cake I had ever seen. It was a round, white layer-cake with chocolate icing, and right in the top she had stuck five little red candles because she knew that red was my favorite color. It was the first birthday cake I had ever had. When Mrs. Wilson brought it out after we had finished supper, Mr. Wilson said I was to make a wish, then blow out all the candles at once.

"All in one blow," he said.

After we had eaten some of the cake, Mr. Wilson gave me a brand-new baseball and bat. And he gave me a glove that looked old and worn. It was funny-looking and far too big for my hand.

"This here is tha glove I used when I was a boy an played baseball," he said.

I said thank you the way Ma'am had taught me. Then Mrs. Wilson handed me a package wrapped in pretty red-and-blue paper and tied with a red ribbon. Inside was a wooden airplane that used rubber bands to make the propeller go around and cause the plane to take off and fly. Mr. Wilson said I couldn't fly the plane until the next morning because it was already dark and, anyhow, it was an outside toy. After breakfast the next morning I ran into the back yard, wound up my airplane, and let it go. It landed on the roof of the back porch, right above the cistern where it was hard to get to. The plane stayed there until the first hard rain finally came in late July and washed it off onto the ground.

Sometimes when Mr. Wilson didn't have a lot of work to do outside the house he played games with me in the front yard where the chickens didn't peck and scratch and make number two. We played catch with the baseball and glove and the glove worked better than I thought it would. He pitched the ball to me and I tried to catch it. At other times I tried to bat when he pitched it to me. He taught me how to throw the ball and catch it with both hands so it wouldn't roll out of the glove.

"Like a man," Mr. Wilson would say, and smile at me.

Although I still didn't fully trust grownups, I soon felt comfortable on the farm. I liked working in the garden with Mrs. Wilson, I liked the pleasant smells of the locust trees in bloom, especially in the evenings, and I wanted to meet the rest of Mr. Wilson's family who lived a mile and a half down the road.

But at night, however, when it was dark, I often dreamed of having to go back to the home and in my dreams I would scream and cry as I was being taken away. I never tried to explain to the Wilsons that I was having bad dreams or that I worried a lot, because I thought they wouldn't understand. Nor did I tell them that when I was alone I daydreamed about their adopting me and making me their very own boy. Although this was something I didn't dare talk to them about, it was always on my mind. More than anything in the world I wanted to belong to somebody again, to have somebody care for me like their own, to have a real mother and father and maybe a brother like Jefferson, someone I could really trust. ✦

Chapter 5 ————————————————————— ‹‹

Mrs. Wilson almost never scolded or looked crossly at me. There were times, I knew, when I did deserve to be scolded, such as when I deliberately disobeyed her. But she seldom lost her temper without good reason and never showed any impatience with my constant questions. Once tears came to her eyes when I said something about how I missed Ma'am and then I wished I hadn't said it. I was, in fact, being honest.

It was terribly hard having to think of being good all the time instead of just being myself. And, no matter how hard I tried to be a good boy, it wasn't long before I got into trouble with the Wilsons.

One noon I refused to eat the meat Mrs. Wilson had fixed for dinner. She called it "chicken-fried steak"—a beef dish—and it was something I had never had. Like the milk she gave me for breakfast every morning, I didn't like the taste, and I had made up my mind that I wouldn't eat it.

"Eat it," Mr. Wilson said. "It's good for you an it'll make you grow big an strong."

After he had looked away and continued to eat his dinner, I pushed the meat around on my plate, hoping he would think somehow that I had eaten some of it. Mr. Wilson soon finished his meal except for dessert, when, again, he looked hard at me and said sternly, "Eat your meat, son, like I told you to."

At that point, I stood my ground, looked right at him and said loudly, "No I won't. I don't like it an I ain't gonna eat it."

"Well, mister fussy, we'll just see about that. You'll either eat it right now or you'll be punished!"

I looked back squarely into his angry face. I was scared but I didn't eat the steak. Then I learned that what I had thought was just a threat from Mr. Wilson wasn't just a threat. He meant exactly what he said. Without another word, he pushed his chair back from the table, stepped around to my chair, jerked me off the mail order catalogs on which I had been sitting, turned me across his knee, and spanked me. I was plenty scared, more scared than hurt by the spanking. But I decided right then never to make that mistake again. What scared me most was the thought that they might take me back to the orphans' home that very day because I had disobeyed Mr. Wilson.

"Now set down an eat yer dinner like I told you to."

I hoped Mr. Wilson wouldn't stay mad at me and I didn't want him thinking I was a bad boy. I quickly replaced the catalogs that had been knocked to the floor, climbed back up, and sat down at my place again. Holding my breath, I choked down the fried beef, now cold and tasting even worse than ever. The Wilsons seemed relieved.

Not all of my punishment came from Mr. Wilson. I hadn't been at the farm very long before I learned from Mrs. Wilson that it was all right to say "heck" but not "hell" and "darn" but not "damn."

"You probably learned those bad words at the home but we don't use them around here."

At Sunday school I heard older boys say "heck fire" and "lordy lordy" when they were inside the church but they always talked dirty and said swear words when they went

into the nearby grove of locust trees to pee. When I used
those words at home Mrs. Wilson would say, "Now those
aren't nice things to say, Billy Joe. You never hear Mr. Wilson
saying words like that."

Once she heard me saying "hee, hi, ho, hore" and she
warned me about saying "whore." "That's a bad word," she
said, but didn't tell me why it was bad.

Although Mrs. Wilson never spanked me over her knee or
whipped me with a switch, she used a very effective way of
breaking me from using bad words. One morning as the two
of us were leaving for church, I accidentally stepped into a
small pile of dog mess on our driveway near the car. Without
thinking, I used some of the forbidden words and Mrs. Wilson
heard me. As quick as a flash, she grabbed my hand, pulled
me back into the house, headed straight for the wash basin,
and washed out my mouth with soap. And when she had finished, she said, "Here, wipe yourself off with this washcloth
an be quick about it or we'll be late for church. An don't you
ever let me hear you talkin like that again."

With Ma'am in Cedar Creek, I was never told I could not
do something or say something. At the orphans' home,
though, everybody told me what to do. Everything was so different again at the Wilson's that I often said or did something
that got me into trouble. Mr. Wilson scared me with his stern
looks and his threats to punish me, the same kind of threats
I used to hear at the orphans' home. If I cried in his presence
or seemed about to, or if I puckered up and began to whine,
he would raise his voice and glare and almost shout, "Stop
that blubberin" or "Stop that whinin" or "If you can't stop
that whimperin, leave the table. You're not a baby."

If Mr. Wilson told me to do something, I did it. But sometimes he would say something I just couldn't agree with. If I
tried to argue with him, he would growl, "Don't contradict
me. I'm tha boss around here an you'll do what I say."

I quickly learned not to cross Mr. Wilson and that once

he said something he didn't want to have to say it again. Mrs. Wilson never argued with Mr. Wilson about me. Nor did she object to his scolding me or whipping me when I did get cross-wise with him.

I became more and more lonely for other children. For as long as I could remember, all the way back to before Pap died, there had been someone for me to play with. Even at the orphans' home there was Charlie, my best friend, and other boys who slept in the same room and who played all kinds of games with us out on the playground, but now, except for those I saw at church, there were no children for me to play with.

One day Mrs. Wilson told me about a little boy who lived across the road and asked me if I would like him to come over and play. I was delighted, of course, and that afternoon Dean Frye and his mother came walking down the road from their house to ours, about a quarter of a mile. Dean was very close to being my age and we spent our time playing in the loose dirt around back between our house and the clothesline. We made roads and drove our wooden make-believe cars and trucks lickety-split from one place to another. We had a great time together and I hated to see him go home. Dean remind-ed me a lot of Charlie, my only real friend at the orphans' home and before long we were together every day or so. After our first visit neither Mrs. Wilson nor Mrs. Frye went with us. But I knew that the two women talked on the telephone before either Dean or I left home. I wasn't nearly so lonely after I got acquainted with Dean.

One thing that really made me uneasy was the way the Wilsons and other adults talked about me when I couldn't help hearing what they were saying. When someone men-tioned the orphans' home or how long the Wilsons planned to keep me, it seemed like they were talking about me as if I were a pet or a thing and not a person. I hated that kind of talk. One night after supper I had gone out to the toilet and when I came back to the kitchen I heard Mrs. Wilson talking in the dining room. She was telling Mr. Wilson about the visit she had had with Mrs. Barrows, a neighbor who lived a quarter of a mile north of our farm.

"Lola hadn't heard about Billy Joe," she said. "She was very curious. She said she had never heard of anybody taking a child from the home. I told her we hadn't adopted him but that we were keepin him for a while to see if we wanted to go ahead with adoption."

I stood at the washstand and, forgetting to wash my hands, waited to hear what Mr. Wilson had to say. From the way they were talking, I knew they had no idea I could hear them. My heart pounded and I kept quiet.

"We're gonna hafta be dealin with this before long," Mr. Wilson said.

"Yes, I know. If we decide to keep him, the first thing we have to do is make a petition to the county judge that we want to adopt him. There's a deadline but it isn't for a while yet. I'll look it up tomorrow morning."

"Have we heard from the superintendent up at the home? Has anybody called to see how we're gettin along with him?"

"No, nobody's called. Maybe it's because your mother works up there. They probably figure that if we were havin any problems she would tell them."

I couldn't stand any more of this talk. I tiptoed to the back screen door, opened it, and let it bang shut. "Are you ready for bed now, Billy Joe?" Mrs. Wilson called to me as I started washing my hands in the kitchen.

"Yes, ma'am," I answered, trying not to show that I had heard them talking about me. But that night I had trouble getting to sleep and I cried some before the Wilsons finished talking in the living room, came to bed, and blew out the coal oil lamp.

The next day Mrs. Barrows and her daughter came to visit Mrs. Wilson and me. I learned that they lived a quarter of a mile up the road. The two women decided that it would be all right for us kids to play together now and then. I could tell Mrs. Barrows was very proud of her daughter's name.

"'Ariwana' is an Indian name," she told me.

Ariwana never wanted to play cowboys and Indians or Dick Tracy or anything like that and I soon discovered that she could whip me any time she took it into her head. It was bad enough that she was a girl, but it was worse that she was a lot bigger than I was. The last time she hauled off and hit me up alongside the head with her open hand I figured I didn't need any more of that kind of treatment from her. When I got back home that day, I said to Mrs. Wilson,"I ain't gonna play with Ariwana any more."

"Why? Did something happen between you two?"

"She hit me on the head so hard I saw stars."

"She probably didn't mean to hurt you."

"Yes she did! She's done it before. I just never said anything about it."

"Did you hit her back?"

"Well, I hit her back the first time she hit me but it didn't do any good. She hit me again."

"Well, I always thought Ariwana was a nice little girl. She'll probably apologize the next time she sees you."

"I bet she don't! Anyway, she always wants to play girl stuff."

"What kind of girl stuff?"

"Well, this mornin she got out a bunch of little toy dishes an put em on the floor, then she told me to sit down because she was gonna serve tea."

"That sounds nice. You didn't like that?"

"No, I didn't! She always wants to play somethin sissy like that. She ain't nearly as much fun to play with as Dean Frye is."

"Well, you don't have to play with Ariwana if you don't want to."

"Well, I don't want to an I ain't never goin up to her house again!"

Ariwana never apologized even though what happened was all her fault, and I never again went up to her house to play and she didn't come to my house either. Besides, because she didn't go to Round Grove School and didn't go to our church and because she and her folks almost never went to Aline on Saturdays, I didn't see much of her, even though we lived only a quarter mile from one another.

After wheat harvest was over, when farm work had let up a little, Mrs. Wilson began teaching me to read and write. I could already say my ABCs but didn't know what they looked like or how to write them. Every day except Saturday and Sunday, we spent several hours together and I worked hard, not only because I wanted to please her, but also because I was learning lots of new things. Reading, I discovered, was my favorite part. Every night at supper Mrs. Wilson told her husband what we had accomplished that day.

"He's doing remarkably well," she said. "He's learning several new words every day."

Then summer turned to fall and before long it started to feel like winter would be coming soon. The locust and black-jack trees had lost most of their leaves and the wind blew cold enough for us to wear our winter coats. My afternoon lessons were going wonderfully well. And day by day I felt more at home with Mr. and Mrs. Wilson. Like always, they spent almost all day apart and did a lot of talking over supper. One evening after a cool and windy day, the two of them talked throughout the meal about how I seemed to be learning so much so soon. Clearly, both were pleased; they smiled a lot as they talked and seemed happy to answer my many questions.

By now I had all but forgotten Pap and Bonnie. And, although I missed Ma'am, I didn't think of her except when I overheard a grownup at church or in town talking about where I had come from and wondering why I had been put in the orphans' home. I would ache at times like this, still wondering why Ma'am didn't want me any more. Maybe, I thought, I was supposed to forget my real family altogether when I got a new one. Maybe that was what Jefferson was trying to tell me that day at the orphans' home right before I came to live with the Wilsons.

After school started in September, Mr. and Mrs. Wilson began taking me to Round Grove School for special PTA programs. It was always after dark when we got there. Whether or not they had kids in school, everyone who lived near Round Grove was welcome at the PTA meetings. Since I had turned five and could carry a tune pretty well, people wanted me to sing. Mrs. Wilson had taught me many of her favorite songs and Flo Hood, who was PTA president that year, had heard me sing when she was visiting at our house. She said she was so surprised that a little boy could carry a tune so well and remember all the words to grownup songs that she asked me to sing at the next PTA meeting. And I did.

People clapped for me and from that time on I sang at every meeting. Somebody always asked for "Red River Valley" or "Strawberry Roan." Folks liked those old cowboy songs and always clapped when I finished singing. When I yodeled they clapped even harder.

I guess maybe I liked best to sing western songs because I had it in mind to be a cowboy when I grew up. I think Mr. Wilson was happy when I performed because he always kept time by clapping his hands and smiled a lot while I was singing. He seemed to like it when people told him what a good singer I was for a little kid. Although two songs were my limit, it soon got to where somebody would offer me a nickel if I would sing a third song or a dime if I would sing a fourth. So I would sing and sing. It was one of the ways I could earn money to save for things I wanted. Even though I didn't always feel like singing, the nickels and dimes and the other goodies I got later made me glad that I did it.

That first Christmas with the Wilsons was exciting for me, very much different from what I had known before. There was a Christmas tree, for one thing. Mr. Wilson and I found a nice cedar growing in the east pasture. "How does that one look to you, son?" he asked. We agreed that it was the prettiest tree in the whole pasture. Mr. Wilson cut it down with his axe, then carried it back to the house over his shoulder and I carried the axe as I walked along beside him. "Now be very careful with that axe," he cautioned. "It's mighty sharp an you could hurt yourself if you're not careful." I was very careful as we made our way through the high grass, plum brush, and blackjack trees back to the house. "Just leave tha axe right here," Mr. Wilson said. "Stand it up there against that gate post."

Before taking the tree into the house, Mr. Wilson carried it into the shed and nailed some boards to the bottom of it so it could stand up straight without tipping over. Mrs. Wilson met him at the door and told him to set it up in the corner of the dining room. She and I spent much of the day decorating the tree. The first thing we did was to pop some corn.

"Why are you doin that?" I asked, and she explained that she would make a long string of the popcorn so that it could be hung like a rope all over the Christmas tree. She said she would show me, and after the corn had cooled, she did. While we were getting the tree from the pasture she had taken a big box out of storage upstairs. It was full of things that we hung on the tree: tinsel, a shiny rope, glass ornaments, and some little red paper balls.

The tree was the most beautiful I had ever seen and it was in our house. It made the whole house smell good. As I stood admiring the tree, I realized that I really wanted very much to become a member of the Wilson family. But I didn't mention it to them.

At breakfast several days later Mr. Wilson told me that

we would be going to a Christmas program at Round Grove
School that night.

"When I was a boy I went to that school and when you're
old enough maybe you'll go there too," he said. Except for
calling me "son," that was the first time he sounded like he
wanted to be my real daddy, and more and more I wanted to
be a school boy. "There's gonna be a Santa Claus who'll have
candy an presents for all the kids," he said, "an I bet he'll
have somethin fer you too. There's gonna be lotsa people
there an we're all gonna have a good time."

He was right. The school was packed with people I didn't
know and there was a decorated tree up front. I wasn't asked
to sing that night. After a program of poems and stories by
older kids and after everybody had sung several Christmas
songs, the back door flew open and in rushed Santa Claus
with a loud "ho, ho, ho, Merry Christmas everybody." He was
big and fat and had a gunny sack over his shoulder.

First he gave each of the kids, including me, a brown
paper sack full of pecans and walnuts and peanuts and candy
and with a big orange in the bottom. I was on top of the
world.

Then Santa started pulling gifts out of his bag, packages
of all shapes and sizes wrapped in bright-colored paper and
each tied with ribbon. Everyone was excited; there was hollering and laughter and most of the kids shrieked with glee
when their names were called to go up to the front of the
room and take their presents from the man in the red-and-
white suit. Before long my name was called.

"Billy Joe Tolliver!" Santa shouted. "Is there a 'Billy Joe
Tolliver' in the house? Where are you, Billy Joe?"

"That's you, son" Mr. Wilson said, grinning at me. "Go up
and get yer present."

I scrambled up the aisle, bumping grownups who were
crammed into seats that were too small for them. I grabbed
the package Santa held out to me, turned, and stumbled back

to where the Wilsons were sitting near the back of the room.

"Did you say 'thank you' to Santa?" Mrs. Wilson asked me.

"No, I forgot."

"Then quick, hurry back an tell him 'thank you' an wish him a Merry Christmas. You need to do that."

So I rushed back down the same aisle, looked right into Santa Claus' happy face, and shouted, "Thank you! And Merry Christmas," then hurried back to my place on Mr. Wilson's lap. Everybody was laughing, even the Wilsons, and I was so happy I hardly knew what to do.

"What's in the package?" Mrs. Wilson asked. Everyone in the room seemed to be watching as I tore open the pretty package, throwing paper and ribbon every which way. It was a little violin and a bow and piece of rosin.

"What's this stuff for?" I asked Mrs. Wilson, holding the piece of rosin up for her to see.

"Well, that is what you have to rub on your bow strings so you can make music on your violin," she said, "but let's wait until we get home to try it out."

By now I was full of the Christmas spirit. And on Christmas morning I discovered that Santa Claus had left presents for the three of us under the tree. He had even hidden some small packages among the branches. Later, the Wilsons and I had Christmas dinner with all of Mr. Wilson's family at his parents' farm a mile and a half from the road. Never in my life had I seen so many grownups in one house and had so many good things to eat. I figured that maybe this was the way a family was supposed to live. It sure was different from the way I lived back in Cedar Creek. ✦

Chapter 6 ————————————————————

Mr. Wilson had blue eyes and Mrs. Wilson's eyes were dark brown, almost as dark as Ma'am's, and her hair was very dark brown, while Mr. Wilson's hair was a sort of mixture of colors, not brown, not blond, but somewhere in between. Mrs. Wilson told me that because my hair was very dark brown like my eyes, many people she knew had said I looked enough like her to be her natural son. That made me very happy. Sometimes the Wilsons talked about family resemblances as we sat around the table and I would listen closely. They seemed glad I looked enough like Mrs. Wilson to be her real son. And I was glad, too. More and more I wanted to belong to a family and it made me feel good to look like one of them.

Mrs. Wilson was kind of fat, and her face didn't look much like I remember Ma'am's looking. I wondered why she was fat, but couldn't ask. Then when I went to church with her one Sunday and looked around, I saw that all of the women were shaped pretty much like her. Mrs. Wilson wore different clothes when we went to church, sometimes twice a week. But Mr. Wilson, who wore overalls even when he went to town, also changed into something else when he went to church on Sunday evenings.

After the excitement of my first real Christmas, the following few weeks weren't very interesting. Many of the toys I had been given for Christmas had been broken and Mrs. Wilson had read to me all the books old Mrs. Wilson had brought from the orphans' home. Mrs. Wilson said she hoped it would snow so we could build a snowman in the front yard. Mr. Wilson said he hoped it wouldn't snow because it was hard on the livestock, especially the milking cows. One day Mrs. Wilson sat down with me and showed me on a big calendar that I had been living with them since April, almost a year.

I was still a little timid around Mr. Wilson. At times he would be very kind to me but at other times he almost seemed happy to punish me, especially if I sassed or disagreed with him. I wanted to ask him why he spanked me so much, but I knew I could expect him to say that he would always punish me if I misbehaved.

By now I was really tired of visiting old Mrs. Wilson at the orphans' home. How I hated it. She lived in that building where Ma'am and Mrs. Collins had left me that dark night when I was four. And I knew I would never, never forget it. In fact, I hated to be anywhere near the orphans' home. Each time we went I wondered if I would be left there, that maybe the Wilsons didn't want me after all but hadn't told me. I always asked if I could stay at the farm and not have to visit old Mrs. Wilson and her daughter again, but I always had to go along. The three women would talk while we waited for Mr. Wilson to cut the boys' hair. The best thing about these visits was when they were over and we could leave to go back to the farm where I was beginning to feel at home and where I could hug the collie who licked my hands and liked me to pet him, and where the black barn cat purred when I held her on my lap and stroked her.

One night after supper Mrs. Wilson started to talk, looking directly at me. There was no smile on her face, she seemed dead serious, and I was afraid she was going to tell me they had finally decided to return me to the orphans' home.

"Billy Joe," she said slowly and carefully, "how would you like to be our little boy and never again have to live at the orphans' home?"

She gave me a little smile and, when I turned to look at Mr. Wilson, I saw that he, too, was smiling. I was pretty certain they were not making a joke at my expense.

"We'd like to make you our real son an change your name to ours so you will become a member of our family, and Mr. Wilson and I will become your daddy and mother."

"You mean I could stay here forever?"

"That's exactly what she's sayin son," Mr. Wilson said.

He almost never called me "Billy Joe," not since the first week or so of the first spring I spent with them. He usually called me "son" and I liked it when he called me that. And I had been wanting to call them "Mother" and "Daddy."

What was happening was what I had worried about, hoped for, and looked forward to. At the same time this conversation came as a surprise. I had no answer ready. My mind was full of questions.

Did this mean I wouldn't be a Tolliver any more? That I wasn't supposed to think of Ma'am and Jefferson any more? That I was to forget all about my life in Cedar Creek? I wasn't sure I could really do that.

The Wilsons were looking directly at me, waiting for my answer. I could tell this was no time to ask any questions, argue, or say anything funny. And I had been thinking about this moment ever since Jefferson had told me how the whole adoption business was supposed to work. He had said, "If somebody wants to adopt you, let em. Being adopted by some nice folks is a hell of a lot better than bein in this place."

I knew I was taking too long to answer, so I swallowed and said, "Yes, ma'am, I'd like to be your boy."

Mrs. Wilson's eyes were moist, "We so hoped you would!" I saw that Mr. Wilson's smile filled his whole face.

"That's good!" Mr. Wilson said. "Right after breakfast in the morning we'll get ready an go up to Cherokee, to tha county courthouse. We'll have to see tha judge an sign tha papers. An we wanna change yer name to Rex Wilson. Would you like to be called 'Rex'?"

"Can't I still be 'Billy Joe'?"

"Well, we thought about that but decided it would be best to just start all over with a new name. You won't be 'Billy Joe Tolliver' any more. You'll be 'Rex LaVerne Wilson,'" Mrs. Wilson said. "We think you'll like that name when you've had it a while. And you'll call us 'Mother' and 'Daddy.'"

That night I lay in my bed saying over in my head, "Rex LaVerne Wilson," "Rex LaVerne Wilson," trying to get used to it. I really hated the "LaVerne" part. I wondered if Ma'am would mind. Would I ever see her again? I was scared, happy and sad all at the same time.

The next morning we climbed the courthouse steps together. I was between the Wilsons, holding their hands. It felt funny because I had never held their hands like that before. We went straight down a long hall to a door that had a name printed on it in big gold letters. Mrs. Wilson read the words to me: "JAMES HARDESTY, COUNTY JUDGE." Mr. Wilson opened the door and we went into a small room. The woman behind the desk said, "You must be the Wilsons. Judge Hardesty is expecting you. Go right in."

The judge was sitting in his black leather chair behind a desk covered with papers. The very first thing I noticed about him was his huge smile, not off to one side, but right in the middle going all across his face. He struggled out of his chair and I could see that he was really fat and the buttons on his vest looked like they could pop right off. He grunted some, leaned over the desk, and shook hands with the Wilsons. The smile never left his face.

"And this is the youngun you folks wanta take as your own? Well, son, I'm mighty proud to meet you an I'm ready to get on with the paperwork."

He patted me on the head. Then he sat down with a grunt, settled into his chair, and handed some papers across for Mr. and Mrs. Wilson to sign.

Watching them write on the papers, I remembered how Ma'am had signed papers for Mr. Collins. Then the judge signed them, mashed each of them with a thing he called a "seal," put one set of the papers in a long envelope, and gave it back to Mr. Wilson. Then he turned to me, shook my hand, and said, "I hope you realize, young man, how fortunate you are that these good folks wanta give you their good name an a good home."

What I realized was that I was Rex LaVerne Wilson now, not Billy Joe Tolliver any more. This would take some trouble getting used to. People who knew me as "Billy Joe Tolliver" would also need to get used to my new name. And another thing: I had to get used to calling the Wilsons "Mother" and "Daddy" instead of "Mr. Wilson" and "Mrs. Wilson." I was sure I could manage that and for the rest of my life call them "Mother" and "Daddy."

Leaving the courthouse a little after noon, we headed straight down the street, had hamburgers for dinner to celebrate, and then started home. All the way my new mother and daddy called me "Rex" and had me call them "Mother" and "Daddy," "just to get used to saying it," Mother said, and we laughed and had a happy time together.

The rest of the day I kept thinking: is this all there is to it? I still felt that I didn't really belong. Wasn't I supposed to feel that way by now? My new mother and daddy treated me the way they always had when I had called them "Mr. and Mrs. Wilson." Nothing had really changed. I still felt a little scared of my daddy and what he could do to me. And they didn't hold my hands any more or hug me or kiss me and say that they loved me as I expected them to do. Ma'am and Pap had done that. Weren't real parents supposed to do that? It was quite clear, however, that Mrs. Wilson meant to be a real mother to me, to take Ma'am's place. And while she didn't tell me she loved me, I believed that the longer I lived with her and the better we got to know one another the more like a mother she would become.

I made up my mind that I would try my best to start my life all over, to pretend that everything that had happened to me up to that day hadn't happened at all. I would try to forget Ma'am and Pap, Bonnie, Jefferson, Mr. Collins, Mrs. Tidwell, the orphans' home. I was determined to do my best to be a good son to my new parents.

I continued to be bothered some by our meeting with Judge Hardesty. It had all happened so quickly and nothing had really changed. Mainly, I guess what bothered me was what had not happened, something I needed but didn't get. My new mother had smiled at me after the papers were signed and she had given me a little squeeze but she hadn't held me tight, kissed me on the cheek, and told me she loved me. Ma'am would have and that's what I really wanted more than anything in the whole world. I was pretty sure that Mr. Wilson had agreed to adopt me because that's what Mrs. Wilson wanted. I think she really wanted to be a mother and here I was needing a mother.

I was left with the feeling that I was supposed to be happy to be adopted and never to have to go back to the orphans' home. I knew I should love, respect, and be grateful to my new parents, as Judge Hardesty had suggested, but that was hard and would take time. I liked my new mother and daddy but the adoption still had not proved to me that I was a real member of their family. ✦

Chapter 7

One day Mother asked me if I would like to sleep on the daybed in the front room. I said, yes, I would. It was very nice, I thought, that Mother had asked me and hadn't just told me that she was moving my bed. I helped her move out of their bedroom the baby bed I had been sleeping in. We rolled it into a corner of the dining room where it would be easy for Daddy and me to carry it out to the car so it could be taken back to the orphans' home. Mother didn't explain why we were moving my sleeping place except to say that I had grown into a big boy, able to sleep alone, now that I was their son. To me it meant that I didn't have to sleep in a bed meant for a baby and that they wouldn't be watching everything I did night and day.

Nearly every day that spring and summer, Mother and I spent time together, "getting ready for school," she would say. By the first of August I was reading first and second grade reading books from cover to cover, often aloud to Mother and Daddy. We even worked on penmanship. From talk I heard at the dinner table, Mother had managed to get hold of every textbook being used by the first and second graders at Round Grove School. And well before I actually started to school in September, I had been through all of the books at last once.

Mother was a good teacher, taking care that I didn't lose interest. Reading was what I liked best to do and Mother made sure I never ran out of storybooks.

By now I was getting used to my new home, and except for an occasional dream, I never thought of myself as "Billy Joe Tolliver." Both Mother and Daddy called me "son" and I liked that. When Daddy called me "Rex" it was to scold me or punish me, often spanking me with his big hand. To hear him growl or shout my name made me feel cold all over.

Some of my whippings were for little things I didn't feel guilty about. But there were times when I knew I had broken a rule and deserved what Daddy called "correction." Once during the summer, Daddy stormed into the dining room where Mother and I had been working on a penmanship lesson, a long, leather bridle rein in his hand. Something had angered him, I could tell, because he stomped over to where I was sitting and glared threateningly down at me.

"Rex," he said loudly, "did you gather the eggs yet?" Of course, I knew exactly what he meant; gathering the eggs from the hen house down by the barn was my part of the evening chores and I had been doing it for several weeks.

"Yes, sir," I answered, too afraid to look him directly in the eyes. I tried to focus on where the belt would have been if he had been wearing his Sunday clothes.

"Did you shut and fasten tha door to tha chicken pen after you got the eggs?" His voice was now more harsh, more terrifying.

"Yes, sir," I mumbled in fear, knowing from experience what was about to happen.

"Don't you lie to me. Them hens is all outta their pen cause you went off without shuttin the door. I ain't gonna have you lying ta me and I ain't gonna let you lie yerself outta somethin you was supposed ta do and didn't."

He yanked me off my chair, held my left arm in a vise grip with his left hand, and began swinging the rein at my bottom and upper legs. It hurt a lot and each time the leather strap hit me I could feel a welt rising and each time it wound around my backsides, it hurt more than the ones before. I didn't scream because I was sure that, if I did, he would only hit harder. But I cried loudly, pleading for him to stop, trying to assure him that I would never leave the door open or lie to him, that I would never do it again.

When at last he had finished, Daddy released me and I stumbled back to where I had been sitting. Through my tears I glanced at Mother. All during my punishment, she had said nothing, and had remaining seated at the table, looking at the floor. But now I could see the tears in her eyes through my own.

Fortunately, most of my soreness had disappeared by the next morning and a kind word from Daddy helped me better understand that, to him, I had no one to blame but myself for getting into trouble. Doing schoolwork with Mother, I was sure, would make me feel better.

My folks showed no sign that they knew how troubled I was about entering first grade as I counted the days until I would start at Round Grove School. I often lay awake at night thinking about it, wondering and worrying. I wondered if the kids at the school would tease me or make fun of me, like the church kids did, because I had been adopted from the orphans' home. Some of the boys at church still called me "Billy Joe" or just plain "Tolliver," even though they all knew that my name had been changed several months ago. They seemed to be having fun at my expense and I hoped they would stop taunting me for something I couldn't do anything about. I hoped the kids at Round Grove would be friendlier.

Some thoughtless word by Mother or Daddy or the hired man at the dinner table could make me break out in goose pimples or become silent or lose my appetite. Once at supper, Daddy whipped me with a bridle rein because I had filled my plate with food but then couldn't eat it. Giving me no chance to explain, he whipped me until I cried, then sent me to bed.

Before he went to work the next morning, Daddy made a hole in one end of the bridle rein and hung it beside the dining room door in plain sight of everyone. He told me it would stay there as a reminder that he would use it on me if I didn't eat my meal and if I needed to be "corrected" for something. He had already whipped me at least a half-dozen times for talking back to him or for finding fault with something he said, and those whippings were almost as hard as the first one I got with the bridle rein. He seemed to hit me hardest if he thought I talked back to him or if I disagreed with him. After a while, I figured out what he meant by "correction." What I thought of as telling my side when I disagreed with him, he considered sassing. It made him mad.

"I'll learn you to contradict me," he would growl as he jerked the rein off the nail with his right hand while firmly gripping my arm with his left. Sometimes the red welts on my legs didn't go away for three or four days.

Neither Mother nor Daddy understood how my worries kept me awake far into the night and why bad dreams made me grind my teeth so loud that sometimes I would awaken the two of them in the next room. They never asked if anything was bothering me; they just scolded me, telling me to stop grinding my teeth.

They didn't know that I was worried all the time. How could I explain to them that I was afraid they had become tired of me or so disappointed in me, that they were sorry they had decided to adopt me? I didn't know how to tell them. The words wouldn't come.

Once, on the way home from Uncle Earl and Aunt Hazel Williams' house, I told Mother and Daddy that my cousin Eldon, who was two years older, said he thought it was peculiar that I was the only one of his cousins who didn't have light hair and blue eyes. He had told me that, just because my mother was a Williams, that did not make me a real member of the Williams family because I was not related by blood and not really her son.

"He didn't mean nothin by it," Daddy said, brushing it off. "I'm sure he didn't mean it the way it sounded," Mother added gently. I could tell she was trying to make me feel better. But I didn't.

"Some kid's always makin fun of me cause I'm adopted! Billy Melrose said he heard tell you were probably gonna take me back to the orphans' home!" I blurted out my worst fear, tears beginning to roll down my cheeks, my lower lip out.

"You'll just have to learn not to pay any attention to kids who say things like that. They don't know what they're talkin about," Daddy said, adding in a loud voice, "an ya can stop that bawling like a little baby, an suck in yer lower lip before somebody steps on it!"

"We're not gonna take you back to the orphans' home an no one is gonna take you away from us," Mother said, a sad and tired look on her face, her eyes misty. "You have nothin to worry about, son," she said. "And please don't cry, we understand."

I heard what she said, but I couldn't be sure she really meant it. I couldn't forget that I had trusted Ma'am and she and Mr. Collins had left me at the orphans' home. And I had heard some people warning my new mother and daddy that they had better be careful or I would end up in the penitentiary or that reform school down at Paul's Valley because adopted kids seemed to turn out bad, stole from their folks and other people, and never amounted to anything. Talk like that hurt me worse than anything I could think of, like somebody had hit me hard in my belly when I was least expecting it. All I wanted in the world was to be accepted, to be like all the other kids, to feel like I belonged.

Around the middle of August, Grandpa Pete Wilson, who was on the school board and was well liked by everybody, asked me if I would like to go with him to take a look at the inside of the schoolhouse. He said the school board had hired a man to come in and give the place a good cleaning before school started and he needed to see if the work had been done to his satisfaction.

It was hot and humid that morning as Grandpa unlocked the front door and we went inside. The large, almost square schoolroom reeked of ancient sawdust sweeping-compound, the kind that leaves the floor greasy, and the musty dust that comes out of nowhere lay heavily on everything. Cobwebs were all over and I reckoned the room had been closed since school had let out in the spring.

"I don't believe that ole boy has come to clean up yet," Grandpa said. "It don't look like anything's been done around here." He ran a finger across the thick layer of dust lying on top of the first desk he came to. "Well, he's got about a week yet so I'll come back again in a few days. But this place has got to be cleaned up before you kids start showin up the day after Labor Day. Now let's take a look outside. There was a lot to be done there, too."

Grandpa Pete seemed to be clamping down hard on his pipe stem as he looked carefully at where school kids would be running around in a few days. Dead limbs had fallen from some of the blackjack trees; one was lying on top of the teetertotters and would have to be taken away. There was tall grass all over the baseball diamond and ragweeds, pig-weed, and Russian thistles growing everywhere else. There were lots and lots of sandburs, especially in the trails between the toilets and the schoolhouse.

"Don't worry about this," Grandpa said, "somebody's gonna come an mow around here a day or two before school starts."

Sometime in late August, just before school started, Mother and Daddy and I went shopping at Cherokee where they bought me several pairs of blue bib overalls and sever-al blue cotton shirts like Daddy wore. They bought most of my clothes—at least those that showed—at the J.C. Penney store. My Big Mac overalls had two big pockets in the back and one big, wide pocket on the bib part that was made into several little pockets: one with a snap on it and one that I could put a watch in. There was a narrow little pocket for my pencil, even. Big Mac brand overalls were made with a buttonhole clear up to the top so that if I ever got a watch it could be tied to my overalls with a shoestring so I wouldn't lose it.

My big red dinner pail was also brand-new. Daddy bought it at Baxter's Hardware store in Aline. It could hold more than enough stuff to eat for a kid my size. Mother made sure I understood that I was not to eat any of the food until noon when all the kids got out of school for an hour. She said that if I ate part of my dinner during morning recess I would be starving to death by the time I got home in the afternoon.

Now that school was almost ready to begin, I could think of little else. But something had happened, shortly after harvest several weeks before, that troubled me deeply. No matter how I tried, I could not put it out of my mind.

At breakfast one morning Daddy told Mother that he needed to go to the John Deere place in Cherokee to have some welding done on the tractor hitch.

"Unless you got something planned for him, I'll take Rex with me. I don't know how long it's gonna take and if we ain't back by dinner time, go ahead and eat; don't wait fer us. We can always get somethin to eat up there."

It had gotten to be dinner time that day and the tractor parts still hadn't been fixed. "Well, son, " Daddy said as we left the welding shop, "it's past our dinner time an them parts ain't gonna be ready for at least another hour, maybe longer. How'd ya like to get somethin to eat?"

"I sure would," I said, absolutely delighted and suddenly feeling hungry. "Can I get a hamburger?"

"I imagine so. Let's go to that place over there where that

there bluebird sign is hangin. I reckon they've got a hamburger in there that's about your size."

Everybody in Alfalfa County ate their dinner at noon and it was past one o'clock, but as we walked up to the Blue Bird Café and opened the screen door, we could see that some people were still sitting at the counter. They all swiveled their heads to see who we were. One man, with red dust all over his blue overalls, who looked like he had spent the morning on his tractor in the field, grinned when he recognized Daddy. His lips were thin and his chin almost touched his nose. "Howdy, Frank," he said cheerfully, "you an that there boy kin set up here with me if ya want to."

"How ya doin, El?" Daddy answered. "We'll just do that." From the way they spoke I figured they were friends. I climbed up onto the stool between Daddy and his friend.

"Say, Frank, where'd ya get that youngun?" El asked. "I ain't seen him before. He one of your hired hands?"

"Nope, this here's ma son, Rex. I guess ya didn't know I had me a boy. Me an Erma got him when he was four."

Daddy's loud words made me tremble. Knowing what was coming I silently begged, please, not again. The man with the funny thin rubbery lips looked me over, head to toe as I sat looking down at the shiny counter. "Seems like I did hear somebody say you folks had adopted a boy. Ya get him up at Helena?"

"Yeah," Daddy said, "got him from the orphans' home up there. He had just come in when we first saw him. Me an Erma was up there one Sunday visitin my mother; she's the head matron at tha home, ya know." It hurt so much to hear grownups talking this way about me, as if I were a cow or a horse, something to be "got," setting me apart from ordinary kids whose mothers and daddys were their real folks. I was sure Daddy didn't have the slightest idea how I felt or he wouldn't have just sat there and talked to this man about things I didn't think were anybody else's business.

"Well," the man said, "I really gotta hand it to ya, Frank. It's a mighty fine thing yer a doin fer this here youngun, givin him a fine home an everthing like that there. Did ya go ahead an change his name ta yers or jus leave it the way it was?"

"Yeah, we give him a new name, got us a lawyer, an went through the court an everything. You could say we legally adopted him."

I wanted to run away and hide until Daddy was ready to go home. But I knew I couldn't do that or I'd be in serious trouble and probably get a whipping. I wished as hard as I could that the waitress would hurry and come and take our order or bring the man his dinner so he could start eating and maybe stop talking about me. The man turned to me again.

"My name is 'Elmer Ferguson,' son. Folks round here always call me 'El' fer short." Turning my head, I looked up at his strange, unshaven, unwashed, caved-in face, and tried to give him the smile I knew he expected. He stuck out his right hand and I shook it because that was what Daddy had taught me to do. His hand was big and brown and looked greasy and dirty. His palm was rough with callouses. I finally realized that Mr. Ferguson looked funny because he didn't have any teeth. Not a tooth in his head that I could see. I had never seen anybody without teeth and I couldn't help staring. No wonder he looks so funny, I thought, and I was glad Daddy didn't look like that.

As we waited for the waitress to come, they stopped talking about me and began to talk about the weather. For a long time I sat there, saying nothing, not looking at either of them. Over my head, Daddy and Mr. Ferguson talked about how dry it was, how the pastures were all dried up and how poor was the wheat crop everybody had had that summer. I had heard it all many times before. I sat quietly and listened to more than I wanted to know about the wheat harvest and the falling cattle and hog markets. With the other ear I listened to rattling dishes and the banging of pots and pans back in the kitchen. I gradually began to feel better and to feel hungry again, because they were no longer talking about me. So I took a good and close look around the café.

There was no doubt that Mr. Ferguson had been in the café for a while before we got there because there was a full ashtray on the counter in front of him and he had already been served a big, white crockery mug of coffee. I figured he had probably already given the waitress his order. I wished she would come to take ours. His dirty, shapeless Mexican straw hat, the kind Daddy wore when he was working in the field, was pushed back on his head, and I could tell he spent a lot of time in the sun. I could see exactly how far down on his head he wore his hat because about halfway up his forehead his skin turned from brown to almost white. Daddy's face had the same line on his forehead, except he never got tanned, and the bottom half of his face would burn in the summer.

As the two men talked, I kept hoping the waitress would hurry up and ask us what we wanted for dinner. By now I was starving for a hamburger with catsup, mustard, pickle, and onion on it, and I could almost taste the cooking smells coming from the grill down at the far end of the counter. I knew it was rude to stare at people, especially if they were crippled or if something was wrong with them they couldn't help, so I tried not to look at Mr. Ferguson's mouth with no teeth in it. But I did keep watching him out of the corner of my eye while I read all the menus and posters and announcements on the wall behind the counter and those that were thumbtacked to the wall behind us. There were notices of farm sales, and Coca-Cola signs, and a Pepsi Cola sign that said you could buy a twelve-ounce bottle for a nickel, and that was a lot. According to one fly-specked poster, the Cherokee High School Senior Class was putting on a play the

14th and 15th of April. The poster was ripped here and there, yellowed with age, dirty with greasy fingerprints. This was August. April had been a long time ago. I wondered why they didn't take it down and put up something else. On a wooden shelf across the counter from my stool there were coffee pots and cups and lots of clean drinking glasses. A blackboard like we had at the orphans' home, except that it was a lot smaller, hung like a picture on the wall above the coffee pots. Somebody had written on it with chalk: "Special of the day— chicken-fried steak, mashed potatoes, gravy, green beans, coffee: 30 cents."

At long last the waitress brought Mr. Ferguson's order: two big hamburgers and a quarter of a thick apple pie. She filled his empty coffee mug, then, turning to Daddy and me, she asked, "What're you men havin?"

"I want a hamburger like that one," I said, and pointed to Mr. Ferguson's plate. The cook had put everything on it that I wanted on mine.

"An whatta you gonna have to drink, sonny?" she asked.

"Gimme a bottle of strawberry pop," I answered.

"An what'd you like, mister?" She smiled at Daddy.

"I'm gonna have that there chicken-fried steak special," he said, "an I'll take a bottle of cherry pop if ya got it. You kin keep the coffee."

"I got it," she said, smiling again. "You fellas gonna have some dessert with that?"

"Yeah," Daddy said. Turning to me, he asked, "What'd you like, son?"

"Ya got any ice cream?" I asked hopefully. The waitress nodded. I didn't get ice cream at the farm very often, and when I did it was homemade and soft. It would be a real treat to buy ice cream in a cone that I could lick. "Can I have an ice cream cone, Daddy?"

"Sure, son." Then to the waitress he said, "What kinda ice cream ya got?"

"We got vanilla, chocolate, an strawberry."

"I'll take a strawberry cone," I said. Daddy told he he would like a dish of plain vanilla ice cream to go with his cherry pie.

I looked over my shoulder at Mr. Ferguson and saw that he had almost finished one of his two hamburgers. It was a complete mystery to me how he could eat a big hamburger like that without any teeth to chew with. I guess he knew I was watching him eat because pretty soon he looked right at me and grinned, his toothless mouth full of mashed bread and meat. "How can ya eat that hamburger without any teeth?" I asked in amazement.

"It ain't so hard as ya might think," he said. "I jus gum it. I just sorta waller it around in my mouth til it gets soft enough an down it goes. I kin chew dern near as well as a man that's got all his teeth, like yer dad there." He could probably see the disbelief showing in my face but he nodded and grinned again before he turned back and finished his dinner. My eyes kept following his mouth. By rolling his tongue he moved the food from one side to the other as his lower jaw moved up and down and sidewise between his loose, flat lips. Then, running his pink tongue between his gums and lips to get out all the food, he would swallow. When the waitress brought our food, he asked her for more coffee.

While waiting for his coffee to cool, Mr. Ferguson unsnapped the pocket of his overalls, pulled out a can of Prince Albert and a little orange-and-black packet of ciga-rette papers, the same kind that Pap used. Within a half minute he had rolled a fat, wet cigarette, twisted it with both ends, and stuck it between his lips. I wondered how long it took him to learn to keep the tobacco inside the paper so the cigarette would hold together long enough for him to get it smoked. From a front pocket he took a wooden match, the kind that Mother used in the kitchen, and struck it on the underside of the counter, lit his homemade cigarette, took a deep drag, blew out the flame, and dropped the smoking match onto the floor. From the way the floor was littered with half-burned matches, it looked like a lot of other people sitting at the counter had done the same thing Mr. Ferguson had.

Before Daddy and I had finished eating, Mr. Ferguson got off his stool, belched, turned to me, and grinned. I guessed he was ready to leave. "Well, Frank," he said to Daddy, "it's shore been good ta see ya." To me he said, "Son, yer one mighty lucky boy to end up with Frank and Erma Wilson as yer folks." I stopped chewing but just sat there on my stool, looking up at him. I knew what he meant and I agreed with him but I didn't like hearing him say it. My eyes followed him as he walked to the end of the counter, paused at the cash register, and paid the man who was standing there waiting to take his money. Even though I was still feeling bad, I had to smile when he took a free toothpick, stuck it in the corner of his mouth, pushed open the screen door, and walked out of the café. I never forgot that day at the Blue Bird Café and I never wanted to go there again. ✦

Chapter 8 ⎯⎯⎯⎯⎯⎯⎯⎯⎯⎯⎯⎯⎯⎯⎯⎯⎯⎯⎯ ⟪

School always started on the first day after Labor Day, and so what Mother called my "formal education" began on Tuesday, September 6, 1932, when, barely six years old, I entered the first grade at Round Grove School. I would be walking to school by myself to meet my new teacher, Miss Mary Francis Downing, and a lot of other kids, aged six to fifteen, who would also be walking from all directions to the school, which started at eight o'clock in the morning.

I got out of bed earlier than usual that morning. I was a big boy now, I thought, because big boys were school boys. I was so excited I could hardly eat my Post Toasties. I liked Post Toasties because the colorful big box they came in had Mickey Mouse cutouts that kids could make into toys.

I was sad that Dean Frye, who had lived with his family across the road and down a little ways south from our place, had moved away with his family in late August. We had been looking forward to being real school boys and we had made big plans, as early as June, to walk the mile and a half to Round Grove together.

Not wanting to be late on the first day, and because my folks didn't know how long it would take me to walk the mile and a half, I decided to start plenty early. By shortly after seven o'clock that morning I was ready to leave home. Mother gave me final instructions.

"Be sure to keep your shoes tied," she cautioned. "They won't let you go barefooted, so keep your shoes on all the time. An don't forget to bring your dinner bucket home with you after school. Don't stop and play with the other kids. You come right home."

"Have you got your pencil in your pocket?" she asked. "Have you got your tablet?" She gave me a quick big hug and a kiss on the cheek, patted me gently on the head, and said goodbye, and I headed down the short driveway to the road. Before I got over the first small hill south of our place, I turned around several times to see if Mother was still watching with shiny little tears in her eyes.

It wasn't until I got down the road a ways that I started to think about why she seemed sad to see me go that morning. Maybe she was as worried as I was about what I would be facing on my first day in school, my first day away from her. Maybe she would be lonely. Since I had come to live with my new parents, Mother and I had always been together around the house and the farm, trading at the store in Aline, going to church. Now, for the second time in my life, I was in a new situation where I was completely on my own. And I was scared. A mile and a half was a long way for a six-year-old kid to walk all by himself, especially when he was scared about what the other kids would say.

From my house I headed straight south toward Round Grove. I knew the way and wasn't scared of taking a wrong turn, getting lost, or being run over by a car. All I had to do was walk straight ahead until I got to the schoolhouse.

When I reached the rutted dirt driveway that led down to the Fryes' vacant house, remembering my friend Dean almost made me cry. As though wishing would bring him back, I stopped and stood there for a minute looking down their old driveway where weeds were starting to come up in the tracks. It made no difference to him that I was adopted. He just liked me. We were good pals. I had counted on starting to school with him, walking the mile and a half with him. But Dean wasn't standing by the Frye mailbox waiting for me that morning. Well, I thought, there's nothing I can do about it. I'll just have to work things out by myself.

Ragweed, gourds, sunflowers, sandburs, and cheat grass grew thick along the sides of the road where they were in no danger of being eaten by livestock or run over by cars. Some of the sunflowers grew so high I couldn't see the tops of the barbed wire fences on either side of the road. From the little sand hill just south of where the Fryes used to live I could see about a mile south down the road, at least as far as the grove of locust trees that marked the edge of Grandpa Pete Wilson's farm. It was just south of the Bailey place on the west side of the road, a little ways south of where the Finneys lived.

I could see the familiar tall poles of the telephone line that ran east and west along the crossroad that went straight to Aline if you turned right and went four miles without turning. If you turned left and went a mile east you would be at the Brethren Church, which Mother and I attended every Sunday and where I had gone to Bible school during the summer.

By the time I got to the locust grove at the north side of Grandpa Pete's farm, I was a little more than halfway to school. By the time I came to Grandpa's house, which was set back from the road on a tree-covered little sand hill, I was less than a quarter of a mile from Round Grove. I looked carefully for Grandpa Pete so I could wave to him but I reckoned he was inside the house.

I loved Grandpa Pete and thought of him as my real grandpa. He never spoke gruffly to me, spanked me, or scolded me, and he was always kind and gentle. Grandpa Pete was quiet and enjoyed sitting by the wood stove on cold winter days patting the little dog that lay curled up on his lap. He

never said much, especially when Grandma Dollie was
around; he just sat there, smoking his pipe and stroking the
little white dog. Grandpa Pete always smelled good because
he smoked that old briar pipe. Sometimes, when he wasn't
holding the little dog, he would hold me on his lap and tell me
stories. One reason I loved him was because he never lost his
temper.

Grandpa Pete didn't have much to say inside the house
because that was Grandma Dollie's territory. In fact, wherever she happened to be, Grandma Dollie was in complete
charge and, unlike Grandpa Pete, she always had plenty to
say. On any subject. The garden, the fruit orchard, the pig-
pen, the livestock. It seemed to me that Grandma Dollie
thought everything belonged to her.

Grandma Dollie was known all over the Round Grove
community. Older people called her "Mrs. Wilson" or "Aunt
Doll." But others, mainly kids who passed her fruit orchard
on their way to and from school and climbed the fence to steal
apples in the fall of the year, referred to her as "Old Lady
Wilson." Just about everybody stayed out of her way, especially kids. She often scolded me, and she still scared me
sometimes the way she had when I had first met her in the
orphans' home, but I had grown to love her, too. In time I had
learned that her scolding, grouchy manner was just her way;
she wasn't mean or mad at me at all. She often fixed me a
slice of fresh-baked bread with butter and marmalade if I
was at her house with Mother and Daddy. "Piecing between
meals," she called it, and said she hoped it wouldn't ruin my
supper. After first spreading butter on the cut end of the loaf,
she would slice it off and finally add the marmalade. I never
saw anyone else do it that way. She would also fry potatoes
for breakfast, something Mother never did. It was always a
special treat for me to have breakfast at Grandpa and
Grandma Wilson's house because I could have all the fried
potatoes I wanted. Just before I started to school, Grandma

Dollie began spending only three days a week at the orphans' home.

At the corner of Grandpa's place, another dirt road ran east and west. When I got there I knew I didn't have much farther to walk. In fact, by then I could see some of the schoolhouse roof and the flag hanging from the flagpole. At this road crossing, just north of Round Grove, I was glad to see the rusty sign hanging on Elza Mills' barbed wire fence at the corner of his field. About the size of a car's license tag, the sign was shaped like an arrow and told people that Enid was thirty-nine miles east. Our neighborhood seemed a little closer to town because of that sign, even if most of the yellow paint had worn off. I especially liked its arrow shape.

Daddy had told me that Round Grove School had been built shortly after the turn of the century. It was on the west side of the road where its playground and outbuildings made a sort of notch in the quarter section of sandy land that Elza Mills farmed. Daddy said it was "school land," and the Nazarene Church and the preacher's house sat on the same quarter. From the school you could see Elza's weathered old gray house and the church buildings through the blackjack trees.

What with the barn and fence on the north side and the little hill on the south that the schoolhouse stood on, and on account of there being a huge blackjack tree on the west end and the road on the east end, the basketball court was laid out sort of in the middle. The court was put there mainly because that was the most level place on the schoolground big enough for it.

From the road and basketball court I climbed up a gentle slope to the front door of the schoolhouse. From the looks of that little hill, I figured that one time somebody had hauled in a lot of hard dirt, maybe from up around McWillie, and spread it all over to keep the ground from blowing right out from under the schoolhouse. Everybody knew there wasn't any hard dirt like that in our part of the county.

Round Grove School sat on what Daddy called "a big pile of blow sand" facing right into the eastern sun. It was a one-room grade school, painted white. Around behind the toilets and coal house was a barbed wire fence, and just inside the fence, on the schoolgrounds, were a dozen or more big black-jack and chinaberry trees.

Although I was familiar with the inside of the school-house, I felt alone and afraid among a schoolyard full of total strangers.

It was already hot when school took up at eight o'clock sharp. Miss Downing rang a bell so we would all know it was time to stop playing and come inside. It was her first year at Round Grove and she didn't know any of the kids or their families, so I figured she felt a little uncomfortable that day. She had parked her black Model A coupe next to the basket-ball court. I wondered if her car had a heater in it. To me it looked a lot like Mr. Collins' car but I didn't mention that to anybody.

After getting the thirty or more kids inside the school-house, the first thing Miss Downing did was to tell us who she was and that she came from Enid. Then she made seat assignments, which took up a lot of time as she sorted us out by name and grade. There were some single desks and some double ones where two kids—either two boys or two girls—were told they would have to sit together. Every desk was old, ugly, splintered, and dirty, and the varnish was worn almost completely off some of the seats. All of the desks were scratched and dented and initials and plus signs and hearts and arrows and dirty words had been carved all over them. My desk was so marred and beat up that I had a hard time finding a smooth place to write on. So I wrote with my tablet under the paper.

A kid named Eddie Talmage and I shared a double desk near the front of the room close to the stove and the slate blackboards. I was glad I got to sit with Eddie. He didn't act like a smart aleck, or a sissy, or anything like that, and sitting with him was a whole lot better than having to sit beside one of the first-grade girls. I didn't know him but could tell right away he was the kind of kid I would like to have for a friend.

Miss Downing put Olive Pritchard and Camilla Tomlin in another double desk right behind Eddie and me. We all faced the front of the room where the American flag, all dusty and old, hung near the ceiling and the big map of the United States on the wall. Oklahoma was colored red and "INDIAN TERRITORY" was printed across it.

Eddie and I sat there grinning at each other. Suddenly Miss Downing's shrill voice snapped at us. "Now just because you two boys sit together doesn't mean you're supposed to play!" The smile disappeared from Eddie's startled face and I knew right away he was as surprised by the teacher's mean words as I was. All we had done was look at each other.

Everybody was sweating, especially us boys in our brand-new overalls that had not yet been washed and still smelled the way I remembered them smelling in the store.

All the windows in the schoolroom were on the south side, and, because the sun shone in through them all day long, we were a lot hotter inside than we would have been out on the playground. Miss Downing kept the front and back doors tightly closed, explaining that she was trying to keep the Nazarene preacher's coon dogs from coming inside after the preacher's children.

When we had all been properly seated, Miss Downing started off the morning with the flag salute, followed by a short Bible reading. Finally, she asked everybody to stand again and join her in singing a song to complete the opening exercises. She called on Melvin Hood to pass out the battered old blue songbooks that were piled in a corner, and we all sang "Swanee River." Mary Rose Clifford, an eighth grader, played the piano. And during all this time Miss Downing never smiled.

There was no relief all morning except at ten o'clock, when we got out for a fifteen-minute recess. Miss Downing said we were not to eat during recess; we were supposed to be going to the toilet and getting a drink of water. Dinner was from twelve to one o'clock. When twelve o'clock finally came, it was with great excitement that I got my red dinner pail from the screened cupboard in a corner of the school's ante-room. My new friend Eddie and I went down to the blackjack trees, where the swings, teeter-totters, and merry-go-round were, to find out what our mothers had sent along in our dinner pails. Inside mine was a peanut butter-and-jelly sand-wich on homemade white bread, wrapped in heavy waxed paper, three oatmeal cookies, and a small orange with a Sunkist label stamped on it. I traded the orange to Eddie for a banana, ate the three oatmeal cookies, and traded the peanut butter-and-jelly sandwich to Mike Tweedy, another first grader, for two sheets of ink paper.

Afternoon recess was also fifteen minutes and it started at two-thirty. Most of the rest of the day was spent in getting acquainted and in getting our study assignments for the next day. Miss Downing gave me a note to give my folks about what books and supplies they needed to buy as soon as they could get to Carmen. She said we could find everything at Fowler's Drug Store. In her shrill voice, Miss Downing care-fully instructed us to bring an orange stick to school so that we could keep our fingernails clean. She explained what an orange stick was by taking one of them out of her purse to show us, and said we could buy them at the drug store.

Even though it was hot that day, Miss Downing was wearing a wool dress and a pair of black leather gloves. Her hair was the color of carrots and she had powdered her face with light-colored makeup like I had seen back in the spring on the face of Mother's Aunt Norah, who had been lying in her casket when we went to her funeral over by Pond Creek. Miss Downing never once smiled, and as the day went on and on she seemed to become more and more nervous. She talked in a high tone of voice that I didn't like very much. I whispered to Eddie that she sounded kind of like a screech owl. He thought that was funny and whispered back that was just what he had been thinking.

By the time school let out at four o'clock, Miss Downing seemed pretty worn out standing there in the front of the room, looking kind of wilted and with big sweat stains under her arms. I felt a little sorry for her because I had seen my mother look like that sometimes. When she told us it was time to go home, the kids burst through the front door in a kind of stampede and headed off in all directions.

I was nearly home before I realized that no one had said anything all day long about my being adopted out of the orphans' home. ✦

Chapter 9 ⟶

Bugs, especially gnats, were bad in the fall in Alfalfa County, and they gave me a lot of trouble when I walked to school and back. Gnats swarmed around my head and got into my eyes, my ears, and my nose. Mother said that maybe they were attracted by the sickly sweet-smelling Brilliantine oil I had to wear on my hair to help train it to grow so it could be combed straight back like Daddy and his two older brothers combed theirs. I hated to have to comb my hair that way because it didn't grow that way naturally. And I felt silly, because, since my hair wouldn't lie down and there were corners on my head, my hair would never look the way Daddy wanted it to. But the worst part of the whole hair business was not the homemade haircuts Daddy gave me with his head clippers or the Brilliantine oil that he bought at the barbershop. Much worse was the skullcap Mother made for me from the top of one of her old black silk stockings. Daddy made me wear it to bed every night to train my hair to grow straight back. I was so ashamed of that thing it made me sick to have anybody see me wearing it. Daddy said I ought not complain, that he had worn a skullcap like that when he was a boy and he didn't mind it at all. He said wearing the cap worked for him and it would work for me. All I had to do was keep wearing it until my hair was trained to grow like his. He figured it would take about six months.

But gnats weren't the only problem I had when I walked to Round Grove School and back. Every time we got a good rain there were mudholes in the road. There was an enormous one about a quarter of a mile south of our house that got deeper and deeper every time a car or wagon drove through it. At the same time, it grew wider and wider as drivers made new ruts to keep their cars from getting stuck while straddling the old ones and trying to keep their engines from getting wet and drowning out. That mudhole was a special problem for me because I couldn't walk through it on the way to or from school without getting myself muddy. I was sure to get a whipping if I came home with my shoes and socks wet. So I walked close to the fence where the sandburs and cheat grass were thickest but where it wasn't muddy. Of course, I could have climbed over the barbed wire fence and walked in the edge of somebody's field but I had learned that I could tear my overalls or cut myself on the barbed wire if I wasn't mighty careful. Sometimes I didn't get all the sandburs and cheat grass stickers out of my socks and Mother would have to pick them out on washdays. But I figured she knew how they got in my clothes and that it wasn't my fault. She never scolded me about it.

Most of the time the road was dry and dusty and, unless I carelessly stepped into loose sand that hadn't blown away, I wouldn't get dirt in my shoes. I usually didn't have to face blowing dust and sand on the way to school. And because I wasn't very big it took me less time to walk back home because by late afternoon the wind was blowing pretty hard. More often than not I walked with blowing sand all the way home. I felt lucky because the wind was at my back.

Even with the wind and blowing sand, there was something about the road that fascinated me. Every day I found broken glass, rusty screws, and old nails in the blown-out places that I hadn't seen before. I reckoned the screws and nails had worked themselves loose from wagons while they were bumping along the old road. Of course, that didn't explain all the broken glass I kept seeing, some of it so old it had turned a purple color. One time I found a silver—I thought it was silver—Belgian coin in the road. It had a 1911 date on it and I reasoned that it could have been picked up by a soldier who had been overseas during the World War. I wondered if it had been left behind by some kid who had taken it from home to show off at school and had lost it through a hole in his pocket.

Most of the broken glass I found was within a quarter of a mile north or south of Finney's house. The people who went to our church, including me, were pretty sure Cecil Finney spent more time with his bootlegging business than he did with farming.

Some people used to live across the road from Grandma and Grandpa south of Finney's place, but by the time I came they were long gone. Even their house was gone. One time I climbed the fence and went over there. I found a cellar that had fallen in, a broken-down old windmill, some iris plants, and several lilac bushes. And there were about a dozen persimmon trees down the hill south of where the house used to be. They were the first persimmon trees I had ever seen. I told Mother and Daddy about the persimmons that were turning yellow. They explained that some people named "Thomas" used to live there and they had probably sent off for the persimmon trees. They said that some outfit in Topeka, Kansas, often advertised in the *Capper's Weekly* that they would send you trees through the mail. Daddy said the trees had to have come from somewhere else. "Persimmon trees just don't naturally grow around here," he said.

Everybody who knew beans at Round Grove knew about the persimmon trees, too, and some of the boys went over there during the noon hour when the persimmons were ripe. They would climb over the barbed wire fence and pick the ripe persimmons from the trees or off the ground where they had fallen after the first hard freeze in November. I learned how good completely ripe persimmons tasted, but I also learned that if the persimmons were even a little bit green, my mouth got all puckered up.

Near the front of the schoolhouse at the end of a concrete walk there was a well with a pipe coming out of the ground with a rusty pump screwed onto it. It looked just like the pump we had at our place hooked up to the windmill down in the middle of the corral that pumped water into the stock tank when the wind blew. I could get a drink out of the school pump only if I could find somebody who would pump the heavy steel handle up and down while I held my cup under the spout. Water would sometimes come out in a big gush, run my cup over, and get my feet and pants legs wet. There was no way to keep from being splattered with water if you were the one who was getting a drink.

If you were the one pumping water and let go the handle before it was pushed all the way down, it could fly up and hit you in the face. Several kids lost some of their teeth that way. Sometimes when the pump hadn't been used for several hours, like the first thing in the morning, it would be dried up and nobody could get any water. When that happened, somebody had to get a bucket of water to prime it from Harry Vealey's stock tank. I learned I couldn't get a drink of water at school just any old time. I liked it better the way we got a drink of water at our house, from a wooden bucket in the kitchen. Mother kept a dipper in the bucket and I could help myself to a drink any time.

A day or so before school started, Daddy had given me a small aluminum cup. He said he had used it as a boy at Round Grove. I'd never seen that kind of cup before and Daddy explained how it worked. "You flatten it out by

squeezin it," he said. "That way you kin carry it in yer overalls pocket." He showed me how I could make it into a cup
that would hold water by taking hold of the bottom with one
hand and pulling up the top with the other. "This is somethin
I'd like you to have fer yer own because it belonged to me
when I was a boy," he said. So I figured that cup was pretty
special because it meant a lot to my daddy.

Some kids brought blue enameled cups to school, like
those I had seen in Young's hardware store over at Aline, but
the ones they brought from home had chips out of them.
Junie Clifford brought a shiny pink enameled cup that he
and his sister Mary Rose drank out of. Some kids didn't bring
cups of any kind. Leonard Tweedy, one of the third graders,
didn't bring a cup to school, even though Miss Downing told
him to bring one. "Well," he told me, "I don't need no cup
when I kin use the hans God give me to get a drink with."
Then he showed me what he meant. He cupped his hands
together something like an open book and caught some water
in them while I pumped. Leonard was pretty good at getting
a drink that way but it didn't work for me at first. There was
never much water left in my hands by the time I got them up
to my mouth or my mouth down to my hands. It took me several tries before I got the hang of it.

Leonard said he figured only girls and sissies like Junie
Clifford had to bring a cup to school to drink out of. "I don't
care what the teacher says, I ain't gonna bring no cup to
school," he said. It wasn't long before I decided he was right
about that. I didn't want him or anybody else to think I was
a sissy so I took my cup home with me one afternoon and left
it in my room in a cigar box under my bed where Daddy
wouldn't find out I wasn't still using it at school. I didn't want
to make him mad over something like that.

It seemed to me that Miss Downing wasn't too happy to
be teaching at Round Grove. Eddie Talmage agreed. He said
she once told his folks she had never lived in the country

where she had to use outdoor facilities but had always lived in Enid where most people had inside bathrooms. Miss Downing said we were to wash our hands after we had gone to the bathroom and before we ate our dinner. But, I wondered, how could we do that when there was no way we could wash our hands unless we held them under the pump spout, the same place we got a drink of water? And we had the same problem washing our hands that we had getting a drink; somebody had to pump for us. I never saw anybody washing with soap at Round Grove and when I got my hands wet the only thing I could do was what all the other boys did: I dried them on my overalls. None of the kids, unless maybe Junie and Mary Rose Clifford, worried to much about keeping their hands clean. Some of the girls may have washed their hands when the boys weren't around to watch, but I don't think the boys ever got their hands wet on purpose. I know I didn't.

Nobody talked much about our toilets, how they were so cold in the winter and they stank awful bad in hot weather. And I never heard anyone complain about the big black flies and different kinds of spiders that lived in there, probably because our school toilets were better than the one-holers most of us were used to using at home. Miss Downing said our school toilets were primitive, then explained what she meant by "primitive."

"We have a sanitation problem here," Miss Downing continued. "We are going to learn to be clean. Cleanliness is next to Godliness. You feel better when you are clean; I know I do. Starting right now, today, you will keep your fingernails clean. That's why I asked your parents to buy an orange stick for each of you." She told us to take our orange sticks out of our pencil boxes and use them. Because several kids still didn't have orange sticks of their own she gave them some out of her desk drawer.

Although she tried, Miss Downing didn't teach us much about sanitation except what we had to read and recite on from our health habits textbook, the same one that explained how important it was to drink eight glasses of water every day. The other important thing I learned from my health book was that all work and no play makes Jack a dull boy. It wasn't long before Miss Downing stopped talking about sanitation. I figured that maybe she just gave up on the whole idea.

As for all work and no play... "What that means," Mother explained at the supper table one night, "is that a person needs to relax once in a while and have fun and not spend all his time workin. That's the reason they have recesses at school."

"But what does it mean by 'dull'?" I asked.

"Well," she answered, "it means that if you just work all the time you get to feelin all tired out, kind of a dull feelin comes over you. Even your head gets tired."

"Oh. I thought 'dull' meant somethin like yer pocket knife bein dull, like it wouldn't cut anything."

After school one afternoon in early October, Twila and Gladys Bailey, Maybelle Finney, and I all happened to leave the schoolhouse at the same time and we found ourselves walking together past Grandpa Pete's place, headed north. This had never happened before. It was a warm and sunny afternoon, the south wind wasn't blowing, the sun was still high in the western sky, and we stopped for a while at the cutout hill just north of Grandpa's house. I discovered girls could be fun to play with, as we all had a good time taking turns sliding down the soft sand on the slope that had been left when somebody dug out the middle of the hill so the road could go through. Because the time just seemed to get away from us, it was later than usual when I got home that day..

The next afternoon Daddy met me as I came out of the front door of the schoolhouse at four o'clock. I looked for our car but it wasn't there, nor was the team and wagon. Daddy was on foot. "I came down so's me and you could walk home together," he said, "sos we kin find out how long it outta take fer you to get home when you don't stop to play someplace." Even though I walked as fast as other kids my size, I had trouble keeping up with him. It wasn't fun to be walking home with Daddy, but we got home well before five o'clock.

"Good time," Daddy said, "maybe a record. Now I want you to try to get home that soon every day. Maybe your mother's never said anything to you, son, but she worries about you when you don't get home when she expects you."

From then on I tried to walk that mile and a half just as fast as we did that afternoon, knowing that if I didn't try hard and get home from school as quickly as I should, I would be in big trouble. And big trouble was getting a whipping with the bridle rein.

On Saturdays my folks and I went to Aline so Mother could do her trading, usually at A. J. Woods' store. Just before we left, she and Daddy loaded up a crate or two of fresh white leghorn eggs and a ten-gallon can of cream that we had separated during the week. They traded the eggs to Mr. Woods for groceries and Daddy sold the cream to Ford's Creamery and Feed Store. When we got to Ford's place on a Saturday afternoon, Mr. Ford or one of his sons unloaded the heavy cream can out of our car and carried it inside. Then, before we went home, Daddy drove by the creamery again, collected a check for the cream, and got the empty, steam-cleaned cream can, which he set back in our Model A between the front and rear seats. Mr. Woods paid Mother what her eggs were worth and she used the credit to get things she had run out of at home, things such as canned peas, compound, flour, and several kinds of breakfast food, especially Post Toasties, which I liked best, and Daddy's favorite, Grape-Nuts Flakes. Though Daddy ate a huge breakfast of chicken-fried steak, two or three fried eggs, and several cream biscuits with thick steak gravy, he would often have a bowl or two of breakfast food before he got up from the table and went outside.

Sometimes when we went to the second picture show on Saturday afternoon, my folks had to hurry to get everything done in town before it was time to start the chores. It depended partly on when it got dark, and often I tried to talk Mother and Daddy into putting off the milking until later on Saturday. They never agreed and we almost always got the cows milked before dark.

Saturday afternoon was also a good time for Mother and Daddy to visit with our neighbors, folks they hadn't seen for a spell and hadn't talked to on the party line. Saturday afternoon in Aline was a special day for all of us, and there was seldom a Saturday that we didn't go to town. We usually left home as soon as we could eat dinner and change into clean clothes.

Daddy and Mother had started to give me an allowance of a nickel a week—only a nickel, no more. One Saturday afternoon I got greedy and asked Daddy for a second nickel and he refused. "One nickel's all you're gonna get," he said. So I found Mother and asked her for a nickel, and she gave it to me. When we got home that day I got a whipping with the bridle rein. It hurt a lot and I cried. "Don't ever do that again," Daddy warned. And I didn't. I never got my nickel before we left home on Saturdays, but only after we got to town and Daddy had parked the car. I guess my folks waited until the last minute because they figured I might lose my nickel if they gave it to me before we left home.

My only other source of pocket money was the nickels and dimes people would press into my hand for singing a song or two. Usually I would save these little windfalls, which Daddy and Mother said I should never ask for, for fireworks or something else my folks approved of. Most of my spending money went to buy Big Little Books because I liked to read when I didn't have anybody to play with and that was most of the time after Dean Frye and his folks moved away.

Going to Enid on Saturday was also special for me. We

didn't go often, partly because Enid was about forty miles away and all but thirteen of the miles were dirt and gravel. But when we did make the hour-long drive over there, my folks would give me an extra dime or fifteen cents for anything I wanted. I usually spent all I had for toys or candy at the Kress five and ten cent store on the southwest corner of the square. I bought my first Life Savers at the Kress store because I couldn't get them in Aline. Sometimes I took a roll of Life Savers to school to prove that I had been to the big city. Eddie Talmage always got some of them but I seldom gave any to anybody else.

One of the strangest things about the Kress store was the drinking fountains at the back. Way at the back. There were two of them, just alike, made of the same white stuff they made public toilets out of. By one of the fountains, a little wooden box sat on the floor for little kids to stand on so they could get a drink without having somebody hold them up to where the water came out.

One time Mother and I were in the Kress store and I got thirsty. It seemed like I was always getting thirsty, especially when we were in Enid and especially if I had been eating candy.

"There's a drinking fountain in the back of the store," Mother said. "Let's go back there and you can get a drink." She walked toward the rear of the store and I followed. Past the glass cases full of all kinds of delicious-looking candy and salted peanuts, past the women's underwear, the shoes, and the hammers and screwdrivers. Finally I saw the two white fountains, almost as tall as I was, in the back of the store. Nobody was getting a drink when we got to them.

"There it is, son, you just stand on the box. Grab that shiny knob there on the side and turn it. Water comes out of that little shiny thing there on the top. Just don't put your mouth on it, and be careful not to get your face all wet."

I wondered why there were two fountains in the store and

when I started to ask she had turned away and was looking at something lying on one of the counters. As I stepped close I could see a little sign on the handle of each of the fountains hanging by a piece of string like pictures on a wall. I could read the signs but they didn't make sense to me. "WHITE" was printed on one, "COLORED" on the other. What didn't make sense to me was that neither of the fountains was colored; they were both white, exactly alike. Because the little wooden box was sitting up against the fountain where the sign said "COLORED," that's the one I drank from. Everything worked just fine, just the way Mother said it would. When I turned the shiny knob on the side the way she had told me to, cool water squirted out gently, in a little stream, just high enough for me to drink. I got all the water I wanted without getting my face wet and was feeling proud of myself.

Suddenly, as I was about to step down, Mother grabbed me from behind, yanked me off the little box, and, as she pulled me away from the fountain, kicked the box over toward the one with the "WHITE" sign hanging on it. "This is the one you're supposed to drink out of!" she scolded. "White folks don't use that other one, it's for colored people."

Later, Mother explained that in Oklahoma white people and colored people weren't the same and that was why we didn't drink out of their water fountains and they didn't drink out of ours. She also said that darkies didn't sit with white people in the picture shows or on trains and busses and didn't eat at the same cafes and restaurants. I don't know how long it would have taken me to find out all that if I hadn't gotten thirsty in the Kress store that day.

But it was clear to me there was no way to tell Mother that I thought it was silly to have two identical fountains in that store. Hadn't I, a white person, been able to get a refreshing drink of cool water from the "colored fountain"? Her fussing made no sense at all. ✦

Round Grove School

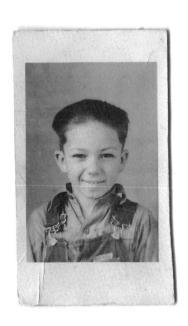

Chapter 10 ————————————————————— ⤙

"Maybelle Finney's got fleas!" I heard it first from Junie Clifford. I could tell he didn't like Maybelle. He said to me, "You'd better not get too close to Maybelle cause she's got fleas." He said Maybelle got them from the coon dogs Cecil Finney kept in their house during the winter. "She shore has got fleas," Junie declared, "an you better watch out or they'll jump off on ya."

"Junie" wasn't his real name; it was Doyle Clifford, Junior. But because he was such a sissy most of us kids called him "Junie." But Junie was about three years older than I, and I figured he probably knew what he was talking about. Besides, he had known Maybelle Finney and her family a lot longer than I had. But why is it, I wondered, that everybody, even the school's biggest sissy, is so mean to Maybelle. When I mentioned it to Mother she told me Maybelle couldn't help being who she was. She said Maybelle was really a very nice girl. Although I didn't think she deserved to be treated mean, I didn't figure I could afford to be too friendly toward her for fear somebody might tease me for being sweet to her..

I would have died if somebody like Marion Hood or Bob

Loudon or some other smart aleck had accused me of liking Maybelle Finney. So it didn't take me long to begin staying as far from her and the Finney place as I could.

The morning and afternoon recesses gave everybody plenty of time to go to the toilet or get a drink of water. Some kids, usually the girls, would play on the teeter-totter or the merry-go-round when it wasn't too cold or wet to be outside. Naturally, us boys let them have that part of the schoolground all to themselves, preferring to play on the other side of the little hill the schoolhouse sat on. On my first day of school, I learned that at Round Grove boys and girls didn't play together unless Miss Downing took charge and asked us all to play Red Rover, a game that wasn't much fun unless everybody played. In bad weather, most of the girls stayed inside the schoolhouse. Some spent their whole recesses at the blackboards drawing pictures of girls with short, turned-up noses, long curly hair, and big eyes and lips like Clara Bow, whom they had seen in posters at the Aline picture show. And every time after recess was over, Miss Downing would ask one of the big boys to erase all the girls' drawings off the blackboards. It seemed to me that she should have made the girls either stop drawing pictures or erase the blackboards themselves. But she never did.

More gray than black, our blackboards were made of real slate and were attached all along the wall on the north side of the schoolroom, across from the windows. During the day we used the blackboards a lot and by late afternoon our felt erasers would be so full of chalk dust that we couldn't clean the blackboards clean.

It wasn't long before Miss Downing began every afternoon to ask two of the younger kids to take all the erasers outside and knock the dust out of them. I figured it was an honor to be asked to dust the erasers. We carried them outside the schoolhouse where the wind would blow away the chalk dust when we slapped them together, then brought them back inside all nice and clean. Sometimes when Eddie Talmage and I got to clean the erasers, we would step back a ways and throw them as hard as we could against the side of the building. We like to hear them go "whap" and see little clouds of dust fly out of them. Throwing the erasers against the schoolhouse worked at least as well as slapping them together and it was a lot more fun.

Eddie and I usually did our eraser dusting at the northeast corner of the schoolhouse. There was a narrow concrete bench there, sort of a little booth built into the side of the building where we could sit down. Eddie and I were always glad to dust the erasers. For one thing, it meant we could get out of school for maybe fifteen minutes, even longer if Miss Downing forgot about us. Whether we slapped the erasers against the bench, pounded them together, or threw them up against the schoolhouse, we always did a good job so they looked like blue felt again and were ready to be used the next day. Sometimes Miss Downing said, "You boys do good work."

While dusting the blackboard erasers, Eddie and I talked about the toys we wanted our folks to buy us next Christmas, how much we hated girls, and sometimes we talked about Elton Baker, one of the most popular boys in the class.

Elton was a rough-and-tumble third grader who talked and acted tough. He wasn't a bully but he was bigger and older and always telling us what to do so we never crossed him. Nobody did. Elton had an older brother, Curt, but he never hollered for Curt's help when he got into a fight. He never got into a fight he couldn't win. He was smart enough not to get into to trouble with Miss Downing. Maybe, I figured, Miss Downing liked Elton because Harry Baker, Elton's daddy, was on the school board. Maybe it was because he brought her a big red apple every morning and carefully placed it in the middle of her desk where she would be sure to find it. The Bakers had lots of apples from their large orchard and a big fruit cellar to keep the apples in during the winter.

It was plain to see that girls liked Elton to notice them. Sometimes they would wait for him around the corner and jump out at him. Sometime they would sneak up behind him when he wasn't looking and grab hold of his shirt like they were trying to pull it out of his overalls, then shriek and run off, daring him to chase them. I decided they wouldn't do things like that unless they liked him a lot.

All the boys who were younger than Elton wanted to be like him and wanted him to like them. One time he told Mike Tweedy to give him some of the peanuts he had in his overalls pocket, and Mike gave him all he had. He once told Marion Hood never to walk in front of him and after than Marion didn't.

On the day before Thanksgiving, Miss Downing asked everybody to think a minute, so we could tell everyone why we were thankful. She said the main reason the Pilgrims observed Thanksgiving Day in the first place was to show that they were thankful for being alive in the New World. I was very surprised whey she called on me first. "What are you thankful for, Rex?" she asked. I didn't have time to think about it so I said the first thing that came into my head.

"I'm thankful that the Finneys' dogs don't bite me when I walk by their place every day."

"That's, uh, an interesting thing to be thankful for, Rex." Then she called out other names but not in any particular order. Frankie Hood said he was thankful that at their place he had all the milk he wanted to drink. Mary Rose Clifford said she was thankful for her little brother, Doyle. Paul Tomlin said he was thankful for the new pair of shoes he got up at Cherokee just before school started. Miss Downing then looked directly at Elton, smiled sweetly, and said, "Now Elton, would you stand and tell us what you're thankful for?"

Elton stood up with a grunt, looked all around the room, grinned at everybody, even at me, and said, good and loud, "I'm thankful for the snow." Continuing to grin as though he was very pleased with himself, he sat down again. That's crazy, I thought. It hasn't snowed since last winter.

"That's nice, Elton," Miss Downing said, smiling. The very next person Miss Downing called on was Eddie Talmage. "And what are you thankful for, Edward?"

"Same as Elton," Eddie stammered, and sat down so hard I was jolted, and everyone could hear his seat squeak because it was old and some of the screws that held it together were loose. Then Harry Lewis Depew said, "Same as Elton," and Mike said, "Same as Elton," and Marion Hood said, "Same as Elton."

I don't know what Miss Downing was thinking by this time, but I could see right through the whole thing and I was plenty disgusted. I knew all those boys probably had something to be thankful for but by saying "same as Elton" they were letting everybody know that they were flattering Elton so they could keep on the good side of him.

It seemed that Elton never ran out of wisecracks that made us laugh. I used to wonder where he learned all that stuff. And the funny stories he used to tell: I never heard stuff like that at home. In cold weather he wore a brown-and-white tweed cap. It wasn't new and I figured his daddy had worn it because it was way too big for Elton's head. No other boy at round Grove had a cap anything like it. There was a brown leather button on top, right in the center, and sometimes he would grab hold of it and yank the cap off his head.

I asked him about his cap one time, when he seemed to be in a good mood. "How come it's so big? Looks like there's a lotta extra room in it." He grinned off to one side of his mouth, crossed his eyes, and snorted, the way he always did when a wisecrack was coming.

"Well, he said, "I gotta tell ya fer a fact, I keep my religion in there." What a great joke, I thought. I'll remember that and tell it to somebody some time and they'll think I'm funny and clever like Elton. Of course I knew that religion wasn't

something you could carry around with you, especially in
your cap. but I was never really sure Elton didn't keep something is his cap, like maybe a small Bible or a folded-up piece
of paper with religious stuff written on it. I knew Elton and
his whole family went to the Nazarene Church. I thought
Nazarene kids were taught to carry religious stuff around
with them.

Another reason I liked Elton was the big red or yellow
apples he brought to school in the fall to trade or sell or give
away to people he liked. Even at dinner I never saw him eat
anything but apples, except in the spring when his folks did-
n't have any left in their cellar. After all their apples had
been eaten up, his mother sent apple-butter sandwiches in
his dinner bucket.

Elton had a really nice, store-bought stick horse that his
aunt in Enid had given him for his ninth birthday. It was
without doubt the handsomest stick horse I had ever seen. It
was a dapple-gray with a mane made of real horsehair. And
it had a black leather bridle with two long reins, the same
kind of bridle you would use on a real horse except it didn't
have a bit to go in the horse's mouth. Elton's horse even had
big brown glass eyes, about the color of mine. Because he
rode his horse to school every day, the paint soon wore off the
underside of the stick end that dragged along on the ground.
But the rest of Midge—he called his horse "Midge"—always
looked new and Elton sometimes teased the rest of us
because we didn't have "boughten stick horses", made in a
factory somewhere, like he did.

Miss Downing wouldn't let Elton bring Midge inside the
schoolhouse so he always leaned her carefully up against the
window frame, near the front door, where she remained,
admired but untouched, until four o'clock, when he rushed
out through the front door, mounted up like a cowboy, and
rode off for home at a fast lope, trailing a little cloud of brown
dust. Because nobody wanted to mess around with Elton, he

would always find his stick horse at the end of the day exactly where he had left her that morning. Some of us were strongly tempted but until now not one of us had ever dared touch her.

"How'd you like to play a trick on Elton?" I whispered to Eddie when we were about half done dusting the erasers one afternoon. Eddie seemed amazed that I'd dare think such a thing.

"What kinda trick?" he asked warily.

"Let's get his stick horse an hide it someplace where he'll have a hard time findin it." Eddie was dumbfounded. He stared at me, his eyes as wide as saucers. Then, all at once, he grinned.

"Okey doke, but won't he be mad at us if we do somethin like that?"

"Naw, he won't know it was us that did it," I said. "Besides, he'll probably just think it's a joke somebody's playin in him an he'll laugh about it." I found myself getting a little short of breath but I felt good, thinking how clever and brave I was.

"How come he won't find out it was us that done it?"

"Well, anybody coulda done it, or maybe somebody came down the road an just came up an took it. If he asks us if we did it, we'll say no, we didn't."

"Yeah," Eddie said, his grin widening at the idea. "No sir," he said confidently, "ole Elton won't be able to guess it was us that done it."

"Wait a minute," I said. "If we hide it he might not find it right away an be late gettin home an get in trouble cause he spent so much time just lookin for it. That'd really make him mad!"

"Yeah, that's a fact," Eddie agreed, suddenly soberly thoughtful. "That's right. An if he's late gettin home his daddy might give him a whippin and that'd be shore to make him madder'n heck."

"I got a better idea," I suggested, "somethin that won't make him mad. He'll know it's just a trick somebody played on him. Let's put his stick horse down at the girls' toilet."

"Yeah, but what if some girls are down there?"

"Aw, there ain't gonna be any girls down there so close to school getting out."

"Yeah, I guess yer right. But which one of us is gonna take it down there?"

"I ain't scared to do it," I said.

"Me neither," Eddie said.

"I know what let's do, let's draw straws. Tha one that gets the short straw takes it down there. Ain't that a fair way to do it?"

"Yeah, that's fair."

Looking around close to the schoolhouse, I found two dead grass stems and broke them so one was shorter than the other, then held them out to Eddie in my clenched fist with the stems sticking out so they looked the same length. He picked the longer of two stems.

He grinned with relief. "Whew!" he sighed. "Looks like yer tha one."

Because there weren't any windows or doors on the north side of the schoolhouse, Eddie and I couldn't be seen from inside the building while we were dusting erasers, so I was sure I could sneak around to the front door and take Elton's stick horse without being noticed.

Getting the horse was no trouble. I scooched down below the window sills, grabbed the horse, and raced around the north side of the schoolhouse, behind the coal house, and straight down to the girls' toilet just the other side of the teeter-totters. Gingerly, at arm's length, I leaned the stick horse up against the little white building, then ran back the way I had come to where Eddie was anxiously waiting, peering at me from around the corner of the schoolhouse. We congratulated ourselves on being so brave and clever, scooped up all the clean erasers in our arms, and went back inside.

I was breathing hard as I stepped through the doorway and the first thing I noticed was Miss Downing. She was standing near the windows, close to the pencil sharpener, facing the schoolroom, and she looked mad. She was almost finished for the day with the eighth graders who were reciting up at the front of the room. As the eighth graders took their seats, Eddie and I returned to ours.

I looked up at the dusty old wooden clock that hung on the wall above the blackboards. Even the brown and gold letters painted on the glass, "I.L. LOOMIS Watchmaker and Jeweler," didn't hide the big hand on the clock pointed right at ten. Ten minutes until four. I couldn't wait for school to let out. I thought Eddie was feeling pretty good, too, about what we had done, but when I glanced over at him he looked scared.

Then, for the first time, I looked toward the front of the room and spotted Elton Baker's stick horse lying on Miss Downing's desk. A knot began to form in my stomach. I knew something had gone wrong. Miss Downing must have seen me down at the girls' toilet from where she was standing by the windows. Why hadn't I been more careful? I looked up at her, hoping the anger I'd seen on her face had gone. It hadn't. From the way she was glaring at me I could guess she was plenty mad. The knot in my stomach quickly grew into a real bellyache. Then, in her clear, shrill voice, she spoke directly to Bob Loudon, who sat in the back of the room. "Robert, have you a pocketknife?"

"Yes, ma'am," he replied.

"Then go and get a good, strong switch and bring it right back in here. Hurry now, it's almost time for school to let out."

In minutes Bob was back with a green chinaberry branch, about three feet long. He had trimmed off most of the small twigs and leaves and it was ready for use. "Thank you, Robert," Miss Downing said, and sent Bob back to his desk.

All the while I was thinking that my overalls wouldn't give me much protection against that big switch.

Immediately Miss Downing turned her eyes on me. "Now Rex," she snapped, "come over here!" Grasping a handful of my loose shirt in the back between my overalls suspenders, she turned me toward the whole school, now so quiet with anticipation of what was about to take place you could have heard a pin drop on the greasy floor.

Whap! She laid the chinaberry switch hard across my hip pockets. Whap! Whap! Whap! Again and again, harder and harder. I looked over at Eddie. He was white as a sheet and had sunk down as low as he could get in his seat. Nobody laughed. Miss Downing kept hitting me until she finally made me cry.

I didn't think I deserved a whipping and wondered why Eddie didn't get a whipping that day I never figured out why. In fact, he wasn't even scolded for having a part in the trick. I didn't think it was fair that she didn't do something to him. Maybe, I thought, it's because his daddy is on the school board and mine isn't. Or maybe it's because I'm adopted and he isn't. People say that adopted kids are supposed to be bad.

That was the first of seven whippings I got from Miss Downing during first grade at Round Grove. More than once she whipped me for no good reason I could think of. Like the time when the only thing I did was accidentally drop the lead out of my new Eversharp onto the floor.

"Rex Wilson, you get up from that floor this instant!" Miss Downing screeched at me. "Get up from there right now!" So loud that everybody in the school stopped what they were doing and turned to watch. "How dare you do a thing like that? You naughty, naughty boy!"

I didn't know why she was so mad. All I had done was get down on the floor to look for the pencil lead I had dropped. Camilla Tomlin had scooted over to the edge of her seat and shifted her legs and feet so I could see better to find it. The floor was dirty, greasy, and splintered, and I was down there on my hand s and knees, careful not to bump my head, facing the back of my seat. Except that I had dropped the lead, I wouldn't have been down there. I needed that lead and unless I could find it I would have to borrow a pencil from somebody and Miss Downing had told us over and over again not to borrow pencils and crayons and erasers and papers from others. "Now young man, you just march yourself up her right now!" I opened my mouth but words wouldn't come out. Some of the kids were giggling. Bob Loudon and Melvin Hood were choking, like maybe they were trying to keep from laughing out loud. Andy McCullen snorted, looking from side to side, enjoying himself.

Miss Downing stood at the front of the room, the same place she stood every time she whipped me, gloved hands on her hips, so worked up she was shaking. There was sweat on her upper lip. Her eyes seemed to be on fire. When I came within reach she grabbed my right arm and yanked me over next to her. For a second I lost my balance and thought I was going to fall on the floor. But she yanked me up and with her other hand reached around to her desk and picked up an old yardstick that said "AMSDEN LUMBER COMPANY" on one side and "Let Us Help With All Your Lumber Needs" on the other.

"You can't get by with that kind of thing in my classroom, you naughty boy!" she screeched again. By now she was not only sweating on her upper lip, her dyed orange hair had partly come loose and a hairpin was about to fall out. The snickering and snorting from the back of the room had almost stopped now.

Whap! Whap! Whap! I twisted a little to one side so she would hit me more on my hip instead of directly on my butt; it didn't hurt so much that way.

The next time she swung, the old yardstick broke into several pieces that went flying out toward the middle of the room where the other kids sat glued to their seats. All Miss Downing had left to hit me with was a short piece that didn't work very well. She hit me a couple of times with it but it didn't even hurt. From the way she was acting, she was just about worn out, I thought. Then, with a little grunt, she threw the short piece of yardstick over toward her desk where it landed on the seat of her chair. She let go my arm and I took a step backward. Miss Downing just stood there, saying nothing, trying to catch her breath, panting like she had run all the way over to Harry Vealy's house and back. I stood there, looking down, waiting for her to speak. "Now, young man, go sit at your desk until four o'clock. And don't you ever try a stunt like that again!"

I still didn't understand what stunt she was talking about. And I was glad she hadn't made me cry. She didn't stoop over to pick up the pieces of yardstick but just left them on the floor where they had landed. I felt like maybe I should offer to pick them up but decided not to. Back at my desk, I sat quietly, looking at my reader, thinking how glad I was that Miss Downing hadn't asked somebody to go outside and cut a switch the way she had done every other time she had whipped me.

I wondered if any of the other boys who had laughed knew why I got a whipping that day, but I never talked to anyone about it, I got more whippings from Miss Downing that year than anybody else in the school. ✦

Chapter 11 ────────────────────────── ⟪

Early in December, Miss Downing announced exciting plans for Christmas at Round Grove School, including the drawing of names for a gift exchange. From beneath her old wooden desk on the stage, she pulled out a pasteboard box about twice the size of a big shoe box. Then she called Lila Hood and Mary Rose Clifford to the front of the room. "There's something very special I would like you girls to do this morning," she gushed, loud enough for everyone to hear. "I want you to use your talents and imagination to decorate this box in Christmas colors. You may also use designs if you wish. I am quite sure that anything you create will be lovely. Then when you've finished your work, each and every pupil will place his or her name on a slip of paper and drop it through the slot you will make in the top of the box. Some day soon we will all draw names from the box for our Christmas gift exchange."

Collecting rolls of crepe paper from the top of the old brown cupboard that stood in the front of the room, the girls lost no time getting started. They worked at a library table standing against the back wall. The rest of us had to continue our regular schoolwork while listening to the rustling sounds behind our backs. The girls were finished before ten

o'clock, so we took a good look at their work when Miss
Downing let us out for morning recess. The box was beautiful,
generously covered with red, green, and white crepe paper. The
girls had even cut out some little Santa Clauses, colored them
with crayons, and pasted them on all four sides and the top of
the box. After recess had ended, Miss Downing passed the box
down one row of desks after another and everybody's name was
slipped inside through the little slot the girls had cut in the top.
No one was left out, which meant that there were thirty-six
pieces of paper in the box. Each had been folded a time or two
so nobody could look through the slot and read the name. I
heard Andy McCullen telling some of the big boys after school
that he had put his name in twice but I don't think they
believed him.

On a Friday afternoon in the first week of December, Miss
Downing took the beautiful Christmas box off the top of the
piano where it had sat all week, shook it hard, removed the lid,
and walked up and down the aisles so each of us could reach
inside and draw out a piece of paper with somebody's name
written on it.

"Be sure you draw one name and one name only," Miss
Downing said sharply. "The idea is to keep secret the name you
draw so that when the gifts are passed out you will be surprised
when you find out who drew your name." She said we were not
to spend more than a quarter on a present and that there were
lots of nice things that could be bought for less than a quarter.

I hoped I would draw Eddie Talmage's name and that he
would be lucky and draw mine. Neither of us wanted girls to
draw our names. Besides, we couldn't expect girls to know what
to get us for Christmas anyway. As much as anything, we did-
n't want to be teased by the other boys for getting Christmas
presents from girls. We figured the worst thing that could happen would be for one of us to have to buy a present for a girl.

Even before school let out that day I had a feeling Eddie
hadn't drawn my name and I tried to let him know without

saying that I hadn't drawn his. We got together after school to trade secrets. He got Frankie Hood's name and I got Twila Bailey's. All that weekend I worried about how I could get hold of Eddie's name instead. Monday morning I learned that Junie Clifford had drawn it. "I'm willin to trade," he said, "but yer gonna have ta give me somethin ta boot." I ended up trading him Twila's name and, although I hated being taken advantage of, I also gave him the four big sugar cookies I had brought in my dinner pail that day. During afternoon recess Eddie told me he had to trade two times before he finally got my name. He said Olive Pritchard had drawn it and he had to give her two sticks of gum before she would agree to tell him what she had done with my name. She had traded it to Camilla Tomlin. But when Eddie tried to trade with Camilla she told him she didn't have my name any more. She made Eddie say "pretty please with sugar on it" before she told him that she had traded my name to Gladys Bailey. Eddie said Gladys was glad to trade him my name for Frankie Hood's. We both knew she had a crush on Frankie anyhow.

The last Saturday before we got out of school for Christmas and New Year's, Eddie Talmage was also in town with his folks, his little sister Pauline, and his baby brother Willie. By the time I saw him, after I had gotten out of the picture show, I had already bought his present. It hadn't taken more than a minute; I knew exactly what I wanted to buy: a beautiful Sally Walker hardwood top. It was painted with red, white, and blue stripes, had a coat of clear varnish on it, and had a brilliant shine when I held it up to the light. Daddy had gone with me to the drug store but let me pick it out. It cost a whole quarter, which was the most Miss Downing said I could spend, but Daddy paid for it. I was sure Eddie would like the top because we both knew the Sally Walker was the best kind to have. With its rounded point, like a little ball, the Sally Walker could move around and spin on hard ground or in loose sand longer than the spiked kind, the kind of top that dug a little hole that got deeper and deeper until it finally stopped spinning. I didn't tell anybody, but I sort of envied Eddie because he was going to get such a fine gift from me, something I wished I could keep for myself. It was much prettier than any of the tops I had. But I tried not to let my envy show, because Eddie was my best pal and I knew it wasn't Christian of me to be thinking like that.

Eddie spotted me sitting in the back seat of our parked car where I was waiting for Daddy. The top was in the little paper sack Mr. Moler had given me at the drug store, so I waved Eddie over and he climbed into the back seat beside me. When I took the top out of the brown sack and showed it to him, I could tell from his grin and the way he sort of gasped that he was overjoyed. I reminded him of what Miss Downing had said, that we were not supposed to tell anybody what his Christmas present was before he got it. We promised one another neither of us would tell.

"I bought your present, too," Eddie said. After reaching into his coat pocket, he pulled out the gift he had bought for me at Moler's, unwrapped the small brown paper package, and proudly showed it to me. My spirits fell. What Eddie had bought was an ugly, brownish-red-colored ink pen holder. Not for a fountain pen but for the kind you had to dip into an ink bottle. It was absolutely good for nothing unless you had a pen point to push into the big end, the end with a screw on it. And there wasn't one. When Eddie learned that his gift hadn't cost as much as the one I had bought for him he rewrapped the pen, then said with strong determination, "I'm gonna go back an trade this thing fer somethin that costs a quarter."

"Okay," I said, "but you don't have to tell me what you get. You can surprise me." He gave me a look that showed me he didn't fully understand what I was trying to tell him.

"I'll be back in a minute," he said, scrambling out of the car, slamming the door closed, and racing off toward Moler's.

A few minutes later Eddie found me in Baxter's Hardware Store, where I had gone with Daddy to leave some shoes to be half-soled. He motioned me over to a corner of the store where Mr. Baxter kept rope and binder twine. Slowly and carefully he untied the white string and unwrapped the brown paper package he was holding. It was the same pen holder he had shown me earlier, but, instead of buying a point for it, he had bought a second pen holder, exactly like the one he had shown me in the car. There was nothing in his package but two ugly red-brick pen holders that were exactly alike.

"What am I gonna do with two of these things?" I asked. "Why didn't you get a point to go into it instead of another one? You can't write with one of these things unless it's got a point in it."

"Oh," he said, "I forgot about that. I'll take em back an trade one of em for a pen point."

"That's okay," I said as patiently as I could, hoping he wouldn't see how disappointed I was. "I'll figger a way to use em. I know Gramma Dollie's got some pen points and she might gimmie one of em." Naturally, I expected Eddie to go right back to the drug store, give back one of the pen holders, and buy a point that would fit the other one. He can figure that out for himself, I thought.

When we had the gift exchange just before school let out the next Friday afternoon, I got my "surprise" Christmas present from my best friend Eddie. Sure enough, it was those same two ugly, brown-red pen holders that weren't worth a darn. And Eddie got the beautiful Sally Walker top from me. We both tried to act surprised and pleased with our gifts because Miss Downing seemed to be keeping her eyes on us as we unwrapped them. We were sure she never guessed that we had traded around to get one another's names. When our holiday vacation was over and school took up again, I gave Eddie one of the pen holders. "Thanks," he said, "but I can't use this thing unless I get a point for it."

There was one other time during the school year when we drew names. Around the first of February Miss Downing announced that we were going to draw names and have a valentine exchange on the fourteenth. "It will be like the exchange we had at Christmastime," she said, "so don't tell anybody whose name you draw out of the box. That way you won't know who has your name until you get the valentine." Allie Tomlin and Loretta Loudon worked all afternoon decorating the valentine box in bright red colors. They wrote each person's name on a little piece of white paper, then gave everybody a chance to draw a name. It was all very secret so nobody would know who had whose name. I figured the reason we had to go to all this trouble was to make sure everybody got a valentine, so ugly girls wouldn't be left out and get their feelings hurt. Miss Downing said we could buy very nice valentines at Moler's Drug Store for a penny or two and that even their fanciest ones only cost a nickel. "You ought not plan to spend more than a nickel, at the most, for a valentine," she advised.

When my folks and I went to Aline the next Saturday afternoon, Daddy gave me a dime to buy valentines, in addition to the nickel I usually got.

"You might also wanta buy a valentine for Miss Downing," he suggested. When he said that, I figured he and Mother probably hadn't guessed that by Valentine's Day Miss Downing had whipped me four or five times and that I didn't like her very much. I didn't have the least idea of buying Miss Downing a valentine, but I took the extra ten cents, figuring I would buy ice cream or candy with a nickel of it. I headed straight for Moler's when we got to town, even before I went to the picture show.

I planned to spend my usual nickel for a candy bar or five pieces of Fleers Dubble Bubble gum, and pick out one of the crazy two-cent gag valentines for Curt Baker, whose name I had drawn. Then I wanted to find a fancy nickel valentine for Sharon DePew, Harry Lewis' big sister, a third grader with bright blue eyes and curly blonde hair. I liked Sharon a lot and didn't even mind when I was teased about the crush I had on her. The three cents I figured on having left were going to be added to the money I was saving to buy the Mickey Mouse watch, the one Mr. Moler kept in a glass case with fountain pens and safety razors at the back of his drug store.

We had the valentine exchange on Thursday afternoon, Valentine's Day, just before school let out. Because Allie and Loretta had done such a good job decorating the inside of the schoolhouse and had fixed up the valentine box so pretty, Miss Downing asked them to come up to the front of the room and give out the valentines.

When they took off the lid, I could see the big box was almost full of white, pink, and red envelopes of different sizes. Each had a name written on it; some of the names were even written in ink. Allie and Loretta drew out the envelopes and passed them out so kids wouldn't be running all over the room at the same time. I could tell that Curt Baker really liked my valentine. It was a funny one, I thought, showing a boy with a huge clothespin on his nose and containing a little poem that read:

Roses are red
Violets are blue
A polecat stinks
And so do you
HAPPY VALENTINE'S DAY

Curt laughed and looked over at me when he read the poem and saw who the valentine was from. And I felt good when he showed it to several of the older boys in the back of the room.

After the box had been emptied and the valentines had

all been given out there was a good-sized pile of envelopes on Sharon's desk. I could see her from clear across the room if I turned most of the way around in my seat but she never once looked at me. Then, at four o'clock, we all marched out of the schoolhouse and headed for home. I caught up with Sharon before she got to the corner, where she and a bunch of other kids would turn east. I walked along beside her for maybe a minute. When she finally noticed me, I asked, "Did you get a lotta valentines?"

"Yeah," she snapped, her big blue eyes looking sort of off into the dead weeds that covered the east side of the road.

"How many did ya get?"

"It ain't none of yer business," she said, "but I got eleven." Now she looked straight at me. "An how many did you get?"

"I just got two. Did you get the one I sent you?" I asked hopefully, watching closely for some kind of appreciation, maybe even some sign that she liked me a little.

"Yeah," she said, her nose in the air. "I got it."

"Well, did you like it?"

"It's okay, I guess."

"It's the prettiest one I could find at the drug store."

"Well, I got some that's prettier. An bigger, too!" Maybe she really didn't like getting a fancy valentine from me, I thought.

"Well," I said, "I went to a lotta trouble to find that valentine just fer you an I spent a whole nickel fer it." I was sure she would be flattered. But Sharon didn't seem to give a hoot that I had spent a lot of money on her valentine. We were now close to the corner where she turned east. Suddenly turning toward me, making her eyes into slits and her lips real thin, she almost shouted at me. Partly, I guess, so the half dozen or more kids who were walking her way could hear her.

"Well, Rex Wilson, you ain't so danged smart as you think you are! Elton Baker gave me a valentine that cost at least a dime an that's twice as much money as you spent, so there!" With that final word she turned east, ran to catch up with the others going in that direction, and didn't look back.

Thus ended my very first schoolboy crush on an older girl. By Friday morning I was completely over Sharon and wondered what I had seen in her in the first place. When I came across Elton at morning recess I told him flat out that Sharon and I were all finished and if he wanted her for his girl he could have her.

Shortly after my valentine experience, Mother began spending spent a lot of time teaching me how I should behave in public or when company came. "If you practice good manners every day you won't have to think about them," she said. "They'll just come naturally."

For example, she lectured, "Never, never, let anybody see you pickin your nose. If you need to blow your nose use a clean handkerchief. Never wipe your nose on your coat sleeve because a gentleman doesn't do that. And besides"—she made a face—"it's nasty!" Although she never said so, I could tell Mother didn't like it much when Daddy taught me how to blow my nose, the way he did outdoors, when I didn't have a handkerchief in my pocket.

"It's real easy when ya know how," he said. "Watch, I'll show ya."

The idea was to press my thumb hard against one side of my nose, bend over a little, aim a few feet in front or to the side so snot wouldn't land on my shoes, and give a quick snort. If my nose got wet I could wipe it with my hand or shirt sleeve, then dry my hands on my pants legs. "If ya get some on yer hand, yer doin it wrong," Daddy said. Later, Mother told me firmly that I must never, ever let anybody see me blowing my nose that way.

Because I learned some of these important lessons at home, I figured that other kids were taught the same things by their folks, so I was surprised when I saw kids at Round

Grove picking their noses right there in the schoolhouse. Usually they did this when they were working arithmetic problems or learning spelling words, as if they had no idea what their hands were doing. One time I just happened to turn my head in time to see Skillet Hanks, a fat fourth grader, roll a little booger into a ball between his thumb and forefinger that was about the size of a BB. Then he flipped it up into the air with his thumb. It almost hit the ceiling before it landed on Maybelle Finney's desk, half the way across the room. To her horror and embarassment, it landed right on her tablet as she was taking an arithmetic test. Then it rolled off onto the floor as Maybelle and I watched.

I just couldn't understand Miss Downing. How come she never even sees anybody picking his nose, I wondered, let alone gives them a whipping? Seems to me that's lots worse than chewing bubble gum in school. And she once whipped me for that. Didn't she see Skillet slip the booger up into the air? Maybelle had seemed upset about what had happened, but she didn't tell Miss Downing. But why wasn't Miss Downing bothered by such things?

At least as bad was a kind of game that some of the older boys used to play every Tuesday afternoon. "They're lettin big poops in the schoolhouse," I told Mother. She said that was something nice people didn't do, especially inside the house or in the classroom.

"You don't even say 'poop,'" she said. "It isn't nice. If you have to talk about it, you say 'break wind.'" What was going on Tuesday afternoons at Round Grove was a sort of tournament to see who could break wind the loudest. At least it seemed to me that's what they were trying to do.

What really amazed me was that Miss Downing never seemed to notice and that none of the big boys who sat in the back seemed the least bit ashamed or bashful about what they were doing. Some of the seventh and eighth grade girls, like Lila Hood and Mary Rose Clifford, looked disgusted and maybe a little embarrassed. Other girls would giggle, not because they were enjoying what was taking place but because they were also embarrassed. Some of the girls would give a little gasp as each boy tried to outdo the other. Sometimes the boys snorted or laughed but not loud enough that Miss Downing noticed. Of course, the boys all kept their eyes on her and wouldn't let one go until she looked the other way.

Windbreaking began about two hours after dinner, almost like clockwork, during the dullest and sleepiest part of the day when everybody had trouble keeping their minds on schoolwork and when the air in the schoolhouse had become thick from overuse. Ventilation was never very good because Miss Downing never opened the windows or left the front and back doors open.

Eddie Talmage and I got to talking about Tuesday afternoons and we decided that maybe washdays on Mondays and windbreaking contests on Tuesdays were somehow connected. Everybody knew the mothers in our neighborhood spent all day every Monday doing the family washing. Every Monday most mothers would cook up a batch of navy beans and have them for supper that night. My mother never washed on any other day but Monday and I remembered that Mrs. Frye, who used to live across the road from us, washed that day, too. Sometimes when she wasn't able to get to it on Monday, Mother would put off the washing for a week. And every Monday she would first put water on the stove to heat for the wash, then put on a big pot of navy or pinto beans. Sometimes she fixed butter beans with a ham bone or a chunk of fatback.

Washing was a hard, all-day job for Mother, but I never helped her and neither did Daddy except to lift the boiler of water off the stove and pour it into the washing machine. She used to get started right after breakfast, before I left for school, and many were the times she would still be at it when I got home around four-thirty in the afternoon. When it rained or snowed on Monday, she would dry the wash by hanging it on lines she would string all over the house, upstairs and downstairs. Mother had it easier than several women I knew. At least she had a washing machine, while many women used a washboard sitting in a tub of warm soapy water.

My mother had almost no time to cook on washday. About the time Mother started the first white load, she started the pot of beans and fatback cooking on the stove. By noon the beans were ready to eat. Sometimes, depending on how long it took her to get the wash done, she would serve beans again for supper.

It was common for some of the kids, especially those from large families like the Hoods, Tweedys, and Tomlins, to show up at school on Tuesday morning with half-pint fruit jars of cold beans in their dinner pails, beans left over from the day before. Unless a family had an icebox—and most didn't— beans wouldn't last very long and nobody could afford to waste food.

Mother said,"When you think about it for a minute, most of the mothers I know don't have a lot of choices in what they can send their kids for dinners. An cold beans and homemade bread and butter make a pretty good meal. At least, it's filling." Most of the kids I talked to figured bread and butter and beans were a real treat, something they looked forward to having for dinner on Tuesdays.

But in my opinion those Monday bean dinners always ended up making Tuesday afternoons the worst time of the week. ✦

Chapter 12 ⟶

While I was in first grade at Round Grove School, Mother and Daddy saw to it that I learned the important things about being a man and a gentleman and why it was important to know and practice these things. "It's more than just tha common courtesies," Mother said. "It's tha things you do and tha things you don't do, or think, or say, or write, because you're gonna grow up to be a gentleman, not just a man." Mother said that "fools' names like fools' faces are often seen in public places." At first I didn't understand what she meant but I figured it out pretty quickly when she went on to say I must not go around writing my name on walls, or my desk, or on the sides of buildings or cement culverts the way some boys did. "It's also important that you know," she said sternly, "that a gentleman doesn't covet something that belongs to somebody else." She said the Bible teaches us that Moses told everybody the Ten Commandments and one of them was that people weren't supposed to covet. I asked her what "covet" meant. "For example, son," she said, "you ought not keep thinkin about how much you would have liked to have that nice top you gave Eddie Talmage for Christmas." She had remembered longer than I had. It had been easy to forget about that top since Daddy gave me one for Christmas that was almost exactly like the one I gave Eddie. But Mother was right about my thinking too much that I'd like to have something that belonged to someone else. I had wanted to keep that top I gave Eddie. From then on, I tried my best not to covet anything.

Daddy said, "Try to be a man, son. An if you get in a fight, fight fair. Like a man." He said it was much more honorable and manly to lose in a fair fight than it was to cheat and win by fighting like a girl or a sissy. "One thing you don't ever wanta forget," Daddy said. "Boys don't pull hair, not if they's real boys that one day's gonna grow up to be men. An they don't scratch or bite, no matter how much they'd like to really hurt the other guy an make him bleed a little." He said boys never squeal and carry on like girls or little babies and don't try to gouge eyes or kick or hit below the belt. So naturally, because I didn't want anybody to think I was a sissy, especially Daddy, I wouldn't do anything that would make him ashamed of me. I followed as closely as I could the code of honor he taught me. Of course, I lost a few fist fights but I always knew I might have beaten the other guy if I had scratched and pulled hair the way he sometimes did. I hoped Daddy was proud of me for always fighting fair even when I lost or when the other boy fought like a girl. Like Junie Clifford did. "An son," Daddy told me, "you never pick a fight with a girl or let one of em pick a fight with you. If any girl tries to pick a fight with you, why you just walk away." That's really good advice, I thought. Even sissies like Junie don't get into fights with girls.

Mother was also proud of her Southern heritage and saw to it that I was well acquainted with Southern traditions, the War Between the States, important places, and outstanding Southerners from the earliest years of our history. She was determined that I be brought up to understand the difference between Southerners and Yankees and that to be

Southern was better and more honorable. She said that a "Carpetbagger" was the worst thing anybody could be and that's what a lot of Yankees were. Mother patiently explained southern values, using words like "gentility" and "chivalry" that she had to explain to me. "Son," she said one time, "never forget to honor and respect your elders." I was taught to say "yes sir" and "yes ma'am" when spoken to by an adult and when I forgot my manners I was scolded.

After most of a year at Round Grove I thought I knew Eddie Talmage pretty well—he was my best pal—but one day he surprised me. It was during afternoon recess when he came looking for me from behind the coalhouse where Mike Tweedy, Elton Baker, and I were building a fort out of some chunks of blackjack wood piled inside to burn in the stove if we ever ran out of coal. He stood over by the open door for a minute, on one foot then the other, looking toward me, trying to catch my eye. After a while he finally moved slowly over to where I was resting on my knees, laying one log on another. "I wanta show ya somethin," he said, and shoved some wrinkled sheets of tablet paper toward me.

"What's this supposed ta be?" I asked.

"That there's a poem I wrote fer Miss Downing." He spoke barely above a whisper, probably hoping Elton and Mike wouldn't hear. He seemed embarrassed, like maybe he didn't want anybody else to know he had done something for Miss Downing that he didn't have to. I knew darned well I wouldn't do anything for her that she didn't make me do, but then, she liked him better than me. I motioned him to follow me around to the front of the coalhouse so Mike and Elton couldn't hear us talking.

"A poem?" I asked. "How could you write a poem, you ain't a poet."

"Look at it an see if you think she'll like it. I wanta surprise her with it." It wasn't long, the poem he'd written, but he had used most of two pages partly because, like me, he wrote in first-grade letters. I looked up once as I read what he had written and could see him grinning. His face had turned a kind of red color.

"The boy stood on the burning deck
Eating peanuts by the peck
When his father called
He would not come at all
He loved them so."

"That's pretty good," I said, trying hard not to laugh. I didn't want to hurt his feelings. "But it doesn't rhyme, ain't poems supposed ta rhyme?"

"Yeah, I guess they're supposed to," he said, "but I been working on it all week an I can't make it rhyme any bettern it does. So I'm gonna give it to her anyhow." I told him if Elton Baker saw him give his poem to Miss Downing he'd tell everybody in school he was trying to be teacher's pet and then everybody would tease him about it. "I'm gonna stay after school so's I kin give it to her," he said. "That way nobody'll see me."

"That's a good idea," I said.

I didn't say anymore to Eddie about it, but something about his poem sounded awfully familiar. I thought some of it was probably copied out of a book. Part of it, I thought, was just plain dumb, like the boy loving peanuts so much that he didn't mind his daddy.

Later Miss Downing told the whole school that Edward had written a fine poem just for her. She said it was just about the nicest thing anyone had ever done for her, that it meant even more to her than a big red apple. She said she was sorry she couldn't read it to us because she had taken it home. And Elton Baker didn't bring her a single apple after that.

Friday, April 21st was our last day of school. A basket

dinner was to be held in the city park up at Carmen and everybody who had anything to do with Round Grove was invited to come and bring a covered dish of something, like potato salad or fried chicken, that could be shared with everybody else. Miss Downing had sent a note home with each of the kids, telling their folks that they ought to arrive at the park no later than eleven o'clock so dinner could be served at noon. She also said in her note that she had reserved several picnic tables for us to use. She said the park people were going to arrange the tables so they would be sitting under some elm trees over between the swimming pool and the oiled road that went by Shoemaker's Conoco filling station and the city power plant. Early Friday morning Mother deviled three dozen eggs, arranged them on a white platter she never used for anything else, and sprinkled paprika all over them before she covered them with a clean dishtowel to keep the flies off. Mother and Daddy and I got to the park a little before eleven. "I don't think Miss Downing is here yet," Mother said, like she wasn't surprised.

"Maybe she didn't read her instructions," Daddy said, and chuckled.

Several families were already there and plates of fried chicken, bowls of potato salad, and several cakes and pies, all covered with dish towels, were sitting on one of the picnic tables. Some women had put out their plates, cups, and silverware to reserve places at the table for themselves and their families and friends.

I looked around for Eddie Talmage but he and his folks hadn't shown up yet. Harry Lewis Depew and Sharon and their folks were there and the Hood family had taken over two of the tables because there were so many of them. Don Paul Calhoun's mother was spreading out a red-and-white checkered tablecloth close to the tables Flo Hood had staked out for her bunch. Don Paul's daddy was sitting on the running board of their old blue Whippet, out of the cool wind, smoking a handrolled cigarette, talking to Cliff Hood. I looked for the Hood boys, but didn't see any of them.

Harry Lewis Depew and Don Paul Calhoun were standing over by the chain link fence that kept people and animals out of the swimming pool. Because it wasn't summer yet the pool wasn't open, even on weekends. Harry Lewis and Don Paul were looking over at me and I could see that Harry Lewis kept spitting between his teeth, something he liked to do to show off because he thought it made him look mean and tough, like a real he-man. I couldn't hear what they were saying but figured they were talking about me. Harry Lewis saw that I was watching them and motioned for me to join them.

I was expecting trouble as I walked slowly toward where the two boys stood, glaring at me. Harry Lewis was always spoiling for trouble, especially with younger and smaller kids like me. The only time he behaved himself was when his older sister, Sharon, was around to watch him. Besides the trouble I had had with him at school, I sometimes had trouble with him in Aline. He was always trying to act like Popeye or Buck Jones or Ken Maynard, especially if he had seen one of them at the picture show. I had never run away from a fight with him. He talked tough and tried to act big but he always backed off when it came to a showdown. Harry Lewis wasn't hard to figure out; he never picked on me or on anybody else unless he was with at least one other boy. I should have known before I walked over to them that Harry Lewis was looking for trouble.

Don Paul Calhoun wasn't saying anything, just hanging onto the chain link fence, looking first at Harry Lewis, then at me. But Harry Lewis was trying his best to look tough, spitting a lot, kicking dirt with the toe of his shoe. "Hey, kid," he growled as I came close, "what's yer name?"

"You know darn well what my name is," I answered. By now I knew for sure he was trying to pick a fight with me. It was two against one, just the way he liked it.

"Don't gimme none a yer smart mouth," he sneered. "Come on, what's yer name?"

"My name's Rex Wilson, you know darned well."

"Get off it, what's yer real name?"

"I told you what my real name is, it's Rex Wilson."

"No it ain't yer real name an you know damn well it ain't an everbody else knows it ain't. Before they took you outta that orphans' home up at Helena you had another name."

"How do you know that?"

"Cause my mother told me, that's how. She read all about it in tha Aline paper once."

"I didn't know they put it in the paper."

"Well, my mother said she saw it in tha paper an she ain't no liar. You callin my mother a liar?"

"No, I ain't callin your mother a liar."

"Well, my mother said she seen it in tha paper once when you come out from Helena ta stay with Frank Wilson, before they adopted you. She said yer real name is Billy Joe Tolliver. That there's yer real name, ain't it?"

That was a hit below the belt and it hurt. It hurt a lot. Probably more than if he had hit me in the face with his fist. I guess he wanted to make me mad enough to fight so he and Don Paul could really clean my plow. But I didn't want to fight either of them, let alone both at the same time. I just stood there as the old familiar hurt knotted up in my stomach. I looked right into Harry Lewis' face but I didn't say another word, just turned around and walked back to where Mother was setting up places for us at one of the picnic tables. I half expected Harry Lewis and Don Paul to come after me, but they didn't. I hoped Mother had noticed what had happened, but she didn't say anything to me. So I never said anything about it to my folks, or to Eddie Talmage, or to anybody. For me the picnic was ruined and I couldn't wait to go home.

Nothing else that happened in first grade bothered me

quite as much as Harry Lewis Depew's meanness that day in the Carmen Park. I couldn't help wondering if any of the other kids at Round Grove knew I was adopted and that my name had been changed.

Everybody except me ate too much. The other kids sailed their paper plates into the little pond on the other side of the swimming pool, and the men beat the socks off the boys, twenty-two to six in the annual baseball game. I didn't play because I was too little but Daddy played third base for the men. Even Mother, who was caught up in the hubbub and excitement and noise of the game, didn't notice that I wasn't joining in the fun.

Mother and Daddy talked all the way home late in the afternoon. But I sat quietly in the back seat of the car, adding nothing to their discussion, glad they didn't ask me if I had a good time at the picnic. ✦

Chapter 13 ⚜

Miss Mary Frances Downing wasn't hired to teach a second year at Round Grove School. Mother heard it at a Round Grove Social Club meeting. We talked about it at supper that night, one of the few times we got the cows milked and sat down to eat before it got completely dark. Like other wheat farmers, Daddy knew he couldn't expect rain until around the first of September so he had quit work early because his wheat ground was too dry to plow.

"Nell Bailey said Miss Downing didn't want to teach at Round Grove another year. She told Roger she couldn't stand to be cooped up another year with all those unwashed little monkeys." From Mother's face and the tone of her voice I could tell she didn't like Miss Downing calling us unwashed little monkeys. "Nell said the school board has hired Glen Ewing to teach."

Well, I didn't know Glen Ewing at all, but by listening closely while my folks talked I found out he was nineteen years old, had finished two years at the teachers' college up at Alva, and was crazy about sports, especially basketball. Mother said he was a good singer, too, but she said that wasn't surprising because all the Ewing kids sang. He was to be paid seventy-five dollars a month starting in September 1933. Daddy said that sounded like an awful lot of money to pay a nineteen-year-old kid without any teaching experience.

Glen Ewing had grown up on a quarter section about a mile and a half northeast of our place, practically on the corner on the north side of the road. He wasn't very big, not nearly as big as Daddy, but he was wiry, Daddy said. I didn't know what he meant by "wiry" until he explained. Mother said he had a perpetual five o'clock shadow. When I asked what she meant by that she said he always looked like he had forgotten to shave and you had to look real close to tell for sure. She said it was kind of unusual for so young a man to have such a heavy black beard.

From the very first day I liked Mr. Ewing and he seemed to like me. I thought maybe it was because he was pretty small for a grown man and I was pretty small for a seven-year-old kid. By the end of the second week of school, the first year he taught, he noticed that I was getting my schoolwork done before the other second graders were. One day he called me up to his desk to talk to me about it.

The next morning he gave me some extra work to do, maps to color and some arithmetic problems. Before long he had me doing some of the assignments he had given the third and fourth graders, but it still wasn't enough. With not enough work to do, I got restless and got into trouble, even though I didn't mean to. I sharpened my pencil a lot, or asked to go to the toilet, or to get a drink, or to speak to one of the other kids. It wasn't until Mr. Ewing had scolded me once or twice for wasting time that he realized I was getting into mischief because, even with the extra assignments he gave me to do, my schoolwork simply wasn't keeping me busy.

Close to four o'clock one day during the last week of September, Mr.Ewing said he would give me a ride home if I was willing to stay just a few minutes after school until he was ready to put the padlock on the front door.

Mr. Ewing drove an old Dodge. It was a dark blue coupe with a rumble seat and fancy upholstery. But I was uncomfortable riding in it because it looked a lot like the car Mr. Collins used to take me to the orphans' home when I was four.

My folks must have been expecting Mr. Ewing because Daddy was in the house instead of working outside and was wearing a clean pair of overalls. We all sat down around our dining room table and Mr. Ewing did most of the talking. He said he had arranged with the County School Superintendent to move me ahead to the fourth grade. I didn't know how he could talk her into anything like that. Mother and Daddy said they were concerned that I would be out of place with the much bigger and older fourth graders. They talked with Mr. Ewing until it was almost dark. But before he left that evening they had agreed that I would skip second grade only and go immediately into third grade. Although I didn't say anything to Mr. Ewing or to Mother and Daddy, the only thing I worried about was that Eddie Talmage and I wouldn't be in the same grade anymore. I thought about that a lot as we hurried through evening chores.

"Correct spelling is one of the most important things about writing," Mr. Ewing told the class. "People who can't spell are called 'illiterate.'" From then on, when the weather was so cold or wet that we couldn't get out onto the basketball court, he would have us choose up sides and have a spelling bee with half the kids on the north side of the room by the blackboards, half on the south side next to the windows. Sometimes he awarded a prize to the winner. I thoroughly enjoyed these contests, partly because from the first spelling bee the year I turned seven, I discovered I was one of the best spellers in the school and I often won. Spelling came easily for me and once I learned how to spell a word, I didn't forget it. Mr. Ewing taught us to break down each word into syllables, then spell it the way it sounded. That usually worked but when it didn't there were a few special rules I could use that he also taught me. I delighted in the challenge of outspelling the older kids. One time when I beat everybody else Mr. Ewing gave me a five-year diary. It had a blue leather cover and a gold little lock that opened with a key.

Because I was small for my age and a year or more younger than most of my classmates at Round Grove, I made friends with a few boys who were a grade or two behind me in school but who were more nearly my age and size. I also had friends who were big and on the basketball team who protected me from other big boys who weren't my friends, boys whose favorite sport was to get little boys into fights with older boys who were bigger, stronger, and in no danger of getting hurt. They would always claim the smaller boys started the fights.

One noon after we had all eaten dinner and kids were mostly just standing around, I heard my name called. "Hey, Rex Wilson, c'mere!" There was the old familiar sneer on Harry Lewis DePew's face as he stood under the big black-jack tree down at the west end of the basketball court. Two of his buddies were with him. As I walked over I could guess what was on his mind. I had not forgotten when he tried to start a fight with me at the after-school picnic at Carmen Park.

"Whatta you want?" I asked as I looked into the hostile faces of Harry Lewis and his buddies, Don Paul Calhoun and Beany Crawford.

"Lissen, ya think yer so damn smart, gettin promoted to tha third grade, outspellin' everbody in school. Just who in hell do ya think you are? Well, I can tell ya who tha hell ya are. You ain't nothin but a orphan kid who oughta not be here in tha first place when everbody knows ya belong up there at Helena in tha orphans' home. An Wilson ain't yer real name, either!"

Harry Lewis was standing, feet planted wide apart,

hands on his hips, now a little farther from his friends, who had backed away. Without saying a word I walked slowly up to him, drew back my fist, and hit him in the face as hard as I could. He was so startled that he ended on his butt end. I had hit him squarely on the nose, the way Daddy had told me to deal with bullies. Streams of blood painted his face red down to his chin. He began to cry as he picked himself up. Without a word Harry Lewis took off for the schoolhouse, crying and running. His pals backed away, mouths wide open, staring at me in disbelief. I figured Harry Lewis would tell Mr. Ewing I had started a fight with him and I was relieved when Eddie Talmage, who had witnessed everything, walked over to me. "C'mon, Rex, I'll go with ya to see Mr. Ewing so he'll know you're tellin' tha truth about what happened."

Harry Lewis almost knocked us down as he came stumbling out the front door of the schoolhouse, Mr. Ewing not far behind. "Come in here, Rex," he said. "I want to talk to you. Eddie, did you see what happened?"

"Yes sir, I was there an saw tha whole thing. It was Harry Lewis that started it. He was callin' Rex bad names an makin' fun of him because he was adopted outta tha orphans' home. I figger Harry Lewis had it comin'."

"Is that right, Rex, is that what happened? Did you hit him?"

"Yes sir, I did. I hit him as hard as I could. That's what my daddy told me to do when I got in trouble with a bully."

"Eddie, you can go back to the playground. Rex and I have some talkin' to do." And Mr. Ewing led me back into the empty schoolhouse.

We didn't talk long because the dinner hour was almost over. But Mr. Ewing was understanding. He told me that fist fighting wasn't the answer to any problem. But he said he wasn't angry with me for hitting Harry Lewis and was not going to punish me. Then, for the first time, he talked to me about my adoption. "Unfortunately," he said very seriously, "there's a stigma of sorts attached to being adopted. I don't know exactly why, there's nothing wrong with adoption, but it seems some people don't understand what is involved and are pretty narrow-minded about it." He explained what he meant by "stigma" and said some folks are prejudiced against others for no good reason. "It isn't right and it isn't fair," he said. Then he explained what "prejudiced" meant. "What Harry Lewis said to you was cruel and completely uncalled for," he said, "and I'm sorry he said it. It makes no difference to me that you're adopted and it shouldn't make any difference to you. You've got to look people right square in the eye, Rex, because you're just as good as the next guy and probably a whole lot smarter. You've got nothing to be ashamed of because you're adopted and I want you to get over lettin people get your goat about it. You've got to stop being so defensive."

I felt a whole lot better, especially when Mr. Ewing said, "Remember, Rex, I'm always here and you can talk to me any time you're having a problem or you get to feelin' down about a crack somebody's made about your bein' adopted. I'm not just your teacher, I'm also your friend and I'm always ready to listen." He stood up and reached for the school bell. "Lunch hour is about over. Now I want you to act like nothin happened out there."

My life seemed to turn around that day and I never forgot what Mr. Ewing said. He was right about everything. And he probably never knew how much better, how much more secure, his kind words had made me feel.

Basketball was Mr. Ewing's first love, his favorite of all sports, and from the talk I heard he had been a pretty good athlete in high school and during his two years up at Alva. Winning the game was very important to Mr. Ewing. We lost a game to Chaney Dell right off the bat his first year, when I was in third grade. He said we were the better team, that we shouldn't have lost, and that we had to practice harder. From then on we practiced our plays over and over until Mr. Ewing was satisfied and we spent lots of time passing the basketball all around to confuse the other team. Once I overheard Daddy telling Mother that some people were grumbling about Mr. Ewing's recruiting practices, how he liked to make up his own standards of sportsmanship, and how he always played the game to win, whatever it took. Well, I think Daddy was right about that. Except for that first game with Chaney Dell, we never even came close to losing during the three years Mr. Ewing taught at Round Grove.

Even though every boy at Round Grove was allowed to use the basketball court, only the older, taller, bigger boys got to play on the school team. All eight of them were much bigger than I, so I was surprised when one day Mr. Ewing asked me to be the team's official mascot.

"I've talked to your folks and they said it was up to you. Would you like to be Round Grove's mascot? You would wear the school uniform and be with the team at all the games. Would you like that?"

I was so thrilled I could hardly manage to say yes.

Having me be the team's mascot was Mr. Ewing's idea and my folks figured it would be all right. He started calling me "Peewee" and often seemed to let me get by with things the other kids got into trouble for. As team mascot I went to every game and tournament we played in, even suiting up and sitting with the big boys on the team.

Mr. Ewing was especially good to me during basketball season. Every time we went to a tournament I rode in the front seat of his 1932 Ford V-8 and when it was cold I could keep my feet warm if the South Wind gas heater was working. I never told Mr. Ewing why I didn't like his old Dodge car and I was glad when he came to school one day with an almost new Model B Ford sedan. Because I was younger and smaller than the regular team players the big boys treated me like a little brother, and often bought me pop and hot dogs or hamburgers at the tournaments. That was probably the best thing about being the team's mascot. But I also liked it when Mr. Ewing sent me into the game when we had a big lead. The other boys would see that I got to handle the ball once in a while and would sometimes let me in on some big plays. Once when I was being guarded by a big kid from McWillie School, and he was waving both arms up and down and hollering at me, I passed the ball between his legs to Dwayne Hood and helped set up a Round Grove two-pointer. The crowd clapped and some of the men whistled. "Atta boy, Peewee!" somebody yelled. I looked over to where Mr. Ewing was standing on the sideline and he was grinning. After he pulled me out of the game he patted me on the shoulder like he patted the big boys to let them know he was happy with the way they were playing.

People said our boys' basketball teams were the talk of the whole county and then some, not so much because we were a winning team, but because of the lengths Mr. Ewing went to in getting big boys to take seventh and eighth grades at Round Grove. His idea was very simple and his methods were no secret. Grade school kids from just about anywhere in Oklahoma could go to Round Grove so long as they actually lived within the school district while school was in session. Mr. Ewing often talked with a boy and his folks, then found somebody in our School District 99, usually kinfolks, that the boy could live with, at least until basketball season was over.

Mr. Ewing taught his basketball players to hustle on the court, to ignore people in the stands who came to watch, and to fight for the ball. "Get hold of that ball any way you can," he'd say. Three of our players were close to six feet tall and were able to get away with almost anything on the basketball court. Smaller kids stayed out of their way to avoid being run over and getting hurt. When I was in the game I tried not to get close to them, especially if one was going in for a layup. ❖

Chapter 14 ────────────────────────────────◄

In many ways, the third, fourth, and fifth grades were my best years at Round Grove School. Under Mr. Ewing's watchful attention, I read constantly, including a good bit about general science, algebra and geometry, and took intelligence tests that he brought from the teachers' college up at Alva.

A multiple choice science question on one of the intelligence tests Mr. Ewing gave to all of us went something like this: "You have a pail half full of water and you swing it rapidly in a circle. What keeps the water inside the pail? (1) Gravity; (2) Velocity; (3) Love; or (4) Centrifugal force." I was one of the few who checked "centrifugal force." I knew what it was because Daddy had explained it to me and I figured everybody else did too. Harry Lewis DePew was the only kid in the whole school who marked " (3) Love" as the answer. Everybody, even Mr. Ewing, laughed and we could all see Harry Lewis's face turn red with embarrassment. I was probably gladder than any other kid in school that Harry Lewis looked so dumb that day because he was always so mean and I figured he had it coming.

All the kids at Round Grove gave Mr. Ewing a lot more

respect that they had given Miss Downing. Even the older and bigger boys like Andy McCullen and Melvin Hood seemed to be scared of him, never sassed, always gave him plenty of room, and almost never broke wind inside the schoolhouse. Several of the boys were bigger and might have been able to whip Mr. Ewing, but I figured that none of them ever had the nerve to try. He also whipped a lot harder than Miss Downing and used a bridle rein or piece of wet rope instead of a switch. Several times he used the bridle rein on me, the same way Daddy did and he finally stopped using the wet rope after Beany Crawford's daddy came to the school one day and told Mr. Ewing that if he ever whipped Beany with a wet rope again he would beat the tar out of him. At about this time Daddy said he was tired of the low marks I was getting in conduct on my report card. "From now on," he said, "I don't wanta see nothin less than a ninety fer conduct on yer report card. An I'm tellin ya that if ya don't turn over a new leaf an start behavin yerself better in school I'm gonna hafta work ya over." Right then my conduct started to improve; I began to work even harder at being good when Daddy promised to pay me a nickel each time I got a ninety or above in conduct. I figured that was a pretty good deal.

My main problem with Mr. Ewing was that he seemed to be in a good mood one day and in a bad mood the next, and when he wanted to, he could be very strict. I was never sure what I could get away with. And because I couldn't always tell how he was feeling before it was too late, I got into trouble fairly often. He whipped me five times the year I was in third grade, mostly for being out of my seat without his permission and one time for trying to grab hold of a big red apple Elton Baker had tied by the stem to a long piece of dirty binder twine. Elton had whispered up and down the aisle on my side that the first one who touched the apple could have it. Then he rolled it up and down between his row and the one I was in. I touched the apple before Paul Tomlin could get his hand on it, but I had to get up out of my seat to do it. It was bad enough to get a whipping from Mr. Ewing, but I didn't even get to keep the apple.

Mr. Ewing also made no bones about his dislike for anyone who stole from other people. After recess one morning, he stood up, whacked his desk good and hard with an eighteen-inch ruler, and told us to listen closely to what he had to say. "It has come to my attention," he announced in a loud serious voice, "that somebody has taken cookies from Trixie Campbell's lunch pail and I mean to find out who took them." Nobody batted an eye or moved a muscle. There was absolute silence. I could even hear the wind blowing through the blackjack trees down by the merry-go-round. It seemed like no one even breathed, that is, nobody but Cecil Moorehead, who had asthma, and as usual I could hear him wheezing. I had never seen Mr. Ewing so worked up before. But then, I couldn't remember anybody just flat stealing something from somebody at Round Grove. "I want the guilty person to raise his hand right now!" Nobody spoke. I looked out of the corner of my eye to see what Homer Harmer was doing. I thought maybe he would be crying because he got scared so easily. But he was just sitting at his desk, sort of rolling his eyes, swallowing, running his tongue over his dry lips, breathing rapidly.

"I'll say it again a little louder in case somebody didn't hear me! Whoever took Trixie's cookies raise his hand. Somebody's guilty and I had better get an answer." Total silence. Nobody was missing from school so if somebody really did take cookies from Trixie's dinner pail, he had to be in the room. I hoped the thief would turn out to be Harry Lewis DePew.

"Well, one of you stole those cookies and I intend to find out who it was. And if the guilty person doesn't own up right now there's only one thing for me to do. You don't give me any choice." Stony silence. "O.K., I'll take you one at a time in alphabetical order. I'll go down the roll and whip every one of you until somebody owns up to taking those cookies. Now all of you stand up and quietly march out of here and wait down at the basketball court. I'll call you when your time comes."

Any thought of special consideration because I was on such good terms with Mr. Ewing seemed to evaporate like the fog that came out of my mouth on a cold morning. I was plenty scared and I could see real fear on the faces of kids all around me. Some of the first graders had begun to cry, especially Bennie Lee Harmer's little brother, Homer. I figured he would be the last person in the world to steal those cookies. Surely, I thought, Mr. Ewing wouldn't whip him. But I knew Mr. Ewing was really mad and that he meant business. I knew better than most that he whipped mighty hard with that bridle rein. But I kept telling myself that, surely, the guilty one would own up before my turn came. It isn't right to whip everybody just to punish the one who stole Trixie's cookies. Mr. Ewing ought to think of that. It made me feel a little better to remember that because my name was clear down at the very end of the alphabet and there were more than thirty-five kids ahead of me, one of them had to be the cookie thief.

Curt Baker was the first one Mr. Ewing called into the schoolhouse. All eyes followed him as he walked slowly to the front door and disappeared inside. All of us were probably thinking the same thing; that Curt Baker never got into trouble. He studied hard, made good grades, was a kid everybody liked. He couldn't possibly have stolen those cookies. And he's going to get a whipping just because the one who really stole them is too much of a coward to own up to it. I don't know how long Mr. Ewing kept Curt inside the schoolhouse because I didn't see him come out the other end of the building. I figured Mr. Ewing had given him a hard whipping and told him to stay away from us other kids so we wouldn't know what was going to happen.

One by one the kids were called into the schoolhouse. Time

dragged on and on. Nobody talked much, just stood around in little bunches looking scared. I hoped that Harry Lewis would turn out to be the culprit, but only a short while after he was called, the alphabet continued. The crowd on the basketball court got smaller and smaller as my turn came closer.

By the time Mr. Ewing worked his way down the alphabet to the Tweedy boys I was beginning to feel sick to my stomach; it was Leonard, Mike, then me, the last name on the list. By then I was resigned to being whipped. But I figured I could stand a beating with the bridle rein if everybody else could. I also reasoned it would be wise to cry because if I didn't, Mr. Ewing might think he wasn't hurting me enough and whip me all the harder. I just hoped I wouldn't be so sick to my stomach that I would throw up.

Leonard Tweedy was called, then Mike, who stayed in the schoolhouse, it seemed, for a good bit longer then any of the other kids. I wondered what was going on in there as I sat all alone on the basketball court, in the dirt, my mouth so dry I could hardly swallow. I was never so relieved in all my life as when Mr. Ewing finally walked out the front door, rang the school bell to signal that it was time for all of us to come back inside. It looked for sure like I wasn't going to get a whipping after all.

During the noon hour we all learned what had happened. Mike Tweedy had told Mr. Ewing he had taken the cookies before recess that morning. Because he had been tardy, nobody was around the screened-in cupboard in the corner of the anteroom where we all put our dinner pails. Clearly, Mike paid the price for his sin; we didn't see him sit down for the rest of the day. He either stood up or leaned on something and Mr. Ewing didn't tell him to take his seat. By afternoon recess we all knew that Mr. Ewing hadn't whipped a single one of the girls and that he had given the boys, especially the little ones, only a gentle swat.

During opening exercises one Tuesday morning, Mr. Ewing

said he had something very important to tell us and that we should pay close attention.

"Some of you probably have noticed Nancy Rose Fleming wasn't in school yesterday." He spoke slowly, solemnly, choosing his words carefully. "Last night her mother telephoned me to say Nancy Rose has a case of the itch and may have had it for several days. She isn't here today because Mrs. Fleming and I agreed it would be better for everybody if she kept Nancy Rose home for as long as it takes her to get over it. Nobody knows how long it will be because, as some of you know, goin to the doctor and takin medicine are against their religion. And we don't know what kind of itch it is, but it's almost certainly contagious and I imagine some of you may have picked up some of her germs. If you have, I'm sorry. But maybe those who have been most exposed can head off gettin the itch if they start right now. I want you all to go straight home this morning and, some time today, take a hot bath in a Lysol solution. Now don't forget, take a Lysol bath before you come back to school tomorrow. Plain soap isn't enough. Use Lysol. I don't want everybody comin down with the itch."

I didn't ask Mr. Ewing how much Lysol to use; heck, I didn't even know what Lysol was. But what bothered me as much as anything was that I didn't like to take baths. Besides, the bigger I got the harder it was for me to fit into the washtub. Another thing, if you're taking a bath in a washtub set right out in the middle of the kitchen floor, anybody who came to the door could see you there all wet and naked. So the idea of having to take a bath in a washtub full of Lysol, whatever that was, was a pretty unpleasant thing to consider and I knew I wasn't going to like it.

"Lysol stinks pretty bad," Junie Clifford was telling everybody before we all started home that morning, "an if ya get any of it on ya, yer skin stinks fer a week even if ya use a lotta soap tryin to get it off." He said Lysol smelled like skunk.

Mother didn't seem to understand my explanation as to

why I had come home from school by nine-thirty that morning and couldn't believe it when I told her what Mr. Ewing had said for us to do. "Now son, tell me again what he said. Maybe you didn't understand him right." So I told her once again what Mr. Ewing had told us. She just looked at me, disbelief showing in her face, slowly shaking her head. She went to the telephone and called Iris Talmage to ask if her kids had brought home any written instructions from Mr. Ewing. Eddie and Pauline had told Iris the same thing I had told Mother. Next she called Nell Bailey, who said her girls had come home with the same story and that she was going to go ahead and bathe them in Lysol. "All right," Mother finally said to me, "we'll get some Lysol and give you a bath in it."

Mother said she didn't have any Lysol, never used it and there were other things you could use to disinfect yourself that smelled better. She said Lysol wasn't good for anything except, maybe, killing red ants or potato bugs. She called down to Grandma Dollie's house and talked with Grandpa Pete. He said he had used up the last Lysol he had to doctor some sores on the back of one of his milk cows. "I used all that was left in the bottle," he said.

Mother said she reckoned there was nothing else to do but drive over to Aline and buy some Lysol. She left a note for Daddy, who was doing some listing out in the eight-acre patch, and left it on the dining room table so if he came back to the house before we got home he would know where we had gone. We drove on over to Aline and parked in front of Jay Woods' store. Mr. Woods told her several people had been in that morning looking for Lysol and he had run plumb out of it. Corliss's Drug Store, the one that used to be Moler's Drug Store, had just sold their last bottle. We tried every store but C.O. Bullard's down at the end of the block. We seldom went there but Mother figured it was the last place in Aline that might have some Lysol. Mr. Bullard looked and found a single quart-sized bottle, the last he had. "Probably enough Lysol,"

Mother sighed, "to disinfect every livin thing in Alfalfa County." Even though it was much more than she needed, she bought it and we went on back home. Mother grumbled all the way. "The only thing I can think of that smells worse than Lysol is skunk," she muttered, "an I'm sorry you have to go through this. But if that's what Mr. Ewing wants, that's what we'll do." By this time I was more anxious than ever to get the bath over with. I knew all the other kids would smell the same way I would on Tuesday morning, but that didn't make the idea any more pleasant.

Mother and I didn't waste any time. The first thing was to bring inside the copper boiler from where we kept it on the back porch over between the cistern and the washing machine. The only things we used it for were to heat water for baths and for washing clothes. I lifted it up onto the cook stove, poured in the water that was left in the wooden bucket we drank out of, while Mother stuck several chunks of split blackjack wood into the firebox at the end of the stove. Using the wooden bucket and making several trips, I filled the boiler about half full of cistern water. While the water heated I refilled the drinking water bucket and dragged inside from the back porch one of the two square galvanized washtubs that Mother used for rinsing clothes on washday. I pushed it to the middle of the kitchen floor. Like everybody else we knew who lived out in the country, we always used one of the tubs for bathing on Saturday nights. I don't know how my folks managed to take baths in that tub. I was never allowed to see how they did it.

My bath was every bit as bad as I expected it to be and the Lysol smelled even worse than Junie Clifford said it did. At the first little whiff when Mother opened the bottle, I recalled exactly when and where I had smelled it before. It was the smell on the floors and toilets at the orphans' home and in the courthouse in Cedar Creek. Mother guessed at the amount of Lysol because the instructions on the label didn't say anything about taking a bath in it. Judging from the smell she had put in plenty, enough, she figured, to kill any itch germs I might have picked up from Nancy Rose. There was a lot of Lysol left over. Mother said maybe she could use it on next summer's potato bugs. Finally it was over. I dried off and put on clean clothes. "Well," Mother said, "you're disinfected. I hope it works." Together we carried the bath water out to the back yard, dumped it so it would run downhill toward the road, wiped up the kitchen floor with old rags, and hung them outside on the clothesline with the wet towels I had used. Daddy seemed surprised when he came home and found all the windows and doors open, and the house smelling of Lysol.

That night I slept on a pallet Mother made for me on the floor at one end of the largest upstairs room where she had piled old magazines and worn-out clothes and where Daddy hung up sides of meat in the winter. Mother said she had me sleep there so I would be as far as I could get from her and Daddy's bedroom downstairs. "Otherwise," she said, "the smell might keep us awake all night."

Everybody showed up at school the next day smelling of Lysol, I guess, although the whole school smelled so strong I couldn't tell for sure. Mr. Ewing said that after he sent us all home he stayed at school for a while, using Lysol to wash off Nancy Rose's desk and anything else she might have touched and left itch germs on. It was several days before the schoolhouse smelled normal again, with the old familiar musty odor of the treated sawdust Mr. Ewing sprinkled around on the floor before he swept every morning.

Nancy Rose was back in school a week later. She seemed to have recovered from the itch because I didn't see any signs of it on her face and hands. She didn't scratch all day long; at least I didn't see her scratching. I kept my eye on her.

Mother told Daddy the whole thing was kind of a bad joke on the Round Grove kids. "It wouldn't surprise me none," I

Chapter 15

Nobody at Round Grove School was rich. Nobody had electricity and not a single family in our community had a refrigerator in their kitchen, nor did anybody have running water or an inside toilet. Maybe some people had battery-powered radios but I didn't know who they were. Most of the girls either wore dresses made by their mothers or clothes ordered out of catalogs. Almost everybody cooked and heated their houses with blackjack wood that grew everywhere. Some families used Coleman lamps like Mrs. Tidwell had back in Cedar Creek that burned white gasoline and furnished a brighter light than the coal oil lamps most people used.

But some families were poorer than others. There were clear signs that even a kid like me could see. Some of the poorest didn't have cars, most lived in small houses that weren't big enough for their families, and several were sharecroppers who didn't own the land they were living on but paid rent with a third or more of their wheat crops.

I guessed that some kids were really poor by what they brought in their dinner pails. The kids in one big family usually brought nothing for their dinner but thick slabs of homemade white bread with lard spread on them and maybe a small apple or homemade cookie. They never brought any lettuce, carrots, or celery or fruits like bananas, oranges, and blue plums. Sometimes the Tomlins and the Hoods brought dried prunes, apricots, or peaches. I knew that because they often tried to trade their dried fruit for something they liked better. Jim Bob Tomlin sometimes had nothing in his lunch pail but a slice or two of homemade bread or cold pancakes or biscuits left over from breakfast. He said the yellow stuff spread on them was plain old mustard.

Time after time I gave Jim Bob some of my dinner. I was happy to share my jelly sandwiches, especially if Mother had also put peanut butter on them. The cake or cookies and fruit were plenty for me to get by on until I got home. So when I gave him something he liked better, Jim Bob would drop his mustard sandwiches into the toilet so his mother wouldn't know he hadn't eaten them.

It wasn't just the dinners he brought to school and the way he always seemed to need a haircut that showed me Jim Bob and his brother and sister were poor. It seemed to me that he wore the same pair of striped overalls every day until they were so worn they couldn't be patched any more. In the bitter cold of January and February, even into early April, Jim Bob's winter coat was never thick enough to keep him warm on the long walk to and from Round Grove, where there was almost nothing to break the strong, bone-chilling north wind. Sometimes the coat he wore was too big and, from the way it hung on him, I guessed it had belonged to one of his three older brothers.

Jim Bob never seemed to wear a new pair of shoes to school. They were always what Mother called "hand-me-downs." His old work shoes were never polished for the same reason mine weren't. You never bothered to polish or even to wash off your work shoes because you were just going to get cow manure on them again anyway. On a farm it couldn't be avoided. All us boys wore the same kind of shoes Jim Bob did, black or brown with high tops. But unlike many of the other boys, I had a pair of dress up shoes that I wore to church or whenever we went to Enid or to somebody's funeral or something special like that.

One day Jim Bob came to school with his shoes all covered with a thick layer of greasy white stuff. He said it was tallow that came off the hide of a calf they had butchered. I asked him why he had put the tallow on his shoes. He said the tallow would help warm his feet and keep them from getting wet when it rained. He said the tallow would also help stop his shoes from squeaking because shoes did that when they got all dried out.

During supper that night I told my folks about Jim Bob putting tallow on his shoes. Daddy explained that it was an old-fashioned way to treat shoes so they would last longer. He said he used to tallow his shoes when he was a boy going to school at Round Grove. I was thankful that I didn't have to put tallow on my shoes or have to wear shoes somebody else had already about worn out. And I always had socks to wear with my work shoes.

It wasn't Jim Bob's fault that he wasn't exactly like the other boys. He couldn't help looking like a little old man, "the spittin image of his daddy," my folks used to say. I liked him anyway and he was my good friend from the time he started first grade at Round Grove. He was younger than I was, but about my size. His sister Camilla was my age and had started first grade at the same time I did. She looked just like Jim Bob except she was a girl.

Jim Bob was next to the youngest of nine Tomlin kids. His daddy was a sharecropper, and the whole bunch of Tomlins lived southeast of Round Grove near Eddie Talmage's house, two miles from the school. Their house was a lot smaller than the one I lived in. It was brown and square and had four rooms. It was surrounded by broken-down farm implements, old cars that wouldn't run, and other junk partly hidden by

blow sand. Unlike most other people in southern Alfalfa
County, the Tomlins weren't related to anybody else. I always
wondered where they had come from, considering Jim Bob
didn't want to talk about it. "How come?" I asked. And he said
his papa told him that where they came from wasn't anybody's business but theirs. I didn't ask again and never found
out.

Jim Bob walked to school with a small crowd of other
kids, including his brother and sister. Eddie Talmage, his little sister Pauline, and three of the Tweedy boys usually
joined the Tomlins as they headed off to the northwest, across
the section, over barbed wire fences, wheat and cowpea fields
of loose sand, and grassy pastures. By going that way they
shortened their walk by about a quarter of a mile. Walking
back and forth across the section wasn't a whole lot easier
than going by the road but it must have seemed a lot shorter
to them.

Eddie told me how the boys used acorns or green plums
in their slingshots, aiming at Harry Vealy's and Bud
Spurgeon's cows any time they came within range, and how
they sometimes hit a squirrel that was trying to hide in a
blackjack tree.

The only times the kids didn't cut across the section was
when the fields had just been plowed or cultivated. They
knew that plowing or other working of the sandy soil left it
so loose that they would have to sort of wade through it and
get their shoes full of sand because they couldn't walk on top
of it. And, of course, if the wind was blowing very hard, dust
would get all over them and into their eyes, even worse than
when they walked down the middle of the road.

Every fall the kids had to cope with sandburs that grew
and ripened during the hot summer months. The older boys
mashed the sandburs down with their heavy workshoes,
eventually causing them to wither and die, making a narrow
path for the girls and younger boys to walk in single file. By

the time school was out in April you could clearly see, where the kids had walked during the school year, a narrow trail, looking exactly like a cowpath, across Harry Vealy's wheat field where wheat didn't grow.

Typically, that bunch of kids from southeast of Round Grove came early to school and most were there by the time I showed up. Sometimes Marvin, the youngest of the Tweedy boys, played hooky and spent the day hiding, out of Mr. Ewing's sight, in a plum thicket about halfway between the school and Bud Spurgeon's house. When the other kids who walked that way came by in the late afternoon, Marvin came out of the plum brush and walked the rest of the way home with them. He was the only kid I ever heard of who regularly played hooky, and I never knew how he got away with it. "Ole Marvin's just like Tom Sawyer," I said to Eddie Talmage one day.

"Who's Tom Sawyer?" Eddie asked.

I could tell that Jim Bob was a complete Christian and took his religion seriously by showing it every day. He was especially sincere about doing unto others as you wanted them to do unto you. I sometimes got the feeling he thought the rest of us were unsaved heathens. He talked about the Golden Rule as though nobody else had ever heard of it.

"Whatta you do," I asked him one day, "if you get so mad at somebody that you haul off and hit him up 'long side the head? Does the Golden Rule mean you'd want the other kid to haul off and hit you?" I meant it as kind of a joke, to tease him a little.

"Naw," he said after thinking on it for a little while, "I don't think that's what it's s'posed to mean."

"Well," I said, "I can tell you what would happen. In a case like that the other kid would hit you back."

Of course, I was just having fun with Jim Bob but he didn't smile and he looked at me strangely. Jim Bob and his family went to the Nazarene Church just around the corner from

Round Grove. For all I know, he may have figured because my folks and I didn't go to the Nazarene Church, we didn't go to church anywhere.

The part about loving your neighbor was also very real to Jim Bob. It was right there in the Bible, plain as day, one of the lessons he was taught in Sunday school. One Monday morning during recess I heard him talking religion with Marvin Tweedy. Marvin was listening but it was clear from the look on his face that he wasn't interested.

Jim Bob explained that you should love your neighbor, then told Marvin that because he was his neighbor he loved him, "just like it's wrote in the Bible."

"I love ya as much as I love myself," he said solemnly.

"Jim Bob Tomlin, you don't know what the Sam Hill yer talkin about! Boys don't love other boys an they dang sure don't go round tellin other boys they love em. Where'd you get an idea like that anyhow?"

"Well, you was in church yesterday, an if ya wadn't asleep ya must of heard the preacher talkin bout love an how Christians are s'posed to love their neighbors like brothers."

"Well, you may be my neighbor but I sure as hell ain't your brother. An I don't love ya, neither. An I don't give a dang what the Bible or anybody says!" Marvin had run out of patience and he stomped away in utter disgust.

A day or two later Jim Bob came up to me during recess and started telling me the very same thing he had been trying to tell Marvin Tweedy. Because I was his friend, I didn't want to just walk away and leave him talking. I said, "You must be some kinda fool cause only a fool would go round tellin people that he loved em, especially other boys. An if ya ain't a fool yer darn sure talkin like one!"

"Oh Rex Wilson, what you said!" he scolded, drawing back in horror, a deep frown on his thin, tired-looking face. "Doncha know what the Bible teaches bout that? Doncha know that if ya call yer brother a fool that yer in danger of heck fire?"

"Lissen here," I said, as patiently as I knew how, "I'm yer friend but I ain't yer brother. I know dang well what the Bible says about that cause my mother told me. Besides, the Bible says you're forgiven seventy times seven fer yer sins so I ain't too worried about goin to hell just cause I said you was a fool."

Right about then Mr. Ewing rang the bell for recess to end and I was glad to put a stop to this argument with my friend. Jim Bob never mentioned the love-your-neighbor stuff to me again. For that matter, I never again discussed religion with Jim Bob or with any other kids who attended the Nazarene Church. Mother said they were a bunch of Holy Rollers and sometimes got all carried away and talked in tongues and did all kinds of odd things like rolling around on the floor of the church. "Things we wouldn't dream of doing in our church," she said.

But sometimes Jim Bob started right out talking about something that would catch me completely off balance. For example, one morning before school started he said, "Has yer papa got a male cow?" I thought he was joking.

"You mean, does my daddy have a bull?"

"Well"—he seemed embarrassed—"a...a male...a bull. Yeah, a bull."

"You know, don't you, what a cow is and what a bull is an how you can tell the difference? You don't call a cow a female so you don't call a bull a male."

"Yeah, but Papa calls a he cow a male."

"Well, yeah, we got a bull. Why do you wanta know?"

"What kinda male is he?"

"I don't know for sure, I think maybe he's a whiteface but he might be a shorthorn. I ain't sure. I know he ain't a Jersey. Why do you wanta know?"

"Cause Papa told me to ask ya today."

"Oh," I said, as though I understood. But I had no idea why in the world Jim Bob was asking about our bull.

Near sundown the same day, Archie Tomlin, Jim Bob's

daddy, drove into our front yard and rolled to a stop down by the barn where Daddy and I were almost finished with the milking. We could see him through the open barn door. He was pulling an old homemade two-wheeled trailer hitched to the rear bumper of his Model T. Mr. Tomlin was alone; neither Jim Bob nor any of his brothers was with him. There was a cow in the trailer, trying her best to get out, yanking on the heavy rope with which she was securely fastened to the front. Her pulling and jerking on the rope made the trailer squeak and bounce. She was struggling so hard I wouldn't have been surprised to see her come crashing out the side of the trailer, through the rickety old sideboards. It looked to me like if Mr. Tomlin didn't get her settled down or get her out of the trailer pretty soon she might hurt herself, maybe even break a leg. I knew that if that happened he would have to shoot her.

Mr. Tomlin opened the door of the Model T on the right side because there was no way to get in and out on the driver's side. As the door came open it made such a loud squeak that it spooked our cows, and the one I was about finished milking became so nervous she tried to put her hind foot into my milk bucket. When Mr. Tomlin slammed the door closed, making another loud noise, my cow jumped again. Slowly, and watching where he stepped, Mr. Tomlin walked over to where Daddy had just finished with a cow and was getting up off his milking stool. "Howdy, Archie," Daddy greeted him, friendly, the way he always spoke to other men. Setting his milk bucket on the ground, he shook Mr. Tomlin's hand, then picked up the bucket again.

"Howdy, Frank." Mr. Tomlin squawked when he spoke, reminding me of a crow. "What's tha chances of gettin ole Daisy serviced by yer male?"

Even though he talked with an accent of some kind, I heard him say "male" as clear as could be so I knew right away why Jim Bob had used the same word earlier.

"Sure, Archie, we're about done here so we'll just open that there big gate by the barn an let her in the corral. While yer gettin her unloaded an lettin her in I'll go up to the other end an let the bull in. He's standin down there in the lane and I spect when he gets wind of yer cow he'll be glad to come inside."

Mr. Tomlin never seemed to stop talking while we finished our milking chores, let the cows out of the barn, separated the cream, washed the separator, the milk strainer, the ten-gallon milk can, and our milk buckets, and put everything away for the night. The last thing was slopping the hogs, giving them some of the freshly separated milk. Mother came out onto the back porch to invite Mr. Tomlin to stay for supper but he said no, thanks, he couldn't stay. He said he had to be heading on down the road just as soon as the male got done with his business.

It was dark before Daddy and Mr. Tomlin were sure our bull and "ole Daisy" were finished with their "business." Getting the cow back into Mr. Tomlin's ramshackle old trailer was not nearly as easy as it was getting her out and I wondered if she wouldn't rather just stay at our place. From the lights in our house and the coal oil lantern I was holding I could see that the trailer floor was covered from one end to the other with fresh, wet, green manure that surely must have been as slippery as a rotten banana skin. And the cow refused to step in even though the floor of the trailer bed was only a few inches off the ground. Daddy got up at the front end, stood on the back bumper of the Model T, and pulled on the rope that was around the cow's neck while Mr. Tomlin whacked her across the rear end with an old broom handle he had brought along. I knew what could happen if I stood too close to the back end of a nervous cow being loaded into a trailer against her will so I kept safely out of the way. Holding up the lantern, I stood where I could watch what was going on and, at the same time, shed a little light on the trailer. With Daddy pulling from the front and Mr. Tomlin twisting her tail and whacking her now and then with the broom handle, the old cow finally decided to climb into the trailer. Her front feet slipped out from under her once, but she got herself back on all four feet and was ready to go home. From the satisfied look on his face, I could tell Mr. Tomlin was relieved and I was sure, from the way Daddy looked, that he was glad to get the whole thing over with. Sweat was dripping off the end of Mr. Tomlin's big nose and his overalls were splattered with fresh manure. But he had a broad grin on his tired face and his eyes were shiny and bright as he closed the trailer's tailgate and looked over at me. "By golly, Rex," he chuckled, "if I'd of been born rich instead of so good lookin, I wouldn't hafta work so dad blamed hard!" I giggled at that and Daddy laughed out loud. Mr. Tomlin was a long ways from being a handsome man and I was sure he knew it as well as anybody. But he was funny, and I liked to hear him talk.

Jim Bob and his papa were the only people I ever knew who referred to a bull as a "male." But Jim Bob and the other Tomlins used several words and expressions that nobody else did and I always wondered why they didn't talk more like the rest of us. Mother knew a lot about words and the English language, so one day we talked about it. She said probably the Tomlins talked like that because they came from Texas or somewhere in Arkansas or southeastern Oklahoma. She said when she was in college up at Alva she had met two sisters who came from Pine Bluff, Arkansas, who sounded kind of peculiar to her. The Tomlins, she said, sounded something like the Arkansas girls did. She said she, too, had noticed that the Tomlins talked differently. From then on, I listened more closely to the way Jim Bob talked.

One time during morning recess when Jim Bob and I came around the corner of the schoolhouse, he got careless and walked a little too close to several girls who were playing with jacks and a little red rubber ball. A bunch of jacks was spread out on the sandy ground. As he passed by Jim Bob accidentally kicked one of the jacks over into some loose sand where it promptly disappeared. Nancy Rose Fleming saw where the jack went and all she would have had to do was pick it out of the dry sand. From the way she threw a fit about it and jumped on Jim Bob, I figured the jacks and ball probably belonged to her. "Why'd ya do that?" Nancy Rose hollered.

"Ah'm sorry," he stammered. "Ah didn't go to do it." "Didn't go to do it?" I wondered, although I had heard him and his sister Camilla say the same thing many times before. Of course, I stayed out of it and didn't say anything, just stood there watching Nancy Rose throw a fit. I sure didn't want to tangle with her because even though I liked her a whole lot, she had sometimes torn into me the same way she was doing now to Jim Bob. I could see she was just pretending to be mad. I knew her pretty well and figured she was just putting on an act, showing off in front of her girl friends and me, taking advantage of Jim Bob's shyness.

"Yer not sorry, ya did that on purpose, I saw ya! Own up, ya did it on purpose, didn't ya? Ya know this is our place to play jacks an boys ain't even supposed to be around here!"

"But ah didn't go to do it," he stuttered, very softly this time, as though he couldn't think of anything else to say. I could see him trembling now and starting to sweat a little. He should have known as well as I did that you never win a fight or a shouting match with a girl, let alone with Nancy Rose.

"Well, I don't know who you think you are, Jim Bob Tomlin, comin around here where us girls are playin an kickin our things around. I'm gonna tell the teacher!" She wasn't letting up on Jim Bob, not a bit.

"Ah'm really sorry, I really didn't go to do it," Jim Bob mumbled for the third time, then quickly turned and ran off

Chapter 16 ———————————————— ◀

Mr. Ewing thought his students should know what was going on in the world and in the United States, especially in the State of Oklahoma. At the same time he knew that almost nobody who lived in the Round Grove School District subscribed to a daily newspaper. He knew because he asked us one day to get out a sheet of tablet paper and write on it the names of the newspapers and magazines that came to our house.

We didn't get the *Enid Morning News*, which was a daily paper sent out from Enid through the mail all over northwestern Oklahoma. Mr. Ewing said it came every day except Sunday, so people couldn't read the colored funny papers until the Sunday paper got there on Monday. There wasn't any paper printed for Monday. Daddy didn't claim to be much of a reader and thought the Enid paper cost too much money. He figured that two weekly newspapers were enough for us.

The mailman brought us the *Aline Chronoscope* on Fridays and the only other paper we subscribed to was the *Capper's Weekly* from Topeka, Kansas, which also came in the mail. I wrote those names on my paper to turn into Mr. Ewing, along with the names of several women's magazines that Mother received. Some students had to turn in blank papers.

Mr. Ewing had a radio in the Model B Ford two-door he drove to school every day during his second and third years at Round Grove School. He also brought the *Enid Morning News* to school every day after he had read it at home. And even though the paper was three or four days old and several people had already read it by the time it got to school, it was a lot better than the weekly papers or no paper at all. The *Enid Morning News* had all kinds of information in it about what was happening in America and in foreign countries around the world. It even had a page of funnies, including those with my favorite characters, Dick Tracy and Okey Doakes. Okey was a silly farm boy who decided to become a knight something like Don Quixote. The strip was funnier after Mother explained to me who Don Quixote was.

Most of the kids at Round Grove weren't interested in reading the newspaper but when Mr. Ewing discovered I was, he encouraged me to read it and I usually had plenty of time to do so after finishing my class work. Sometimes he would say to me, right in front of the whole school, "Rex, what's goin on in the world?" and I would tell him what I had been reading about in the *Enid Morning News*. I learned a lot of new words from reading the paper and learned all about things like the trial of Bruno Hauptmann, the birth of the Dionne quintuplets, and Mussolini's one-sided war against the Ethiopians. Several times Mr. Ewing and I spent part of our dinner hour talking about something we had read in the *Enid Morning News*, especially when we couldn't play basketball on account of the weather.

It seemed that almost nobody in our neighborhood had radios because they figured they were either too expensive to own and operate or thought radios were more trouble than they were worth. But it could have been that they figured they didn't need to know about everything that was going on in the world. Jim Bob Tomlin said only rich people had radios.

When I was in the fourth grade Mr. Ewing had a talk with my folks and they decided I could sing well enough to enter the Alfalfa County Fine Arts Music Contest. Preliminary contests were to be held in several communities around the County, including Aline. I had about a month to get ready for the first round of competition being held in the Aline High School auditorium. Mr. Ewing told Mother and Daddy he thought I also had a good chance of placing in the reading competition.

Twice a week after school Mother drove me over to Aline to practice my songs with Miss Jane Fields, a high school senior who had studied voice and piano for a long time. She coached me on how to stand, where and how to breathe, and how to project my voice without straining my vocal cords. Mother and Jane's folks sat and watched and offered suggestions. All this help and attention improved my self-confidence. Besides, it was fun to sing with piano accompaniment.

About a week before the preliminaries we drove over to Enid. The main reason for going, Mother and Daddy said, was to buy me some clothes so I would look nice for the Fine Arts Contest. Before starting to shop, we drove by to see another of Daddy's sisters, Aunt Dolly (she was named after Grandma Dollie except her name ended in "y" instead of "ie"), and Uncle Floyd who lived on South Van Buren. Uncle Floyd was a miller at Pillsbury Mills on the north side of town. Aunt Dolly was a registered nurse at the Enid General Hospital. Because they had different work schedules she and Uncle Floyd sometimes weren't home. We never knew until we got to their house if they'd be there. Nobody was home when we got there this time and we went on downtown.

We parked on the square and went straight to Herzberg's, a two-story brown brick building on the east side of the square where, Daddy said, they sold nothing but clothes. I had never been there before; everything I wore either came from Penney's up at Cherokee or was ordered out of the Sears Roebuck catalog.

Mother and Daddy got me a grownup-looking single-breasted, black wool suit with a vest and an extra pair of pants. Our clerk found a navy blue felt hat that was just my size. "I'll throw in a white shirt and a necktie for free," he said with a grin, "cause I like this young man." Taking a tape from around his neck, the Herzberg's tailor measured me every which way, then said he would have my suit ready by five o'clock. After we found a pair of black oxfords that fit pretty well, Mother wrote a check for a little more than fifteen dollars that covered everything. "You're a lucky boy," the clerk said to me. And to Mother and Daddy he said, "He's gonna look mighty spiffy all dressed up in his new clothes."

I felt like a million dollars! Not only did I now have a real wool three-piece suit with an extra pair of pants and everything that went with it, but Mother and Daddy had bought me my first ever black oxford dress shoes. If they could spend all that money just for me, they for sure didn't plan to take me back to the orphans' home, I figured .

Mother tried to call Aunt Dolly on the Herzberg's telephone but no one answered. It was getting close to noon so we left the clothing store to find someplace to eat dinner. We had hamburgers and pop and pie at Max and Rex's hamburger stand in the alley behind Herzberg's. I liked that place. Their food tasted real good and everybody behind the counter was nice to me.

All the way home I was feeling pretty special because I didn't know anybody else who had such fine Sunday clothes. And those new clothes probably helped me win the two blue ribbons in the preliminary voice and reading competitions at Aline High School. At least, it hadn't hurt for me to look good on the stage. Later, in the Alfalfa County finals up at Cherokee, I won a blue ribbon in voice for "Soap," accompanied by Miss Fields, and a red one, second place, for my reading.

"You're really enjoyin school, aren't you son?" Mother asked me later. "I'm glad you're learning so much from Mr. Ewing." She was right, but I was also feeling more and more comfortable with my parents and our big farm.

I was beginning to understand what growups meant when they talked about how lucky I was, to be adopted by good people like the Wilsons. And, I thought, if this is what adoption was supposed to be like, it was a whole lot better than anything I had known before.

From the beginning of fourth grade, I had a good saddle horse I could ride any time I wanted. Old Charger was gentle and smart but not young anymore. He and I were both eight years old when we got to know one another. He was the most patient horse I knew of, never reared up or tried to throw me. I rode him to school nearly every day until the end of fifth grade.

For Charger Daddy had traded a pretty good Jersey milk cow, worth maybe twenty dollars, with Homer Davis, who lived two miles west of us. Daddy figured Charger would be gentle enough for me to ride to school and I soon learned how to take care of him. Learning to stay in the saddle was the hardest part because it was made for a full-grown man; and because the stirrups were much too low for me to use, I had to keep my knees squeezed together to keep from falling off Charger's back.

Daddy saw O'Dell Watkins in Aline one day about a month after he had traded the cow for old Charger. O'Dell was about twenty and had been our hired man off and on for several years, from about the time my folks took me out of the orphans' home. We all thought of him as kind of like a member of the family.

"Hear ya traded Homer Davis outta that gray geldin he had," O'Dell said.

"You mean ole Charger?" Daddy answered. "Yeah, I traded a milk cow even up fer him. He seems like a nice ridin horse."

"Fer gosh sakes, Frank!" O'Dell spluttered. "Don't let Rex get on him!"

"How come ya say that?"

"Well, maybe Homer didn't tell ya, but ole Charger gets the idea he's a race horse ever time a car goes around him, an he'll try to outrun it. He's hard to handle when he gets passed by a car on the road. I heard Homer say one time he checked him with his car speedometer an he was runnin better'n forty miles an hour!"

"Well, gosh, O'Dell, Rex's been ridin that horse to school fer about a month now an is just gettin along fine with him."

Lucky for me, I guess, I never had to ride old Charger where there were any cars. So I never found out if he could run as fast as O'Dell Watkins was saying he could, but I did know he could run faster than any other saddle horse I knew of and I used to brag to the other boys about his being part race horse. No one else rode a horse to school, but the Hood kids had the next best thing; they came to school every day in an old-timey one-horse buggy that Frankie hitched up to a bay mare who was blind in one eye.

Frankie Hood was a good driver, careful not to overwork the old mare or to let her go so fast that there was danger of wrecking the buggy or turning it over and hurting somebody. Frankie made the old mare walk or let her trot, depending on how many kids he had loaded onto the buggy. When they got to school just before eight o'clock every morning the buggy riders would jump off and run up the little hill. Frankie then unhitched the horse, tied her up in the barn, took off her harness, and hung it up on a couple of two-by-fours that had been nailed onto one side of the stall she was left to stand in. Hay cut from the schoolyard just before school started was stacked inside the barn high in the rafters above the stalls, and every morning as long as the hay lasted, Frankie gave some to the old mare. Once Frankie felt sorry for old Charger and gave him some of the hay to eat. In wet weather Frankie and his brothers pushed their buggy inside the barn to keep it from getting rained or snowed on, then climbed the little hill to the front door of the schoolhouse. When school let out at four o'clock in the afternoon, Frankie hitched up the buggy to the bay mare in nothing flat, loaded up the kids, and headed off for home.

The barn where the Hoods and I kept our horses was down close to the basketball court. The two horses stood there all day without a drink and often with nothing to eat. I figured the bridle and saddle were uncomfortable for Charger, especially the bit he had inside his mouth all day. So I usually let him lope as fast as he wanted on the way home. That might explain why old Charger and I practically flew home every afternoon after school. Maybe he figured the sooner we got home the sooner he could get the saddle off his back, have something good to eat, and get a drink of water out of our big cement stock tank.

Charger was a "gray" even though he had white hair and a white mane and tail. He didn't look gray to me but Daddy and everybody else called him a gray so I guess that's what he was. Because Charger was a full-sized horse and all we had was a full-sized saddle, when I was mounted my legs were more than a foot too short to get my feet into the stirrups and I never once used them except to get on and off. I only fell off Charger one time, and that was down by the basketball court when Harry Lewis DePew flew a paper airplane at him and he got spooked. Charger jerked sideways, and I was thrown out of the saddle and landed under his feet on the soft, sandy ground. I was mighty shook up and scared, and felt lucky not to be hurt. From where I was on the ground it seemed there were horse legs in every direction, and between two of them I could see Harry Lewis standing off to one side, his face white, his mouth open, his wide eyes staring at me. After that first lunging jerk, Charger stood very still and I was able to roll out from under him without getting stepped on.

When I got home that day and told Daddy what had happened he said he guessed old Charger knew I was under his feet someplace and was careful not to step on me or kick me. He said Harry Lewis had done a mighty reckless thing and ought to get a good hard whipping for it. Later I got to thinking: that was one time when I should have grabbed hold of the saddle horn to keep from falling off. I didn't because Daddy had taught me that a real cowboy never, ever holds onto the saddle horn. "That's not what it's for, son, it's only dudes an sissies who do things like that." He said a cowboy holds the bridle reins in his left hand so he can use his right hand for roping. He said if I wanted to be a cowboy when I got big I would have to learn to ride like one. So I always rode the way real cowboys do, holding the reins in my left hand.

We had a hired hand most of the time to help Daddy with the work on the three-quarter sections we farmed, the home place, Grandpa Pete's place, and the quarter a mile north of McWillie. If it wasn't O'Dell Watkins, it was somebody else. During wheat harvest Daddy might hire three or four more hands. Mother usually kept a teenaged girl during June and July to help with the housework and the extra cooking for the harvest hands.

Most of our hired hands were boys in their late teens but some were in their early twenties; a few were married. From the way most of them talked they figured on going into farming for themselves someday, getting married, and settling down, but they weren't old enough to do either and were too hard up, generally, even to buy a car, let alone the land and machinery needed to make a living at farming. Like Daddy, some had dropped out of school after finishing eighth grade.

The only bad thing about having hired hands was the way they liked to tease me. It was even worse when Daddy and Uncle Hubert, Mother's brother, joined in. I even stopped eating sweet pickles because they said my eating sweet pickles was a sure sign I was sweet on the girls. Mother almost never took part in the teasing but she never said anything to stop it either and there was never anybody to take my side. And I knew that if I let them get my goat or make me cry, they would tease me for being a crybaby in addition to everything else.

"What's the matter?" they used to ask. "Can't ya take it?" It was a lot worse to be teased at home than at school. At least at school I could hit back and win a fight once in awhile, but I always lost at home.

It seemed to me that a lot of people thought drawing good wages for farm work made more sense than spending valuable time getting an education, and a high school education was the most schooling anyone could possibly need. Going to college, according to some people I knew, was nothing but a waste of time and money. One of our hired hands once told me if a man was going to spend his life farming, raising crops and milking cows for a living, a grade school education was plenty.

Unless our hired hand lived within easy walking distance of us, he took room and board at our house. Mother was a pretty good cook and there was always plenty of food. For breakfast she usually fixed bacon and eggs, coffee, beefsteak, and homemade bread, pancakes, or biscuits. At every meal the hired man ate all he could hold. Mother even washed his clothes, cooked things he especially liked, and made his bed, as though he were a member of our family. The hired hand seemed comfortable with us and there was joking, storytelling, and even some gossip around the table, usually after a good supper when he didn't have to get right up and go back to work. The hired man never talked dirty or took the Lord's name in vain at our house and Mother and Daddy were treated with great respect. Of course, I liked some of the hired men better than others. Like Gerald McWilliams, whose daddy was the Nazarene preacher for a while. I liked him even if he was always calling me Flunky Butt. He never told me why he called me that or how he came up with that name.

Some of the men Daddy hired had table manners that made Mother uneasy; if they had been children she would have corrected them. Maybe that was why, about this time, she began coaching me on good table manners. Sometimes I saw her frown or look like she had taken a bite of something that she wanted to spit out when the hired men didn't know how to behave. Maybe she worried that I might be influenced by their sloppy manners. It wasn't just because he was so downright lazy that I didn't like Orville Tatus; it was also because he didn't have any table manners.

One afternoon Mother had gone to a lot of trouble to bake a big, juicy pie from wild blackberries she and I had gathered along the little creek in our east pasture. We were almost finished eating supper when she brought the pie in from the kitchen. She set it on the dining room table, then stood at her place, spatula in hand, ready to serve the pie.

"Orville," she asked, "would you like a piece of fresh blackberry pie?"

Pausing for a moment in wiping his plate clean with a slice of bread, he blurted, "Does a hog like slop?"

Mother forced a weak little smile but she was offended and it showed in her face. She served him first, sliding a quarter of the pie onto a clean plate and passing it over to him, then served Daddy in the same way and cut smaller pieces for herself and me. While Daddy and I waited for Mother to sit down and pick up her fork, Orville grabbed hold of his pie, held it in both hands, and, as though he were starving, began eating greedily. He reminded me of our hogs when we slopped them at the end of the day. Before the rest of us had any more than gotten started, Orville had wolfed down more than half of his share of the pie. "This has gotta be the best pie I ever et," he slobbered, showing a mouth full of blackberries, then crammed in the rest of the pie. While still chewing he wiped his mouth with his shirtsleeve. Letting go a long, rumbling belch, he leaned back in his chair, pulled the makings from the bib pocket of his overalls, and rolled a wet and lumpy cigarette. He lit the cigarette with a kitchen match struck on the sole of his shoe then sat there in a cloud of smoke while Mother, Daddy, and I finished our supper.

"What a horse's ass!" I thought to myself, but wouldn't have dared say so aloud. Mother was angry and it showed. Daddy put up with Orville's laziness for less than a week that spring, then fired him. ✦

Chapter 17 ⸺⸺⸺⸺⸺⸺⸺⸺⸺⸺⸺⸺⸺⸺ ❧

From what Eddie Talmage was saying—and I figured he knew because his daddy, Cap Talmage, was on the school board—the county didn't have nearly enough money to keep small schools like Round Grove and McWillie open and running for eight months every year. He said he'd heard his daddy talking about it on the telephone.

There was always coal for the stove, chalk for the blackboards, and maybe a few other things the school board thought we couldn't do without. But one item the county didn't spend any money on was toilet paper, or if it did, none of it came to Round Grove. Maybe the girls had toilet paper, but I never saw a roll of real toilet paper like the kind people in Enid used. The toilet paper in the boy's toilet at school was always an out-of-date Sears Roebuck or Montgomery Ward catalog for us to tear pages out of and use when we needed it. I never thought much about it because that was what we used in our toilets at home.

I didn't guess what was on Mr. Ewing's mind when he gave me an arithmetic problem to work on. "For extra credit," he said. He wanted me to figure out how much paper we would need for the toilets next year. "Figure," he said, "that we'll have forty kids here every day for eight months. And I'm not talkin about the kind you buy in rolls in a store. I'm talkin about the kind most of us use—mail order catalogs. And don't tell anybody what you're workin on; this is just between you an me."

So I figured and figured, then figured some more, based on how many pages the average kid needed to tear out of the catalog every time he had to do a number two at school. Although it was a little awkward, I asked some of the boys about how much they used. Eddie said he usually used maybe two or three pages, depending on whether the paper was still stiff and slick or limber and softer after he had roughed it up in his hands. Mike Tweedy said he used four pages, and Frankie Hood told me he always used no more than three pages out of the catalog. "I always tear every page into two pieces. I figure that's plenty to do the job," he said.

When I had finished the problem and was pretty sure of my figures, I reported back to Mr. Ewing. I said we would need at least three dozen of the big catalogs, the kind Sears Roebuck and Montgomery Ward mailed out twice a year. I reminded him that in every issue of the catalogs some of the paper wasn't fit to use in the toilets. "That's a fact," he agreed. I told him that maybe those pages could be used to start fires in the schoolhouse heating stove in cold weather. "That's good thinkin, Peewee," he said, and thanked me for my work. And I liked it when he said, "You've done a real good job Peewee, just what I wanted you to do."

Before school let out that afternoon, Mr. Ewing announced that he wanted all the members of the basketball team to stay for a second. Mr. Ewing never meant a second or even a minute but that's what he always said. What he meant was he wouldn't keep us very long after school.

"We've got a big problem," he said, "but we can handle it if you all are willing to give me a hand. The fact is, we've clean run out of paper in the boys' toilet and for all I know, the girls may be out, too." There were eight of us boys, including me, the team mascot.

"We're gonna have a contest," he said, "and see how many big mail order catalogs we can come up with over at Aline next Saturday. I figure a lot of people over there don't have any use for their old catalogs but we do. We'll divide up into teams of two, and the team that brings in the most catalogs will win the prize." He went on to explain that it wouldn't matter which mail order catalogs we collected just so long as they were the big, thick, spring-summer, fall-winter catalogs. Now I knew why he had given me the arithmetic problem.

Mr. Ewing said he had decided the best place to look for out-of-date catalogs was Aline because that was where most of our folks did their trading and the people over there knew a lot of us. He said around twenty percent of the Aline population, or about twenty houses, had indoor toilets. He calculated that we would only need to collect two big catalogs from each house to have enough paper to last the school the rest of the year.

"We can save ourselves a lot of time," he said, "by identifyin the houses that have indoor toilets and eliminatin those that don't before we start knockin on doors. It stands to reason that people who have outdoor toilets won't have any catalogs to give away. I've made a map for each team. With four teams of two boys each, I figure we can scout out the residential areas in about an hour and a half, so all you'll need to do is follow your map and call at those houses where they don't have an outdoor toilet around behind."

Mr. Ewing separated the whole town into four sections and assigned each team to one of the sections. "You'll need to get your folks' permission on this," he said, "and if it's okay with them, either I or my brother Herb will be by to pick you up between eight-thirty and nine o'clock next Saturday morning. Let me know tomorrow if I can count on you."

"I'll be drivin my brother-in-law's pickup truck on

Saturday," he said, "and I'll park next to the drug store and stay there until we load up the catalogs. If we get real lucky we might collect as many as a hundred usable ones. I'll stay with the pickup in case any problems develop. As soon as you've got all the catalogs you can handle, bring them right on over and throw them into the back of the pickup. I'll make a separate stack for each team. Anybody got any questions?"

Mr. Ewing ended the meeting by saying we would start from the front of Corliss' Drug Store. He figured we would be finished by noon and we would all be back home by early afternoon. He also said he would treat each of us to a hamburger and a bottle of pop at Henderson's Café after we got all done so we wouldn't be starving to death by the time we got home.

Except for a few problems we hadn't counted on, the collection went pretty much as Mr. Ewing had planned. Clarence Reaves' big brindle dog refused to allow a team anywhere near their house and the boys weren't even able to see if he had a toilet in the back yard, let alone collect any catalogs. But because everybody else on the block had an outdoor toilet, the boys decided the Reaves family did, too, and, naturally, wouldn't have had any catalogs to give away anyhow. So they continued on to the next block.

One team was invited into Fred Nelson's house and treated to all the cocoa and homemade donuts they could hold while the Nelsons rummaged through their house from top to bottom, looking for old catalogs. Finding none, Mrs. Nelson apologized and pressed four rolls of real toilet paper into the boys' hands and insisted they take them. "I went to school out in the country when I was a little girl," she said, "and I know how important it is to have some toilet paper." She promised to save all her most useful catalogs for next year's collection.

Paul Tomlin and Frankie Hood went well out of their way to call at Slim Rogers' house down by the Co-Op grain elevator where Slim, one of Aline's good old boys and a regular customer at Loomis' beer parlor, worked six days a week as a kind of jack of all trades.

"Boy howdy," Frankie told us all later, "we was plumb scared half to death by ole lady Rogers." Frankie was a great storyteller and as the rest of us hung on every word, Frankie related the adventure over and over, each telling coming out a little differently, more exciting than the last. Having seen no toilet in the Rogers' back yard, Frankie and Paul had walked right up onto the porch and stepped up to the closed front door. As Frankie raised his fist to knock, he happened to glance through the thin curtain that covered the large pane of glass in the door. He could see clearly across the front room and directly into the open bathroom where Mrs. Rogers, a large woman, was sitting bolt upright on the commode, her brown cotton bloomers draped loosely around her ankles, right there in plain sight. "Ohmagosh!" Frankie had whispered to Paul. "Let's get the heck outta here!" According to Frankie, it was already too late for with lightning speed. Mrs. Rogers snatched up her bloomers and, despite her enormous bulk, stormed straight toward the front door, sending a small table skidding across the living room floor as she smoothed down her feed sack housedress. Jerking open the door, she stumbled onto the porch, hair a tangled mess, face flushed with embarrassment and rage at this invasion of her privacy. Frankie said she loomed over them like a mountain of quaking fat. With chest heaving she planted herself in front of them, bare feet set far apart. Paul and Frankie couldn't move. Their mouths opened but they were unable to speak; their shoes stayed rooted to the splintery wooden porch.

"Who are you boys? What'er ya doin peekin in my house?" she had yelled, showering them with warm spittle.

"We wadn't doin nothin," Frankie stammered.

"We wadn't peekin," Paul tried to explain.

"Jus what tha heck'er you boys adoin here? Whatta ya want anyhow? Ya dang well better have a good excuse or I'll have my husband call the sheriff on ya!"

"We're jus collectin up old catalogs fer Round Grove School, that's all," Frankie had answered, "an we thought you might have some cause you ain't got no toilet out in tha back."

"Well, I ain't got none, specially fer no Peepin Toms who sneak round lookin in peoples' houses. Now you boys git outta here right now an don't ya never let me see ya hangin round here ever again, ya hear? Now git! I said git!"

Frankie and Paul took off as fast as they could run, not stopping for breath until they were out of Mrs. Rogers' sight, although they could hear her hysterical shouts of "Git! Git! Git!" following them. Collecting the catalogs they had stashed on the corner near Cecil Woods' garage, they headed back toward Corliss' Drug Store. Riding home in the back of the loaded pickup, Paul and Frankie went on and on about their run-in with Mrs. Rogers and how they couldn't believe that a woman who was almost as big as a milk cow could move so fast and they couldn't.

The next Monday everybody at school was talking about how the basketball team had collected a big batch of cata- logs, now piled in one end of the coalhouse. But by Tuesday we were pretty much back to our favorite subject, WPA jokes. Eddie Talmage, the Hood boys, and I had a lot of fun telling each other new jokes about the WPA, a federal gov- ernment program to make jobs for folks who couldn't get steady work because of the hard times people were having all over the country. Everybody at Round Grove knew some- body or knew of somebody who had a WPA job of some kind so he could get paid by the government.

"Workin for the WPA's somethin like bein on relief," Daddy said once when I asked about it, "and I'm mighty thankful I don't hafta do that for a livin."

One day I told Daddy a joke I had heard at school from Eddie Talmage. He didn't laugh. "Son, ya gotta be fair. This whole country is goin through some hard times an not every-body's as fortunate as us. Some of them people on WPA ain't got any better way to make a livin. An I reckon most of em would a whole lot druther work for themselves. So be fair. Most of them folks is doin the best they can ta get by till times get better."

Uncle Earl, Mother's oldest brother, worked for the WPA. He lived with Aunt Hazel and their two boys on a run-down quarter section up by Carmen that wasn't much good for farming. Like most other Oklahoma land, it was mainly red clay. Daddy said you couldn't even raise a good crop of weeds on that place. Uncle Earl rented the farm from Grandpa Williams. Mother said Grandpa bought it real cheap right after the crash of 1929. Because farming the land was such hard work, Uncle Earl signed up with a WPA outfit that had been organized to do maintenance and bridge repair on the dirt roads in his part of Alfalfa County. "The work's easier and the pay's better," he told Daddy and Mother. Every day Uncle Earl drove to work and back in his old Ford hoopie with high pressure tires; it was a 1925 or 1926 Model T, about as old as I was. When the weather was so bad that Uncle Earl's crew couldn't work on the road, they all climbed onto the back of a flatbed truck and rode over to Carmen where they worked in a hay barn, building two-hole privies, what we called toilets. Uncle Earl said the privies had been designed by an architect who worked for the WPA.

The government sold the new toilets for a few dollars apiece. All the toilets looked just alike and I could recognize one from as far away as I could see it. From hearing my folks talk I got the notion that anybody who bought one of the toi-lets was either too lazy to build his own or was just trying to show all the neighbors and anybody who might drive by on the road how high-toned his family was. It looked to me like the toilet was always put out in plain sight so everybody who came anywhere close could see it and say to themselves,

"My, ain't that there a nice toilet, with a door latch an everthing!" I wasn't ashamed because Daddy didn't buy one of the WPA toilets for us. I didn't think it was anybody's business.

"We ain't tryin to keep up with the Joneses," Daddy said.

It seemed every time I saw Uncle Earl he had a mouthful of chewing tobacco, except at church. I was dead sure he was chewing some tobacco when I saw the little brown trickles oozing out of the corners of his mouth. His work shoes and the legs of his blue overalls were often splattered with tobacco juice. "Ya gotta spit purty often when yer chewin tobacca," he used to say to me, "so be careful ya don't get in the way." Sometimes he chewed inside his house, but because Aunt Hazel wouldn't let him keep a spittoon there was a permanent brown puddle right outside the front door and another by the back door. The puddles were slimy messes that I had to be careful not to step in every time I went to their place. When he was finished chewing a cud, Uncle Earl used to spit it into one of the puddles.

It seemed impossible for Uncle Earl to talk and work at the same time. I was sure he would rather talk than work. Daddy liked to work and often kept busy while other men were standing around talking. But Uncle Earl never seemed to be very interested where work was concerned, and that always worried Aunt Hazel because it took him so long to get anything done, especially if there was someone around to talk with. I decided that many people in the WPA were like Uncle Earl, and Eddie Talmage probably had someone like him in mind when he told me the best WPA joke I had ever heard. One day during recess he motioned me away from where I was just starting to get into a marble game with some other boys. "Hey Peewee," he said. "I heard a new WPA story, wanta hear it?"

"You bet!" I said. I picked up my marbles from out of the sand, dropped them into my overalls pocket, and walked quickly over to where Eddie was now waiting under a blackjack tree out of earshot of the marble players.

"Okay," I said, grinning, "tell me the story."

"Well, here's it," Eddie started off, with a grin so big and wide he could hardly get any words out. "There's this here buncha WPA guys workin on the road over south of Carmen. It was a really hot day, bout a hunderd an ten in tha shade, an the boss he looks around an sees this here ole boy justa leanin on his shovel an chewin on a plug of tobacca. So tha boss he walks over to this here guy an he says, 'Lissen here,' he says, 'if ya don't stop leanin on that there shovel and get to work yer gonna be alookin fer another job.' Then tha boss he walks off to check up on some of tha other guys who was supposed to be workin. Well, it wadn't very long before tha boss he comes back around an he sees this one ole boy, tha same one he seen before. But this time tha ole boy was workin a little or tryin to look like he was workin. An this time he had his shirt off an was all covered with sweat. Then tha boss he looks a little closer an notices that this ole boy's peter was ahangin outta tha front of his overalls. So tha boss he says, 'Say, how come yer peter's ahangin out thatta way?' So this ole boy just looks tha boss right square in tha eye an he says, 'Well, I figger if I'm gonna hafta work like a dad blamed horse I might as well look like one!'" I laughed so hard I thought I'd die.

In my mind I could see Uncle Earl just standing around, leaning on his shovel, talking to anybody who would listen, spitting tobacco juice somewhere downwind, while everybody else was working.

Uncle Earl was a smart man and knew a lot of good stories. We liked to have him and Aunt Hazel and their boys Hugh and Eldon come to visit us, but every time they did Mother would watch to see where Uncle Earl spit out his tobacco juice so she could be careful not to step in it before Daddy got around to cleaning it up. And because Uncle Earl might get tobacco juice on you if you got too close, I stood well back when he was talking or when he spat. I once asked him why he always kept the cud of tobacco in his right cheek instead of his left one. "It's cause I'm right handed an I just naturally chew on that side," he explained. After they left, Daddy would get a shovel and carry the mess over to the corral and throw it over the barbed wire fence. Sometimes he just threw a shovel full of dirt on top of the mess.

"I wish," Mother grumbled to Daddy one time after they had gone, "that once, just once, Earl could visit us without having his mouth full of tobacco!" ✦

Chapter 18 ⟶

Every year the Round Grove PTA raised money for things the
school needed that the state or the county wouldn't pay for,
like sports equipment, blackboard erasers, or new books for
the library. I knew we could buy a pretty good leather basketball for nine or ten dollars and those of us on the
basketball team thought that the PTA should use some of its
money to buy us a new one every once in a while. A basketball didn't last long on a dirt court and the only one we had
was about worn out. Mother said the PTA didn't have more
than a few dollars in its treasury and she couldn't guess how
much money they could raise or if they would be willing to
spend some of it for a new basketball.

We didn't even have nets on the goals of our basketball
court so when you took a shot you had to watch closely or
you couldn't tell if the ball went through the hoop nor did
we have a way of marking off the court, no tape or anything
like that. "You can't paint dirt like you can a hardwood
floor," Mr. Ewing said. So instead we used a pointed stick to
scratch lines for the boundaries, free throw lines, and other
places where lines were supposed to be.

Finally Mr. Ewing said, "The basketball court is in awful

shape. It's an absolute disgrace. Nobody wants to play us on our home court, not even Chaney Dell, because it's so uneven and isn't marked off. Now we can't do anything about the sandy surface, but we can put down some lines so we know a little better where we are during a game." That day he had come to school with a ball of binder twine and a sack of long nails. He told us he wanted everybody in s.chool to help with the project. "It's going to be something we all can be proud of," he said.

Making drawings all over the blackboard he laid out his plans in detail, including measurements. He was sure that we could get our court into good enough shape that other schools would want to play on it. We had four days before our next game with McWillie. "If it isn't ready by Friday, we'll just have to go up there to play," he said.

Right after dinner Mr. Ewing asked Wanda Hood and Twila Bailey to keep all the girls over by the merry-go-round and see that they had something to do. Then he took us boys down to the basketball court. We got right to work with the hoes and rakes and shovels Mr. Ewing had brought from home in the back of his car. It wasn't as much work as we thought it would be, but we made the job last until four o'clock so we wouldn't have to do any more schoolwork that day.

By the time we were finished we had smoothed out most of the rough spots on the court and filled in the low places where water always stood after it rained. We even filled some holes that had been blown out by the wind, using some black mud we brought over in a milk bucket from a low place in Harry Vealey's driveway. We left Harry's mudhole a little deeper but he wasn't home and we didn't think we needed to talk to him about it anyway. We didn't figure he would mind because it was plain to see he had been driving around the hole all fall. Leonard Tweedy shoveled a pile of blow sand out of where it had collected in one corner of the court and threw it out into the road. When the time came for school to let out came, the court looked better than anyone had ever seen it and all it had cost was some binder twine, about fifty spike nails, and a little elbow grease. Mr. Ewing asked the Hoods to keep their horse and buggy off the court. He told me not to let Charger get on it because if there were any damage I would have to fix it back up the way it was all by myself.

We all were mighty proud of our fine basketball court and right away we started talking about how bad we were going to beat McWillie's team when they came down to Round Grove on Friday afternoon. Mr. Ewing said he hoped the wind wouldn't fill the court with blow sand before the game. He also said he didn't want to catch people walking around on the basketball court unless they were wearing tennis shoes and that went for the girls as well as the boys.

Friday came and the court had held up well during the week even though we had practiced hard every day between noon and one o'clock. It hadn't rained and the wind hadn't blown hard so by Friday afternoon the court was still in pretty fair shape. At noon that day Andy McCullen and Curt Baker got a couple of hammers and pounded in the spike nails that had worked themselves out of the ground during the week.

At two o'clock the McWillie team drove up with their teacher, Wilfred Higgenbotham. He offered their basketball which was newer and in a whole lot better condition than ours.

We beat McWillie 33 to 26 and right after the game was over they loaded up and headed back. As they were leaving I heard Mr. Higgenbotham telling Mr. Ewing that it was a real pleasure for his boys to play on such a well-maintained dirt basketball court. I could see Mr. Ewing was proud when he told Mr. Higgenbotham that school spirit at Round Grove had never been higher. He said the Round Grove boys deserved all the credit because they were the ones who got the court into shape especially for the McWillie game.

The Round Grove PTA had planned a box supper for the same Friday evening we beat McWillie's team on our nice clean basketball court. I hoped very hard that enough money would be raised to buy us a new basketball; I was embarrassed when we had to use McWillie's ball because ours was in such bad shape. Eddie Talmage and I did some figuring on how much money might be raised by the PTA. We had both been to box suppers at Round Grove and knew that thirty-five cents was about as much as anybody ever paid for a box. Bob Loudon paid seventy-five cents for Allie Tomlin's box last year, but I had never heard of anybody paying more than that. Eddie and I thought that if we raised maybe twelve bucks we would be doing pretty darned well.

People looked forward to the box suppers and enjoyed themselves. The rules were that simple; women and girls brought the boxes, men and boys bought the boxes. They also knew that what was in the box wasn't half as important as eating with the girl who brought it. The main idea was to be sure somebody else wouldn't outbid you during the auction and end up sharing a box of cake, candy, pie, cookies or fried chicken with your girl.

As families arrived that Friday evening, the women and girls placed decorated boxes on Mr. Ewing's desk before finding seats. There was a PTA business meeting and talk about buying a new basketball with the money that was being raised. Then Earl Dean Shelton, who had been especially invited out from Aline because he knew how to auction, was introduced and stepped onto the stage. He called for everybody's attention. Talking in a loud voice, Earl Dean reminded us that nobody was to start eating until all the boxes were auctioned off and paid for. He said the first thing you did after you bought a box was open it and see who brought it. Then you were to go to where the lady was waiting and sit with her before you started eating the goodies that were inside. When he was sure everyone understood, he went right into his auctioning spiel.

The first package he held up was about the size of a small shoebox and wrapped in bright red paper. Tied with white satin ribbon, it made a "thunk thunk" sound when Earl Dean held it over his head and gently shook it. I didn't bid on it because I knew it wasn't Nancy Rose Fleming's box. Nancy Rose had caught my eye the first year she came to school. I liked her spunk and her brown curly hair and pretty smile. Everybody at Round Grove knew I thought of her as my girl. She had told me earlier that her box was yellow and tied with green ribbon. Before the auctioneer ever got started, I had spotted it among the stack of pretty boxes piled high on Mr. Ewing's desk.

Every girl or woman who came to the program, even the little girls, had brought a box, but because they always outnumbered the men and boys, some men bought more than one box and sat with more than one girl or woman to eat what was inside them. Marvin Hanks, Skillet's daddy, sometimes bought several boxes even though his wife had probably told him exactly which one was hers. Mr. Hanks was both colorblind and nearsighted and for that reason couldn't be sure from the back of the room which box was which. So to be on the safe side, he usually bought more than one box. I figured maybe Mr. Hanks wanted to help raise money for the school because he had gone to Round Grove when he was a boy. Mother said he did it because he wanted to be nice to the homely girls who brought boxes most of the men and boys didn't want to buy. Mother also said Mr. Hanks wasn't really nearsighted and colorblind, that he just pretended to be.

Every year Eddie bid high on Nora Hood's box. He said they had a system worked out so he would know for sure which one was hers. Either their system always worked or he traded for her box after the auction was over. Anyhow, they always sat together to eat. Eddie said she made the best oatmeal cookies he had ever eaten and didn't have any help from her mother either.

I figured Nancy Rose would be thoughtful enough to fill her box with chocolate covered cherries or other chocolate candy I especially liked to eat. But she had ideas of her own that were also pretty good. She brought a big box, expertly wrapped, that she had packed with fried chicken and bread and butter sandwiches. What made it really special was the pound cake and strawberry preserves. She had even thought to include paper plates and silverware. And because she brought several paper napkins I didn't have to wipe the chicken grease on my pants. That Friday night I had to pay more for her box than I had planned on, a whopping four bits. It wouldn't have cost that much except for Junie Clifford who kept outbidding me because he thought it was the box Wanda Hood had brought. I was really lucky that night because Daddy had given me a half-dollar before we left home so I didn't have to spend any of my own money.

When the program was over and everyone was stuffed with goodies, Elaine Fleming, Nancy Rose's mother who was the PTA president, stood up and announced that the box supper had been a huge success, raising fourteen dollars and thirty-five cents. Everybody clapped and cheered, and then just went back to talking with their friends.

By now it was uncomfortably warm inside the schoolhouse even with some of the windows open, because of all the people packed inside. So after we finished eating Eddie, Jim Bob and I excused ourselves and walked out the front door of the schoolhouse to get some fresh air. Men were standing around outside shooting the breeze and several were smoking cigarettes. Bud Spurgeon was smoking his pipe. They didn't seem to notice us and we didn't speak to them partly because if we had they would have teased us about how much we liked girls. We headed down the little hill toward the basketball

court. We were surprised and plenty mad when we saw somebody had parked their Model A right square in the middle of
our nice smooth court. In the moonlight we couldn't tell for
sure whose car it was but we could see the tires had made
deep marks in the softer places where we had filled those fairly big blowholes with mud. And if that wasn't bad enough, oil
had leaked out of the crankcase onto the dirt court; in the
bright moonlight I could see the dark spot under the running
board. It's going to be hard to clean it up, I thought as I
motioned Eddie and Jim Bob to step over to look at the mess.
"Some stupid son-of-a-bitch had to go an park on the court,"
Eddie sputtered, so mad he could hardly stand it.

"I don't know whose car this is," Jim Bob added, "but he
ort not to of did this. Anybody'd do somethin like this ain't
nothin but a piss ass!"

"Let's teach the son-of-a-bitch a lesson he won't forget," I
suggested.

"We could pour some water into the gas tank, that'd fix
him fer sure," Eddie offered.

"Yeah, or we could let the air outta his tars," Jim Bob said.
"He's gotta learn he caint get by with doin this."

"Or," I said, "we could stick a corncob up the exhaust pipe
if we had one."

"Trouble with that is they ain't no corncobs round here.
Maybe we could get a hedgeapple from Harry Vealey's place
an jam it into his exhaust pipe. I heard if ya do that the motor
won't run," Eddie suggested.

"I got an even better idea," I said, "let's just pull off his
spark plug wires. I saw somebody do it in a picture show once.
That way we can teach the son-of-a-bitch a lesson without
doin any damage to his car. When the bastard comes out to go
home it'll take him forever to figger out why the damn thing
won't start."

"Yeah," Eddie agreed, "that oughta teach the son-of-a-
bitch a lesson he ain't never gonna ferget!"

So while Eddie and Jim Bob carefully stood between me and the group of men clustered around the front door of the schoolhouse, I very quietly unlatched and raised the hood of the Model A, laid it over like Daddy did with the hood of our car, disconnected all four of the spark plug wires and left them hanging. Easy as pie. I lowered the hood but didn't fasten it for fear of making too much noise. Then the three of us sneaked around behind the parked cars and went back inside the schoolhouse through the back door. The room was still filled with people standing around, talking, eating and drinking coffee, nobody noticed as we came back inside.

Mother and Daddy liked to visit so we were almost the last people to leave that evening. Daddy had parked south of the schoolhouse on the baseball diamond and as we drove north by the basketball court I could see it was Harold Loudon who had the hood up on the Model A, trying in the moonlight to see why he couldn't get it started.

So it was ole Harold Loudon who had parked on the basketball court. He should have known better. One of my favorite people to be around was Harold Loudon. Probably because he was such a good-natured guy, always telling jokes and making funny cracks. Just watching the changing expressions on his face and the sparkle in his eyes sometimes made me laugh. He was nineteen and everybody liked him. Girls, especially, were attracted to Harold like flies to honey and it was the talk of the neighborhood that Harold cut a wide swath with young women. Daddy called him a "ladies man"; Elza Mills said Harold was a "sheik"; Cap Talmage called him a "dude"; Mother said Harold was a "dandy"; I just called him "Harold."

But it served Harold right, what we did to his car, I thought as we drove on up the road toward home. Maybe he came late to the box supper and was in a hurry but that was no excuse for messing up our nice basketball court after we had worked so hard on it.

"Ya figger Mr. Ewing taught ya anything 'sides basketball?"

Daddy asked me at the breakfast table on the last day of school, the middle of April 1936. "You think he'll promote ya to the sixth grade?"

"I figger I'll get promoted," I answered, "cause if I wadn't gonna be promoted he would have said somethin to me a long time ago."

"How come you say that?"

"Well, for one thing," I said, "Leonard Tweedy told me Mr. Ewing had kept a bunch of kids in after school a while back and he was one of them. Mr. Ewing told them if they didn't get busy right away he wadn't gonna promote them to the next grade. And I wadn't one of those kids so I reckon I'll get promoted."

"Of course you'll be promoted," Mother said with a little smile.

"But like I was askin," Daddy said, "you figger ya learned anything from Mr. Ewing?"

"Well, I learned a lot more from him that I did from Miss Downing."

"You like him better, don't you?" Mother asked.

"I like him a whole lot better and he's a lot better teacher than she was."

"When do we need to be down at the school?" Daddy asked Mother, changing the subject entirely.

"Well, I guess we should get down there by eleven. That will give me time to finish baking the pies I'm taking to the basket dinner."

Without much to do after breakfast and before we left for Round Grove, I got a lead pencil, sharpened the point with my pocket knife, then sat down in the front room to work the *Capper's Weekly* crossword puzzle.

For some reason I couldn't concentrate on the puzzle even though it was an easy one. I couldn't help thinking about what Daddy had asked at breakfast. I could still hear him: "You figger Mr. Ewing taught you anything 'sides basketball?" And I hadn't given him a very straight answer. What had Mr.

Ewing taught me? What had I learned from him during the last three years? Why did I like him so much?

Because of him, I knew I had what he called native intelligence and I could do anything I set my mind to, and I should never, ever again, be ashamed of being adopted. I was as good as anybody. He taught me the fine points of spelling, writing, and correct use of the English language. My best grades were in those subjects. Because of him I had learned to read the newspaper and become interested in geography and what was going on in the world. I could talk to grownups about the war in Spain, who was planning to run for President and the kinds of things the United States was importing from Japan. Because of him, a whole new world was opening for me. Perhaps as important as anything, he taught me that the way to get things done was to work together. I was especially proud of being a member of our championship basketball team, and having been asked by Mr. Ewing to help with the toilet paper problem. ✦

Chapter 19 ———————————————————— ≪

Farmers in our part of Alfalfa County worked harder to make a living than anyone else in the State of Oklahoma. Most figured they were lucky if their wheat crops made fifteen bushels to the acre and if they did better, maybe twenty bushels, they felt like the good Lord had been unusually generous and they could be heard bragging about what a good crop they had.

But most years farmers I knew or heard my folks talking about barely hung on. Many families, mainly sharecroppers, pulled up stakes, moved out west, and were never heard from again. Those who did leave usually had kinfolks who had jobs on the coast. Others read and believed the notices that came out in the *Aline Chronoscope* or the *Helena Star* or the Carmen or Cherokee newspapers. The same notices were often tacked onto walls or telephone poles all around the towns telling about the good life and big wages you could earn if you moved out to California, Oregon, or Washington and picked fruit or worked as unskilled labor on a truck farm.

It was especially hard for a farmer to make it in Oklahoma if he had a wife and a house full of kids. "It's been that way ever since the Cherokee Strip was opened for homesteading by white settlers around the turn of the century,"

Mother said, "an so far as I know, except for hunting, even prehistoric Indians didn't spend much time in our part of Alfalfa County." I couldn't help wondering why she said that. I was surprised she knew anything about Indians. I had heard some talk once about Charlie Singree finding a couple of arrowheads on his place between the Aline Cemetery and the east bank of Eagle Chief Creek. Charlie figured the arrowheads were proof that Indians had at least passed through, maybe even camped there for a while. Old Man Pearce, editor of the *Aline Chronoscope*, was so excited about this find that he wrote and printed a long article about it alongside the "Happenings of Local Interest" right on the front page where you couldn't help seeing it. He said it stood to reason that some Indian shot a couple of arrows at a buffalo or some other big game animal, missed, and just walked off and left his lost arrows where they landed, right there in Charlie Singree's wheat field. Mr. Pearce also reckoned the arrowheads Charlie found were all that remained of the arrows after the rest of them had rotted away.

Sharecroppers' kids came and went at Round Grove School. And even some families who owned their places left without telling anybody why, although there was talk that the bank had taken their land away from them because they got too deep in debt. One day they would have a sale and auction off practically everything they owned, and the next day they would be gone.

Mother was concerned about a family who had moved into the little three-room house a quarter mile north of our church. Their name was Banks and they had two boys and a girl. The older boy, Donald, whom I called "Donnie," started third grade at Round Grove in 1936. Sometimes we walked north together after school. A half mile south of our place he turned east and walked alone the rest of the way, a little more than a mile if he cut across the churchyard. People said Mrs. Banks had lost her mind worrying about how they were going to get along when Mr. Banks—people called him "Ed"—didn't have any work and didn't even farm the quarter section they lived on. Somebody said the reason he couldn't get a job with the WPA doing road work was because he was a Republican.

"Them folks ain't got nothin ta live on," I once heard Daddy say to Elza Mills, who used to live with his wife Alice in the same little house before they moved down to the school land near Round Grove.

"No they ain't," Elza agreed, "an I doubt they even got a pot ta piss in."

I never set foot in their house and didn't know how they lived. But I was curious. Donnie mentioned a time or two on the way home from school that his daddy sometimes talked about getting a job in Oregon or Washington and moving them out there just as soon as his mother got well enough to make the trip.

Nearly every day of the summer the Banks family moved in, Donnie showed up at our house about the time we were eating breakfast. Mother would ask if he was hungry and he often ate with us. Then he would stay all day unless Mother told him to go home. His folks couldn't call around the neighborhood to find out where he was because they didn't have a telephone, and Mother thought they might worry about him. Usually I had work to do that I couldn't get out of just because he had come to visit. Like chopping Mexican sandburs or hoeing the garden. Donnie didn't just stand and watch; he would pitch in and help me out even if I hadn't asked him to. I was glad to find a hoe for him to work with.

Donnie liked Mother's cooking and usually ate more than I did. Mother said she liked to feed people who had real appetites. He even ate fried liver and happily ate my share as well as his own. He especially liked milk, which I thought was pretty odd, because I still hadn't learned to like it. He said most of what they had to eat were commodities they got from the state. "Commodities" was a new word for me but Mother explained it after Donnie went home. She said some people were so poor they didn't even have money to buy groceries. So the state government would give free foodstuffs, called "commodities," and a little money each month to those who signed up. "The Banks family must be on relief," she said, "or Donald wouldn't have used the word 'commodities.'"

"Oh," I said, then asked, "What kinda stuff do they get?"

"Well, I can't say for sure," Mother replied. "We Wilsons have never and will never go on relief. But I think they probably get rice and beans, maybe flour. Things like that."

Daddy said he knew folks who were no poorer than we were who were getting help from the county government. Mother told him to be careful. He just looked at her and shrugged. "There's one bunch I heard of that's on relief that even drove up ta Cherokee one day an come back with a double-bed mattress tied to tha top of their car. Some relief outfit up there give it to em fer nothin."

I could see Mother relax a little, but she didn't smile. "Don't forget, that family you're talkin about has seven children at home, and until they got that mattress two of their little girls had to sleep on the floor of an unheated room."

People had to work hard from sunup to sundown, sometimes six and a half days a week. "There's always more than enough work around a farm ta keep everybody busy," Daddy said. Like us, everybody had milk cows, hogs, and chickens to care for. We usually got out of bed by five-thirty in the morning, winter and summer. Daddy might get up even as early as four o'clock during harvest so he could get into the field as soon as the sun had dried out the wheat stalks. He once explained that the sickle needed to cut the wheat stalks easily so the combine could do its job. But harvest season didn't last more than about three weeks so he didn't lose much sleep unless he decided to plow or disk the fields he had just cut. Mother and Daddy agreed that he really deserved to sleep Sunday mornings because he worked so hard the rest of the week. Fat and pompous John Thomas Everhart, one of the church deacons, asked me on Sunday, a smirk on his face, "Where's yer daddy this mornin, is he sick?"

"No sir," I replied, "he ain't sick. He's home sleepin." Then Mr. Everhart, a farmer himself, looked all around to see if anybody else was watching and listening, and went "har, har, har," as though he had made a funny joke. On the way home from church I told Mother that Mr. Everhart asked me almost every Sunday where Daddy was. "I'm gettin sick an tired of him askin me about that!" I said.

"Don't pay any attention to him," she said. "He knows very well where your daddy is. He's just trying to make it seem like a real sin for your daddy to catch up on his sleep instead of coming to church. And besides, all three of us go to church Sunday evenings. I imagine if the truth could be known your daddy is a better Christian than John Thomas Everhart. Christianity is a lot more than just showin up for church on Sundays." I could tell that she, too, was sick and tired of Mr. Everhart always acting like he was better than other people. "Holier than thou," she called it.

She's right about that, I thought, and I would have bet anybody Daddy was a lot harder worker than Mr. Everhart was. I was glad Mother said what she did about Mr. Everhart. And I knew from the way she acted she didn't want me to repeat to anybody what she had said about him. She didn't have to tell me, and I never mentioned it to another soul.

Daddy gave me a bull calf that was born in the spring. He was a cross between one of our Jersey milk cows and our shorthorn bull. He almost died of scours right after we weaned him from his mother and made him learn to drink separated milk out of a bucket. I decided to call him "Ed."

I was really glad to have the calf. Until he got well we kept him in the brooderhouse between our house and the toi-

let. I fed him, cleaned up his messes, and took good care of
him. We finally got Ed over his scours by giving him medicine Daddy bought at Corliss' Drug Store.

Having the scours wasn't the last bad thing that happened to Ed. He had no more than gotten over the scours
and begun putting on weight when Daddy castrated and
dehorned him along with several other bull calves that were
about the same age. What Daddy and I had in mind was that
I would sell Ed when he got bigger and maybe make enough
money to buy a bicycle, which was exactly the kind of deal
Eddie Talmage had made with his daddy. "That's the only
way yer gonna git that there bicycle," Daddy said, "you just
gotta save up enough money fer it." Naturally, I began wondering when Ed would be big enough to sell and how much
he would bring.

I guess one of the reasons Mother and Daddy kept reminding me I needed to save money was that I had never
been able to save enough to buy the Mickey Mouse wrist-
watch for sale at Corliss'. They said if I wanted it badly
enough I'd just have to save my money. I kept hoping I would
get the watch for Christmas but I never did.

"Well, if ya want that there watch you'll just hafta earn
the money or save up ta buy it," Daddy told me every time I
mentioned that Mickey Mouse watch. One of my problems
was that I didn't have any way of earning money. Now that
I was bigger, people no longer asked me to sing for money.
For a while I considered hiring out to one of the neighbors
during harvest when everybody seemed to need extra help.
Mother and Daddy didn't think it was such a good idea.

"Everybody but me gets paid durin harvest," I reasoned,
figuring that Mother and I were doing Daddy's share of the
milking and his other chores every night and morning as
well as our own. We were milking twelve or thirteen cows
then.

It would have been nice, I thought, if the hired girl and

one of Daddy's hired men would help with the milking. But they never showed up early enough in the morning and always left before milking time at night. Mother said she would rather have the hired girl fix breakfast than help with the cows anyway.

"Well, maybe I could pay you. How much you figger yer milkin is worth?" Daddy asked one day while we were having breakfast.

"Well, Mother an I've been talkin an we decided that two cents a cow would be about right," I suggested.

"O.K.," Daddy said, "you got yerself a bargain. You an yer mother keep track of the number of cows each of ya milks, mornin and night, an when I settle up with the harvest hands I'll pay ya both whatcha earned."

Before the end of the first week I knew I should have asked for more than two cents a cow. Milking was pretty hard work and I was having to milk several more cows than I'd been used to. But I had offered to milk for two cents a cow and had made a bargain with Daddy. We had even shaken hands on it. I would have been embarrassed to go back on my word. "A man's as good as his word," Daddy used to say. And he was right. Daddy was that kind of man and everybody knew it.

The week before the Fourth of July, on June 29th, Mother made me a three-layer chocolate cake with thick chocolate icing and put ten red candles on it. It was the best birthday cake she had ever made for me, but I could tell she was sorry the harvest hands and hired girl ate so much of it that I didn't get a second piece. Eddie Talmage probably could understand how I felt because his mother used to bring his birthday cake to school around the middle of February every year, and, because there were so many kids to share it with, he was lucky to get one piece, let alone a second or third. Eddie never complained and sometimes I wondered if maybe his mother baked another birthday cake for him so the rest of his family could have it at home.

The Fourth of July was just about my favorite day of the year, next to Christmas. That was because Daddy, who liked fireworks, bought lots of them every year at the drug store and brought them home in a big brown paper sack. Daddy wouldn't let me light some of the things he bought, like the four-inch firecrackers or cherry bombs or skyrockets or fountains, any of the ones that had "light fuse and GET AWAY" printed on them. Every year we heard about kids being burned by fireworks they didn't know how to handle and shouldn't have been playing with. Some even got burned on Roman candles; I never did because Daddy always lit them for me.

And it wasn't just kids who got burned on the Fourth of July. Fred Barrows burned his hand pretty bad one year. Mother heard about it by listening in on the party line. She heard that Fred had been drinking beer all day long and had lit a skyrocket with one hand while holding on to it with the other. If he hadn't been drunk he would have had enough sense to lean it up against something or to stick it into a fruit jar or something like the instructions said you were supposed to do. Mother said she had overheard Lola, Fred's wife, talking on the telephone, telling Flo Hood that Fred had done this really dumb thing. "Lola told Flo she was completely disgusted, and it wouldn't have happened if Fred hadn't been boozin on the Fourth," Mother said.

Like lots of other people, as soon as we had finished milking we drove up to Carmen the night of the Fourth of July to see the free fireworks display out at the City Park. It was the closest place we could see fireworks other than the ones Daddy shot off at home, and even though it was about a twenty-five-mile round trip, we always went because neither Aline nor Helena did anything special on the Fourth. The *Aline Chronoscope* announcement made it all seem exciting and I couldn't wait to get there.

Come to Carmen Park

Big Band Concert each Tuesday at 8:15 P.M.
Big Program with Band Concert
each two weeks on Tuesdays at 8:15 P.M.

Old-Fashioned 4th of July Celebration in Carmen Park
Bring baskets and enjoy lunch in this restful park
❖ *Rides for the Children*
❖ *Two Big Band Concerts*
❖ *First-Run Picture Show*
❖ *Big Baseball Game*
❖ *Plenty of Shade and Free Ice Water!*
❖ *Free Street Dance in Evening*

Welcome All!
Spend the 4th in Carmen Park

In addition to the fireworks there were airplane rides that cost five dollars for fifteen minutes, little stands set up with electric lights where you could buy food or ice cream cones, and other places where you could get a sno-cone in a white paper cup for a nickel. You had a choice of orange, grape, or strawberry flavor.

Yellow lights had been strung on trees and poles all around the picnic tables over by the swimming pool and there was a strong smell of the insect repellent that had been sprayed on the tables and on the Bermuda grass and rag-weeds. People were eating picnic suppers and many had homemade ice cream. Others were just talking and smoking cigarettes. People were everywhere, even bunched up around an old-time fiddler who was playing familiar ditties under some locust trees where a small, square platform, about the size of our dining room, had been set up for people to dance.

Even though I got several chigger bites that itched like crazy, I enjoyed the Fourth of July maybe even more than Christmas.

Later that summer we went to the rodeo down at Cleo Springs. It lasted three days, starting Friday night and ending Sunday afternoon. We tried to get to the rodeo grounds as soon after dinner as we could, to get good seats in the grandstand. On Saturday, Uncle Clyde from Arizona, who had come to visit Grandma Dollie and Grandpa Pete, went to Cleo with us. While I had some of Weibel's orange sherbet and vanilla ice cream, which came together in the same little cardboard cup, Uncle Clyde drank a can of Progress beer he had bought for fifteen cents at one of the stands set up just outside the grandstand. I wasn't surprised that he bought Progress brand beer. It was practically the only kind I ever saw advertised. But I was surprised that it came in a can. When Uncle Clyde finished drinking the beer, he let me examine the can. It had a funnel-shaped top with a cap on it, like on a pop bottle. Uncle Clyde had taken it off with a bottle opener that was like a blade on his old-fashioned pocketknife.

To me, the rodeo cowboys were real live heroes, brave, strong, and one hundred percent he-men. They seemed to lead a pretty good life, what with their fancy cowboy boots folks said were made to measure for them. Most wore fine-looking chaps that seemed like they, too, had been made to order. I was fascinated by the way most of them talked with a drawl, like they came from somewhere in Texas or from the Oklahoma Panhandle. They didn't sound anything like the actors in western picture shows and not a single one of them wore a white hat. I figured real cowboys, who worked with horses and cows and got all dirty sometimes, probably didn't see any sense in wearing white hats. I changed my attitude toward Gene Autry, Ken Maynard, Roy Rogers, and Hopalong Cassidy. I knew they and their fancy white hats weren't in the same class with the real cowboys down at Cleo.

I hoped that someday I could be a rodeo cowboy myself, ride broncs and steers, and wave to the crowd in the grandstand as they clapped and cheered for me. But first, I imagined, I needed to look like a cowboy. I had already convinceed my folks to buy me a cowboy hat, a dark brown "Carlsbad" out of the Montgomery Ward catalog. On the way home from the rodeo, I asked my folks if I could get a pair of cowboy boots.

"We could get a good pair in Enid," I said, "or we could order them out of the catalog."

I told my folks they had some really nice boots in my size that would suit me just fine and they came in both brown and black calfskin. I even suggested that my grades and conduct at school would improve if only they would buy me a pair of cowboy boots.

"Ya can't wear cowboy boots until ya learn to stop runnin yer heels over on tha inside," Daddy said. "You've gotta learn to walk straight in regular shoes first." Mother nodded in agreement. "An it'd be even harder fer you ta walk right if you was wearin high-heeled boots. A pair of boots would ruin yer feet fer sure," Daddy said sternly. "Yer gonna hafta do some more growin up before ya start thinkin about havin cowboy boots." From the tone of his voice I could tell that he didn't want to talk about it any more.

So I gave up that idea for the time being. I didn't say anything, but that very day I made up my mind to train my feet to hit the ground so that my shoe heels didn't wear down on their insides. I'll prove I can do it, I told myself, then I'll ask again if I can have some cowboy boots. Every day from then on I worked at it, trying to walk straight. Within a week I thought I could see some improvement. But I didn't say anything. I figured I would just wait until the time was right, like when I needed new shoes in the fall, to show Mother and Daddy that I was wearing out my shoe heels the way I was supposed to. ❖

Chapter 20 ⟵

One morning Mother sat facing me at the breakfast table after Daddy had left for the field. "Son," she gently asked, "do you remember your brother Jefferson?"

Her question caught me completely by surprise. I was so stunned I couldn't look her in the face. I sat there, slumped in my chair, filled with dread. Were Mother and Daddy planning to take me back to the orphans' home after all? Were they going to go back on their promise to keep me? Of course I remembered Jefferson. And Bonnie and Ma'am and Mr. Collins and the trip to Helena, and the first night at the home. I remembered every detail. My throat went dry and my head felt like it would split open. After all these years, why was she asking about Jefferson?

Since my adoption, I had tried my best to overcome the pain of being abandoned by my real mother. I had tried hard to overcome the awful terror I had felt that night in Helena when I was left at the orphans' home with no explanation, no hug, no kiss goodbye. It hurt too much to think about it again. I had lived five years with the shame and humiliation of my adoption, of being different from the other kids, of being a curiosity, of being treated like a prize cow. I had performed at the PTA programs, won prizes in county competitions, managed to look happy every time someone reminded me how lucky I was or when Mother and Daddy showed me off. But it was hard. Year after year I had tried my best to feel more and more a part of the Wilson family, tried to think of them as my real family. Now Mother was asking about Jefferson? Why was she doing this?

"Sure," was all I could manage to say. Didn't she understand that I couldn't belong to her and Daddy and be a real brother to Jefferson at the same time? If Mother noticed my discomfort she didn't show it in her face.

"Would you like to see him again?" she asked.

No! The word seemed to explode inside my head. I had closed that door behind me forever. That was the only way I could try to be a real son to the Wilsons. Besides, I didn't even know where he was. "Where is he?" I asked.

"He's still at the orphans' home." Why hadn't Grandma Dollie or somebody told me? All these years they had known he was there and nobody had ever said anything about it to me! The unfairness of it all hit me hard. I wanted to cry. Mother kept on talking. "Your Daddy and I thought maybe we could bring him out here for a visit one of these days. You've been such a good boy lately that we thought you deserved a special treat, like seeing your big brother again."

I could tell she had no idea what I was feeling. A new thought crossed my mind. Maybe it would be good to see Jefferson after all. At least by talking to him I could learn more about my true family: what Pap looked like, what happened to Ma'am, whether she was really part Pawnee Indian, what her name was. I could ask him again why Ma'am had left Bonnie and me and him at the orphans' home. He was several years older than I was and if anybody knew about these things he would. My goosebumps and dread gradually left as I thought about Jefferson. From what Mother had just said, I felt almost certain she and Daddy didn't plan to take me back and leave me at the orphans' home. But would Jefferson want to see me? Would I know him when I saw him? Would he remember me? "Yeah, I'd like to see Jefferson again," I finally answered.

I remembered that when I last saw my older brother he looked a lot like me. It was on the playground at the orphans' home before the accident with the horn, before I went to live in the upstairs apartment. Then the Wilsons took me home with them and I didn't get to say goodbye. I also remembered that until I was adopted by the Wilsons he had been the only person in the whole world I could trust before I met Mr. Ewing, and I realized that he was the only one who could answer my questions about my real family. As I sat there with Mother, I remembered how Jefferson and I had talked the last time we had been together. That was five years ago, and I had forgotten much of what he had told me. But I had not forgotten Jefferson, how he talked and how he smiled.

"Jefferson must be around twelve or thirteen years old now," Mother said, interrupting my thoughts.

"All I remember is that he's bigger and older than I am."

"And you'd like to have him come and visit with us for a few days? You're sure that'll be all right with you?"

"Yes ma'am, I'd like him to come." By now I was feeling better, more relaxed; my head had stopped throbbing. But my mind raced from one thing to another: Will he look different? Why hadn't he been adopted by now? How were they treating him at the home? I passionately hoped he could help me answer some of the questions that had troubled me for so long. I was sure he would understand how I felt because he was my big brother.

"Your daddy and I have been thinking maybe we could go over to Helena next Sunday after we get home from church. We can drive up and have dinner with Grandma Dollie at the orphans' home. And after dinner we can bring Jefferson back with us. Grandma Dollie said it would be all right."

I still hated Helena and the orphans' home. But on

Sunday I went with Mother and Daddy to eat dinner with Grandma Dollie and Aunt Edith at their apartment in the orphans' home. Being there made me feel uneasy but no one seemed to notice. After we talked an hour or two about things Grandma Dollie wanted to talk about, she said she would go find Jefferson and get him ready to go home with us. "He's plumb tickled to death," she said, "he's rarin to go."

Grandma wasn't gone long. Before I expected her she came through the door to her apartment and held it open wide. There stood Jefferson looking scared. I figured his pajamas and toothbrush were inside the big paper sack he held in one hand. He was bigger than I had remembered.

I looked him over, head to toe, and it was almost like I was looking into a mirror. He was skinny, like me. His hair was cut short, the way they used to cut mine at the orphans' home, and it was the same color as mine. Like me, he had high cheekbones and his eyebrows met in the middle of his nose, but his eyes were darker than mine, almost coal black. And, like me, he didn't have a single freckle that I could see. He stood there, looking right back at me.

Then he eased timidly into the room and pulled the door closed. Everybody was looking at him. I could tell he was uncomfortable; it showed in his face and in the way he sort of dragged his feet when he walked. For a long time we couldn't take our eyes off one another—saying nothing, not smiling or laughing, not crying. We just stood there looking.

Finally he spoke: "Hi Buster, how ya doin?" Nobody had called me "Buster" since I had seen him more than five years before. Jefferson was the only one who ever called me that.

But I couldn't think of anything to say to him. Although we sat together on the back seat of the car all the way home, he talked only to Daddy. "Ya got any horses I can ride on your farm?" he asked. His question seemed to break the ice. And for the next several minutes they talked about what it was like to live on a farm and to ride a horse any time you wanted to.

Neither Mother nor I interrupted Daddy and Jefferson; they seemed to be enjoying themselves. Jefferson seemed excited, sitting on the edge of his seat and leaning forward, his face close to Daddy's ear. He paid no attention to me. I sat there quietly, looking out the window of the car, glancing back at Jefferson then out the window again, not at all sure his visit was going to turn out the way I hoped it would. I knew it was important for Daddy and Mother to be comfortable with him but I needed to feel comfortable with him, too. I was certain there was a great deal more he could tell me about myself and our real family and I was aching to ask him. But it would have to wait until we were alone. The things I wanted to talk about were private matters having to do with my real family and not with the Wilsons. And besides, no matter how fond I had grown of them, I still wasn't sure where I stood with the Wilsons. Just when I had begun to think everything was fine, one of them would say something to throw me off balance. Like when Mother had asked me if I wanted Jefferson to visit. Or when Daddy would say, "Now Rex, you must learn to remember your station in life and not try to make yourself somethin you ain't." I was never really sure what Daddy meant by that. But I always felt put down, especially by the tone of his voice, reminding me that I came from the orphans' home, that my real mother had abandoned me there. Was this supposed to make me not as good as everyone else? This bothered me a lot, to be told "remember your station in life" or "don't try to be better than you are," when all this past year at school Mr. Ewing had told me "aim high, the sky's the limit," and "you can become whatever you want to be because of your keen intelligence and grasp of reasoning."

All of this left me right in the middle, and I wanted to listen to Mr. Ewing and ignore Daddy, but I knew that would lead to trouble.

So I counted on Jefferson's visit making a difference for me. For one thing I really wanted to know more about being part Indian. We were finally able to talk that evening. "Were you tellin me the truth when you said we're part Indian?" I asked as we walked out to the east pasture to bring the cows in for milking.

"Yes Buster, I wasn't lyin about that or anything else I told you," he said. "It's like I said that time when you was four years old, that time up at tha home when we were together on the playground. We ain't full-blooded, though."

"I never figgered we were," I said, "cause our skin ain't any darker than it is. But how much Indian are we?"

"Well, tha last time I saw Ma'am we talked about that. She came to see me about two years ago. She said she was a quarter Pawnee which means that us kids are an eighth. She said she had enough Pawnee blood to be enrolled as a member of the tribe but us kids didn't, so none of us belongs to tha tribe." She also told him she had gone back to live with her Pawnee kinfolks over by the Arkansas River and that her Pawnee family wouldn't have let her stay there except that Pap was dead and she had given up all her children. He reminded me that the night Ma'am left me at the orphans' home she also left Bonnie. I wanted to ask him what happened to our sister but I was more concerned about things that seemed, at the time, more important.

"Was Pap part Indian, too?"

"No, he was a white man. Didn't look anything like an Indian. We look a lot more like Ma'am than we do like Pap."

"What was Pap like? I can't remember anything about him except he was old an wore an old army overcoat in cold weather."

"Well, about all I can remember is that he was about as tall as yer adopted daddy but was slimmer. He had brown hair and eyes and was a lot older than Ma'am. Oh, yeah, there is one other thing you might wanta know. Ma'am told me he worked for tha railroad an had come out here from Tennessee, when Oklahoma was still Indian Territory, before it even became a state. She said he was the only one in the Tolliver family that had come out this way."

I never got a chance to ask Jefferson why Ma'am had to leave us at the orphans' home, but just before the end of his visit he told me that Bonnie had been adopted by a nice family and he wished he could have been adopted, too. But now that he was bigger, he didn't think anyone was going to adopt him.

Later, when it seemed the right time, I thanked my folks for inviting Jefferson to visit, but I didn't say I wanted him to come again. His visit proved to me beyond any doubt that I could not belong to both families. To be honest, I wasn't sorry to say goodbye to him. In fact, I had come to realize that to the extent I had a choice, I only wanted to be a real son to Mother and Daddy and have them be proud of me. By now I felt I was a part of the Round Grove community, that I belonged where I had been for the past five years. Most of the kids I knew at school accepted me and I was comfortable among them. People in Aline recognized me as being the Wilson's son and smiled when they spoke. And I felt right at home with Grandpa and Grandma Wilson; I would have bet that no other kid at Round Grove had nicer grandparents. I never saw Jefferson again and never again did I lie awake at night thinking of where I had come from

During the summer it sometimes got so hot in the picture show—it was called "the Aline Theater"—that I sweated a lot and my shirt stuck to the back of my seat. Mother was pretty upset the first time it happened because there was brown stuff all over the back of the new shirt I was wearing that day, one she had just bought for me to wear to school. I wondered why our picture show wasn't air-conditioned like the Strand over in Enid, where for about six months every year they hung out a long banner-like strip of canvas across the front of the building that had "COOLER INSIDE" printed on it in big letters drawn to look like icicles. But I always went to

the show on Saturday even if it was hot inside and even if the
picture wasn't a western. "It's tha only show in town," Daddy
would say. The comedy was always good, featuring Our Gang
or something like that, and most of the time there was a ser-
ial to make up for a show that was just a lot of love stuff. So
if we ever got to town early during the summer, I found something to do right up until time for the show to start at two
o'clock.

"Say, aren't you Frank Wilson's boy?" It was the man sitting on the other end of the bench and he was talking to me.
I didn't know who he was but it was a familiar question. The
next thing he would say, I supposed, was, "Boy, Frank an
Erma's really done right by you, givin ya a nice home an all
that there, takin you outta tha orphans' home an takin you as
their own." It was the kind of talk I was tired of hearing. I had
to think a moment before answering his question.

He was sitting on the far end of the unpainted, splintery
old wooden bench bolted to the sidewalk in front of Dewey
Webster's barbershop on the west side of the street. The reason they put the bench there instead of on the other side of the
street, I figured, was so people who didn't have anything better to do could sit on it most of the day without having the sun
shining right into their eyes. It was a long bench. I had seen
as many as four old men sit there all afternoon on a Saturday
when it wasn't too cold. The reason I sat down on it that
Saturday was because I couldn't find my friends, it wasn't
time for the picture show to start, and I was eating a double-
dip strawberry ice cream cone I had just bought at Corliss'
Drug Store.

There was just the one man sitting on the bench with me
and when he spoke I was caught by surprise. I never visited
with anybody, especially men whom I didn't know pretty well.
I was just minding my own business and I figured the man on
the other end of the bench wouldn't want to talk to a kid anyhow. Turning my head just a little to the left, I could see he

was looking right at me and he didn't appear mean. He had even taken the cigarette out of his mouth. I didn't want to talk but at the same time I couldn't ignore him.

"Yeah," I answered, and went on with licking the ice cream cone.

"You ought not say 'yeah' to your elders, son," he said patiently. "It isn't polite."

"Yes sir, Frank Wilson's my daddy," I said, sort of choking because my mouth was full of ice cream. And I was feeling a little ashamed for being rude to an adult. "Why are ya askin?" I said, wanting to get the orphans' home business over with.

"I thought that's who you were. I've seen you with your folks a time or two here in Aline." He put the tailor-made cigarette back between his lips, inhaled for what I thought was a long time, then blew the white smoke out of his nose. I waited for him to tell me how lucky I was, how grateful I should be that Mother and Daddy had taken me out of the orphans' home and given me such a good home.

"I knew your daddy when I was about your age," he said. "We were good friends in those days. We were in school together at Round Grove. I'll bet you go to Round Grove, don't you?"

"Yes sir," I said, surprised by this turn in our conversation.

"Well son, I've always thought a lot of your daddy. I reckon he's one of the best men I ever knew."

By this time I was about half-finished with my ice cream cone. It was melting faster than I could eat it, running down on my hand, the cone getting all soggy. Besides, it was almost time to get on up to the picture show. I didn't want to miss the start of the comedy. I hoped the man would stop talking.

"You don't know who I am, do you son?"

"No sir, I don't think so. Do you live around here?" I still couldn't figure out where our conversation was headed.

"No, I live up at Cherokee. I run one of the wheat elevators up there. But once in a while I hafta come down to Aline on business. One time I stopped by your folks' place. It was a year or two ago and that's when I first saw you and found out Frank had a son. You may not remember when I was there, but I remember you. Maybe you remember something you did that day. While we were sitting in the shade of that big mulberry tree out in front of your house, you threw a clod up at the windmill while it was turning in the wind and little pieces of that clod flew everywhere. You thought it was funny and we all laughed."

"I remember doin that. Your wife was with ya that day, wadn't she? I remember what she said when that clod hit the windmill fan."

"What did she say?"

"She said, 'Boys will be boys,' I think it was."

"That's probably exactly what she said, all right, but she wadn't mad at you. She likes kids, especially boys; we've got boys of our own."

"After you and your wife left that day," I said, "Daddy told me you were a pal of his when he went to school at Round Grove. Funny, I still remember him sayin that."

"Your daddy grew up to be a pretty big man. I remember he was small for his age when we were boys. But he grew up to be pretty good-sized." The man paused, turning to gaze at nothing in particular, like Mother used to do when she said she wasn't looking at anything. He had almost finished his cigarette. I watched as he inhaled deeply for one last time, then flipped the burning butt out into the street.

He's right, I thought, Daddy is pretty big, bigger than Eddie Talmage's or Frankie Hood's daddy. My daddy was heavier and taller. Not fat. Grandma Dollie told me that my daddy didn't have an ounce of fat on his body. I noticed his belly didn't hang out over his belt buckle when he got dressed up in his Sunday clothes the way John Thomas Everhart's belly did. Because Daddy was almost six feet tall and weighed around two hundred pounds, he just looked big. And he was strong, too. He could do all kinds of things other men couldn't do, like hold a calf down with his bare hands while somebody dehorned and branded it in the spring. To show how strong his grip was he would sometimes grab hold of one of the horizontal pieces of one of our dining room chairs, the piece between the two back legs, and lift it straight up without letting the chair turn in his hand. I never saw anybody else who could do that. He said Ott Dew, Grandma Dollie's cousin, could do it, but he was the only other man he ever knew who had a strong enough grip to do it with one hand.

"My name's Charlie Dobson, son," the man said with a smile, holding out his big right hand toward me as he would have to another man. He could see I had finally finished my ice cream cone and was ready to leave. "I've enjoyed talking to you, son; tell your mother and daddy that I said hello." Then, shaking my sticky hand still wet with ice cream even though I had wiped it on my overalls, he smiled and watched me head off north in the direction of the Aline Theater. I turned once and looked back after I had crossed the street. The bench was empty now; the man was gone. I couldn't see him among the people on the sidewalk and I never saw him again.

I liked Mr. Dobson and wished there were more men like him. He treated me just like a real person, maybe even like a man, and he never once mentioned the orphans' home or how lucky I was to have been adopted. ✦

A Larger World

Chapter 21 ————————————————————— ⟪

At breakfast one morning around the middle of August, Mother told Daddy it was time they bought me some new school clothes for the coming year. She said if he didn't have something else in mind for her to do, she and I would go up to Cherokee as soon as we could get around. Like every year, Mother and Daddy waited until August to buy me school clothes so I could get all my summer growing done. Doing it that way, they said, the shirts and overalls, and especially the shoes they bought, would need to be only one size instead of two sizes too big. Buying new clothes was one of the things I liked best to do and I was glad they didn't expect me to start out a new school year in worn-out clothes I'd outgrown. I was ten years old.

Way back in first grade, Eddie Talmage and I had agreed that Big Mac overalls were the best money could buy, the only kind of overalls that were worth having. We sometimes talked about how glad we were that we didn't have to wear overalls with "SR" or "MW" stamped on the brass buttons, where everybody could see they had been ordered from Sears Roebuck or Montgomery Ward, instead of "BIG MAC."

While having her second cup of coffee that morning

Mother asked Daddy if he needed anything from Cherokee. Great, I thought. Going to Cherokee means she's planning to take me to the J.C. Penney store where they have Big Mac brand overalls and shirts for sale. "No," Daddy replied, "but I'll be doin some diskin down at the folks' place most of the day so if you'll pack me some dinner an a gallon of lemonade before you get goin ya won't hafta hurry back to fix me somethin to eat at noon."

"All right," Mother said, "if you're sure you don't mind having a cold meal."

"No, I don't mind a tall," he said. "It's a lot less trouble than eatin at the folks' place."

"Well then," Mother said to me, "let's hurry and get cleaned up. Be sure you wash your face an hands and don't forget to brush your teeth."

"Daddy," I asked, "can I have a dime for a Big Little Book?"

"Well, I reckon I kin spare a dime; ya been purty good lately. An I don't mind spendin money fer books."

He's right, I thought, I have been good, haven't had a whipping in at least a month. Maybe I should have asked for fifteen cents. But I didn't want to push my luck and I didn't want him to think I was greedy. And a dime, after all, was a lot of money to me and all I really wanted was another Big Little Book. Besides, I thought, I might talk Mother into giving me a nickel after we got to Cherokee. With a nickel I could get one of those big, thick ice cream sandwiches they had at the ice cream parlor a block north of Penney's. Daddy gave me the dime plus a nickel I hadn't asked for. I was happy. I thanked him and dropped the coins into my pocket. We didn't leave that morning until around nine o'clock, not until Daddy had left on the tractor for Grandpa Pete's place.

It didn't look to me like the road that ran north and south past our house had ever been graded with a real road grader. And it was so narrow that if one car met another one coming from the opposite direction, the cars had to pull over and drive close to the fence until they got by one another. There weren't any ditches along the road until you got two miles north of our place, where the loose, light brown sand ended and the red clay began, and I assumed they had the ditches there so rain could run off and the road wouldn't stay muddy and slick for so long. Then, continuing for more than ten miles, as far as you could see in every direction, the land was red clay and the road became so soft and slick when it got wet that it was easy to get stuck on it. Daddy said the road was "soapy" when it was slick like that and I thought that was a good description. I knew exactly what he meant.

Cherokee, the County Seat of Alfalfa County and its largest town, was about fifteen miles north of our place and it took a half hour or more to get there in our Model A. Daddy once said you ought not drive a Ford more than thirty-five miles an hour, even on pavement. Mother didn't drive more than about twenty miles an hour on the ten or eleven miles of dirt road, but when we got to the cement highway a few miles south of Cherokee she mashed down on the foot feed and we raced along at forty, which in a Model A was, as Eddie Talmage liked to say, "goin lickety-split!" I sat on the forward edge of the seat so I could see out the car window and the windshield. Even though it was a hot day and we were both sweating, we kept the windows rolled up until we got to the pavement so the dust wouldn't blow inside and get us dirty.

Everybody always said that Alfalfa County could be more than just hot in August; it could be very hot. On most days the fly-specked thermometer Mother had hanging on the back porch on a nail just outside the kitchen door read more than a hundred degrees in the shade, even before noon. Mother said the humidity that blew in from the south made it seem even hotter and in August she would rather sit in the shade drinking lemonade than be out in the sun. On the day we went to Cherokee together the whole country was dry because it hadn't rained since May, at least a month before wheat harvest began. By August all the farmers had cut their wheat and were hoping for a good rain so they could get their fields plowed and ready to drill to wheat again in September. While waiting for rain, about the only thing they could do was to disk the ground like Daddy was doing down on Grandpa Pete's place, to chop up the wheat stubble and the weeds that were coming up everywhere. In some fields, you could hardly see the stubble for the ragweeds, thistles, and pigweeds that had just about taken over. Here and there, as we drove along, we could see great plumes of dust rising against the bright blue sky where other farmers were out disking their dry fields.

Mother and I could see Cherokee a long time before we got there, mainly because the country was so flat and the wheat elevators stuck up so high. There wasn't much traffic and we didn't have any flat tires or other trouble on the road.

Mother drove north on Main Street and parked in front of Keye's Drug Store across the street from J.C. Penney's. "I never have any trouble parking in Cherokee," she said, thankful, I was sure, because she was a heavy woman and wouldn't have to walk a long ways to get to Penney's.

Although Cherokee wasn't as big as Enid, it was a whole lot bigger than Aline, where Mother usually did her trading. She never took eggs to Cherokee to trade for groceries or to Carmen or Helena, but always to Aline. Compared to Aline, Cherokee was kind of a wonderland for me. Besides the J.C. Penney store there was a variety store where I could find Big Little Books, and an ice cream parlor, and a Safeway store. At Jack's Bakery I could get a big sugar-coated donut for a penny or a big sack of potato chips, made right there, for a nickel. Jack's even had a tray of pure milk chocolate in large chunks on a shelf beside the cookies. The clerks would take an ice pick and chip a piece off a big chunk, put it in a little paper sack, weigh it, and sell it to me. I thought this was wonderful.

I hoped Mother and I would be in Cherokee long enough to eat dinner there, maybe even at the same café where I had my first hamburger when I was five, the time I wouldn't eat it until the cook took off the slice of raw onion. Knowing Mother pretty well, I didn't think she would want to eat at the Blue Bird Café even though it was in the same block as the Penney's store. For one thing, they didn't have tables and chairs and she didn't like to sit on a stool up at the counter. The main reason I didn't want to eat there was because I remembered before I started to school when Daddy and I had come to Cherokee to get some broken parts of our tractor welded back together, and had eaten our dinner at the Blue Bird Café with some old friend of Daddy's. I had been humiliated by the way Daddy had talked to him about me over my head, as if I didn't have ears and couldn't understand what they were saying. I hated it and knew I would never forget that day in the Blue Bird Café.

I held the screen door open for Mother, then followed her into Penney's. Although it was very hot out in the sun, the store was nice and cool because it was air-conditioned with a very large water cooler. You could see it sticking up from the roof if you went around to the back of the building and looked up. Uncle Clyde, who lived in Arizona, said that out there in the desert they called it a "swamp cooler." I asked Daddy why they called it that and he explained that that kind of air conditioner didn't work right unless the excelsior in the sides of it was kept wet all the time. "Maybe," he said, "it's called a 'swamp cooler' because the wood shavins inside that big metal box get moldy an rotten after a while an start smellin like a swamp." Of course, I didn't mind a little moldy smell when it made the store so much cooler. I wished we could have a swamp cooler at our house but Daddy said it wouldn't work without electricity.

But that day, instead of smelling musty, it smelled surprisingly good inside Penney's as I followed Mother right past the ladies' underwear counters. She paused, picked up something white and frilly, then a pink corset, and felt them with her fingers and laid them back on the counter. We were headed for the boys' clothing, which was over in the southwest corner of the big room, next to where they sold shoes.

A nice woman clerk told Mother that the boys' sizes were between the mens' work shoes and the little kids' departments. Piles of brand new clothes were stacked high on tables and counters in every direction. The highest stacks were kids' stuff, probably, I thought, because it was the time of year when everybody was buying their kids school clothes. I was too short to see over some of the stacks of shirts and overalls so I followed Mother, who was tall enough to see where she was going.

We were pretty close to where they had stacked boys' overalls when I heard a familiar voice. Turning a corner I saw Eddie Talmage. I hadn't seen him since school let out in April and he looked like he had grown two or three inches. He was with his mother, little sister, and little brother. The little kids were picking at one another the way I had seen other kids do.

"Eddie!" I shouted. "What're you doin here?" I was sure glad to see him. Eddie and I never got to play together during the summer because the Talmages lived three and a half miles from our place and there were other kids over that way for him to play with when school was out. Another reason I hadn't seen Eddie since school got out was because his folks did most of their trading in Helena and went over there more often than they came to Aline.

"Hi Peewee!" From the big grin on his face I knew he was glad to see me, too. But I figured he was probably embarrassed to be seen with his mother and the two little kids.

Eddie's mother said Cap was home getting everything ready so he could get started plowing his wheat ground just as soon as we got a little rain. Like Daddy, Cap Talmage was a hard worker and didn't spend a lot of time hanging around town drinking coffee, shooting pool, or chewing the fat with other men when there was so much work to do on the farm.

While Mother visited with Iris Talmage and the two little kids continued to quarrel with one another, Eddie and I walked around the end of a counter to get caught up on what had been going on all summer. He said that, same as me, he had worn out all his school clothes and had to have some new ones before school started. His mother had told him he could have Big Mac overalls again this year and he was feeling on top of the world.

"You bring any money with ya?" I asked Eddie. "I've got fifteen cents. When we get through here I'm gonna go over to the variety store an get a new Big Little Book I've been wantin. Maybe yer mother'll let you come with me." I didn't know if Eddie read any books he didn't have to read in school, but figured he probably liked Big Little Books that had a picture on every other page.

"I only got a dime," Eddie said. "I been savin it fer some ice cream."

"Well," I said, "you can buy a Big Little Book for a dime. I got a nickel to buy one of those ice cream sandwiches at that ice cream place right up the street north of here."

"I'm spendin my money fer some chocolate ice cream," Eddie said. "Les go up there when we get done here. No, I got a better idea. We kin stop there right after we go to tha variety store an you get yer book."

"Okey doke," I said. I could see in my mind a thick slab of vanilla ice cream between two brown chocolate cookie-like crackers that tasted a lot like cake. Just then a clerk came over and spoke to Mother and Mrs. Talmage. She was wearing Sunday clothes. A little sign on her flowered dress said "J.C. Penney" on it.

"Can I be of help to you ladies?" she asked.

Eddie and I heard her speaking and we walked back to where our mothers were standing.

Because the Talmages got to the store before we did and had been waiting longer, Mrs. Talmage had Eddie try on new clothes first. He slipped on some dark blue Big Mac overalls, then a larger pair. When his mother was satisfied with the size and fit she asked the clerk for three pairs. Next she had Eddie try on blue work shirts until he found a size that fit right—which was at least one size too big—and Mrs. Talmage told the clerk she'd like three shirts in that size. Next came two pairs of long underwear and five pairs of brown and white cotton work socks, the same kind Daddy wore, with a red toe and red heel. Eddie was embarrassed for his mother to buy underwear for him right there in front of me and my mother. I could tell. His face turned red, and he acted ashamed and wouldn't look directly at me. Pretending not to notice, I asked him, "You gettin some new shoes, too?"

"Naw," he said, "not this time." He seemed relieved that I didn't tease him or laugh because his mother had bought him the long underwear. I knew he didn't like to wear long winter underwear any more than I did. "I ain't gettin any new ones till I wear out tha ones I got on right now."

While a clerk from the girls' and little kids' departments helped Mrs. Talmage buy clothes for Pauline and Willie, Mother and the clerk in the flowered dress got me fitted out in overalls and blue shirts just like Eddie's, except that Mother bought me four of everything. She said she did that so she wouldn't have to wash quite as often. Like Eddie, I didn't get a pair of work shoes. Mother always ordered my long underwear out of the catalog so I didn't have to be embarrassed the way Eddie was right there in the store in front of everybody.

The Talmages were still in Penney's when Mother finished buying my clothes. After the clerk wrapped everything in a big brown package tied with white cotton string, Mother wrote a check and handed it to her. Then she told me she had other shopping to do in Penney's for herself and Daddy, so I asked, "Can I go over to the variety store while you're busy here an get that Big Little Book I've been wantin?"

"May I, not can't I," she answered. "Yes, you may go if you promise to be very careful crossing the street and don't get run over by a car."

"I'll be real careful," I promised. "Is it all right if Eddie goes with me?"

"You'll have to ask his mother about that. She's over there in the girls' clothing department. But if you're going, be back in fifteen minutes."

"Yes ma'am," I said, and went to find my pal. Mrs. Talmage said it would be all right for Eddie to go to the variety store with me. "But don't fool around comin back," she cautioned. "We gotta be gettin on home soon as we can."

"Okey doke," Eddie said, and the two of us rushed out of the store.

Having only fifteen minutes, we walked as fast as we could to the street-crossing a half block north of Penney's, checked for cars coming from north and south, then turned right and ran across the street. If there had been more time I'm sure we would have paused for a few minutes to enjoy the sweet spicy smells of cakes, donuts, bread, rolls, and other good stuff coming through the open door of Jack's Bakery.

I had been in the variety store before, and had even been there alone. I knew exactly where they kept the Big Little Books. Eddie followed me to the rear of the store, straight to a counter where a huge assortment of Big Little Books was on display, spread out neatly so I could easily read their titles. They had several I wanted that I figured I would buy just as soon as I had saved up enough money. But the main one I was looking for was *Chester Gump in the City of Gold*. It took me at least two minutes to find it. Stretching up and over the counter, I could reach it without having to ask a clerk to help me. Upon returning to the front of the store I handed the clerk the book along with my dime and a mill, an aluminum coin worth one-tenth of a cent. She opened the cash register, dropped my money into the drawer that slid out, put the book into a paper sack, and handed it to me with a smile. She could tell I was tickled to have the new book. Eddie looked around but didn't buy anything. I decided he meant it when he said he was saving his money for ice cream. With less than ten minutes left we hotfooted it across the street to the cool and inviting ice cream parlor.

The vanilla-and-chocolate ice cream sandwich tasted even better than I had remembered. Eddie said he would try it and got one, too. He said he could always get a plain old chocolate ice cream cone at the drug store in Helena. With handfuls of paper napkins we sat down at one of the little white tables, like the kind they had in Corliss' Drug Store. Between bites Eddie asked, "Say, did ya hear we're gettin a new teacher this year?"

"Heck no," I said, "I didn't hear that." I was surprised and shocked. "You mean Mr. Ewing ain't comin back?"

"Naw, Dad told me he's gonna be teachin at the high school up at Helena an coachin their basketball team." I listened carefully so I could tell my folks and I pressed Eddie for information on the new teacher. I figured this would be some news I could tell Mother and Daddy that they didn't already know.

"Who's the new teacher gonna be?" I asked, acting nonchalant, taking a big bite of my ice cream sandwich.

"Well," Eddie answered, his mouth full of ice cream, "she's a woman. Lives over at Aline. Her dad runs one of them creameries, the one right there by the picture show. Ya know where that's at, don't ya?"

"Ya mean the Ford creamery?" I asked. "We take our cream there all the time."

"Yeah, that's tha one. Our new teacher's name is Tam Ford." I had never known anyone named Tam before.

"What does she look like? I hope she's better lookin than

Miss Downing." I wasn't sure I'd like another woman teacher.

"Well, I figure she is but I know fer a fact she's a lot prettier than Mr. Ewing." Eddie grinned. Then, swallowing the last bit of his ice cream sandwich and wiping his hands with paper napkins, he added, "I only saw her once. She's kinda young an kinda purty an she ain't very big. An she ain't married, from what I hear." Well, I thought, wiping the sticky mess off my hands, it'll sure be different, having a pretty young woman teacher.

"I wonder if she knows anything about basketball," I said. Eddie just shrugged his shoulders.

"I don't know nothin bout that," he said.

We kept our eyes on the clock behind the counter in the ice cream shop and saw we had just about used up our fifteen minutes. Eddie's tongue found the last wet crumb of his sandwich at one corner of his mouth. Then we got up, dropped our used napkins into a big wire wastebasket, and walked out into the hot August sun. We watched for cars as we hurried across the street and headed back to J.C. Penney's.

Our mothers were waiting by the front door, still talking. Mrs. Talmage looked and acted a little peeved with Eddie even though I was sure we hadn't been gone more than fifteen minutes. She told Mother she was in a hurry to get on back home so she could fix dinner for Cap. Then she said goodbye and that she was glad she ran into us, and charged off down the street to where she had parked her car. Eddie, Pauline, and Willie, all loaded down with packages, followed her, having trouble keeping up. Eddie looked back once and I waved. I couldn't wait to see him again.

As we loaded our packages into the car, Mother told me she needed to go to the drug store, get me some school supplies, and then buy some groceries before we left town. She asked if I would like to find a café and have some lunch before we finished our business. "I imagine you're gettin pretty hungry by this time," she said. She didn't know I had just finished eating an ice cream sandwich. "How hungry are you son?"

"I reckon I'm hungry enough to eat a dime-size hamburger," I answered, "an have a bottle of pop to go with it."

"Well, the café will have a menu I'm sure, and you can order anything you want. It's too bad the Blue Bird Café never put in any tables; it's the closest one."

"I don't like that place anyway," I said. "Let's go to the City Café. It's up there by the variety store." I didn't tell her why I didn't like the Blue Bird Café, and I already knew why she didn't.

"That'll be just fine," Mother said. "We'll finish shopping after we've eaten."

There was no talk about what Mother would have to eat at the café or what I would have. My folks never expected me to tell them what I was going to have before the waitress came. I was glad they liked me to make up my own mind about such things instead of expecting somebody else to make up my mind for me. This was just one of the many ways Mother and Daddy taught me to be independent.

Safeway was my favorite of all places to buy groceries, partly because they had so much more of everything than A.J. Woods or Paul Shembeck had in their Aline stores. Safeway was a store where we walked around, looked at and felt things, took what we wanted, and put everything into a wire basket. When we finished we took our basket of stuff up to one of the check-out stands where a clerk wearing a white paper cap and a Safeway apron took everything out, calling the name of each thing and the price as the checker punched keys on an adding machine. Then Mother paid for what we got and a man put our groceries in big paper sacks along with a free copy of their store magazine, *Family Circle*. Then he carried everything out to our car for us, even though it was parked across the street. *Family Circle* was a great magazine. The best thing was a page in the back with dibs and dabs of information called Food for Thought. I always read that part first.

On the way home I told Mother what Eddie had said about our getting a new teacher at Round Grove School. She hadn't heard about it. She said she didn't know Tam Ford personally but she knew who she was. All I knew was that we took our cream to Ford's Creamery and Feed Store on Saturdays and sometimes we bought chicken feed there. I had been in Ford's several times but I couldn't remember ever meeting a pretty young woman in there, just several men wearing canvas aprons over their blue overalls.

Eddie's news about our new teacher was a complete surprise and it bothered me greatly. I couldn't imagine having a teacher I liked better than Mr. Ewing but there was nothing to be done about it. "I know you're shaken up, son," Mother said on the way home from Cherokee, "but I'll bet Miss Ford will be a wonderful teacher. This way you'll have a couple of weeks to get used to the idea."

I was glad Eddie had told me about our new schoolteacher. And now that I had new clothes and the school supplies we had bought at Keye's Drug Store, I was eager to get started in the sixth grade. ✦

Chapter 22 ————————————————— ◄

Late in the summer before I started sixth grade, I decided I would rather walk to school than to ride old Charger; two years of that were enough. But mainly I wanted to walk with my new friend Donnie Banks, who, along with his family, had moved to the place just north of our church, a mile east of the corner a half mile south of our house. And, I figured, old Charger could use a rest. He was getting old, and besides, I could ride him on weekends or even to school sometimes if I wanted to.

School began the day after Labor Day, the same as usual. I was delighted with Miss Ford, our new teacher. Eddie Talmage had said she was pretty but she was more than that. She was lovely to look at, probably the prettiest woman I had ever seen anywhere, even in magazines, and she was wonderful to listen to. Her soft voice was warm and sweet in contrast with Mr. Ewing's brassy baritone. She wore beautiful clothes, mostly skirts and blouses in nice colors, and had curly brown hair cut short and eyes the color of the western Oklahoma sky on a cloudy summer day. And she smelled good, even at the end of the day.

We hung on her every word. The girls adored her and

immediately began trying to be as much like her as they could. All the boys, except a new kid, the Nazarene preacher's oldest boy, Emmett Simpson, quickly developed crushes on Miss Ford and most got red in the face when she spoke to or smiled at them. It looked to me like we were going to have a pretty good year and for several weeks I didn't even think about whether we would have a basketball team without Mr. Ewing being there to coach us or who would be the starting five.

A strange thing happened around the first of October, which gave me something to think about besides basketball and Miss Ford. It was late afternoon, dry and windy like most days in early fall, when I heard a truck being driven into the schoolyard. It finally came to a stop just south of the schoolhouse where I could see it through the windows. The driver and another man got out and moseyed around to the back of the truck and, leaning against it, got out their makings and rolled cigarettes. The sound of their voices floated through the open windows, and I could smell the burning tobacco. The license tag showed that the truck was owned by the State of Oklahoma so I figured it was at Round Grove School for some official reason. Who the heck were these guys, driving that truck right up into the schoolyard? I wondered.

Through the truck's sideboards I could see stacks of pasteboard boxes with black lettering but the writing was too far away for me to read. I looked over and saw Miss Ford also watching the two men. When she saw they were just standing there she told us to continue our work and said she would be right back. Through the window by the pencil sharpener I could see that as she approached, the men stood up straight, dropped their cigarettes, and ground them out under their shoes. They tipped their hats. One of them spoke, but so softly I couldn't hear what he said. But I clearly heard Miss Ford tell him, "You can stack the boxes in the cloakroom." When she offered the help of some of her big boys, they said they could handle it all right and wouldn't be long unloading. One of the men told her their next stop was McWillie School and they had to hurry to get there before Mr. Higgenbotham locked up and went home.

We could hear the two men stacking the boxes in the cloakroom. They soon finished and without another word they got into the truck and drove away. The rest of the afternoon I wondered what those boxes contained, and when Miss Ford dismissed us, I took a quick look on my way out of the schoolhouse. Stenciled on their sides I read: "State of Oklahoma, Department of Agriculture, Surplus Agricultural Commodities, Not To Be Sold." Other boxes were labeled "Clothing." Like the commodities, the clothing was marked "Not To Be Sold."

That night during supper, I told my folks about the truck and all the boxes that had been unloaded at school and what I had read on their sides. Mother said she couldn't say for sure but the stuff left at the school was probably free food and clothing that the State of Oklahoma was giving to people in the neighborhood who were on relief, like Donnie Banks' family. Daddy said there were people in our neighborhood who were so hard up they couldn't buy even some of the commonest things they needed to get along.

"Are we gonna get any of that stuff?" I asked.

"You know we ain't," Daddy said firmly. "We ain't on any kinda relief, we ain't never gonna be on relief, we don't get nothin from the State, an we never will!"

The words just poured out of him. "We ain't no strangers to hard times like some people's havin but we never got anything from the government. Now I'm gonna tell ya somethin, son, an I don't want ya to go repeatin it to nobody cause it ain't nobody's business but ours." He had my complete attention. He had never talked to me like this. I gulped, swallowed hard once or twice, and looked him straight in the eye. He

wasn't smiling and I could tell he was dead serious. I didn't
have any idea what he was going to tell me but I was proud
Daddy thought I was old enough to keep a family secret.

"Well, son, two or three years before me an Erma took you
outta tha orphans' home, I was well started in farmin; I wad-
n't a millionaire but I was gettin on my feet ta where I
thought maybe I could make a down payment on a farm. So
in the fall of 1929 I decided to buy me a used Model A car, tha
one that's settin out there in the yard. It was just a year old
at tha time. In those days you'd buy things like that on time
if you didn't have tha cash money. Then tha next spring I
traded in my old tractor on a brand new John Deere an give
a thousand dollars difference. But I had to borra the thousand dollars.

"Well, when I harvested my wheat in 1930 I got a good
crop, but when I went ta sell it they only paid me twenty-
eight cents a bushel. Now that there was tha best wheat crop
I had ever had but I only got twenty-eight cents a bushel for
it. Tha note on tha Model A come due after harvest and I
went up to Carmen to pay off what I owed to the Robins
Motor Company. Well, I walked into their place of business
an there was Mr. Robins settin in a swivel chair with his feet
up on his desk. He was talkin with some men so I just stood
around till he wadn't busy any longer. After a while he looked
up at me an asked if they was anything he could do fer me.
So I says, 'Well,' I says, 'I guess they ain't nothin you kin do
fer me but I thought they was somethin I might do for you. I
come up ta pay you for tha car I bought from you last fall.'

"Well, his feet dropped off of his desk an he just looked
plumb shocked. He says, 'Man,' he says, 'do you know you're
the first man in months who's been in here ta pay me for anything?'

"Well, son, I didn't have enough money left to pay off tha
thousand dollars I owed on my tractor but I paid as much as
I could on tha note. I had counted heavily on a lot more

money for my wheat than I got but the bottom had plumb fell outta everthing an I wondered if I would ever be able to get a holt of tha money I needed. So ta get the money I did just about everthing. I sawed wood fer people fer a dollar an hour. I furnished tha tractor, tha saw, tha tractor fuel, an myself. I worked as hard as I could because I thought that a dollar an hour was more'n I was worth.

"Then I got another job for a while workin on tha road where I worked three horses an a Fresno movin dirt from one place to another. I drove tha horses back an forth from home to tha job up north of McWillie. Tha next year I hired out to cut wheat fer several people around here. I plowed an listed an drilled wheat fer people who didn't have any machinery of their own.

"It took me three years an just about broke my back, but I paid the bank ever cent of that thousand dollars I borried. Son, that was one of the best feelins I ever had, finally bein able to pay off what I owed the bank. An I'm mighty proud of what I did. Since then I ain't never bought nothin else on time an I ain't goin to. An we ain't takin any charity from anybody. They just ain't no way we're gonna do that!"

Never before in my life had I heard Daddy talk so long without stopping. Hearing that story made me so proud that I could hardly stand to keep quiet about it. But as I promised him, I never told a soul. Our talk around the supper table that night helped me understand the hard time people were having and how my family was dealing with it. It was the first time Daddy had talked to me like an adult and I began to feel like I was his real son. Mother and Daddy said they knew several other families who were too proud and honest to go on relief. Like us, they were working hard to make it on their own.

My education in relief and commodities and the Depression continued the next day at school. When I went over to put my dinner pail in the cloakroom cupboard, I saw that all the pasteboard boxes were gone. Somebody must have come for them after school let out the day before. During the opening exercises, I looked around the room and could see that several boys were dressed in matching black corduroy jackets and pants. Some of the girls wore matching skirts and jackets of maroon-colored corduroy. I figured that at least five families had been given relief clothing. It all looked the same, like a uniform.

Walking home from school that afternoon, Donnie Banks told me his family got some of the commodities. "But," he said," we didn't get no clothes."

"What did you get?" I asked.

"Well now, let me think for a minute. We got some flour an some rice an some cans of meat an some navy beans an some corn meal an some peanut butter an some lard an, oh yeah, we got some dried milk."

"Dried milk?" I asked in disbelief. "You got dried milk? What's dried milk? I've never heard of such a thing!" I thought he was joking.

"It's real milk. We really like it."

"How do you fix it? What do you do with it?"

"Well, ya see, it's real easy. Ya just get a glass or cup or somethin like that there an ya put a spoonful or two of dried milk in it an ya pour in some water. Then ya stir it all up real good an ya got milk!"

"Well, that beats anything I ever heard. Why don't you just use milk right outta the cow?"

"Cause we ain't got no cows."

"Oh," I said, a little embarrassed, wishing I hadn't asked. I had heard enough. The hungry people, right in our community, folks Mother and Daddy had been talking about, included my friend who lived only about a mile from our house. For some time I had known that several Round Grove families were poorer than we were. But until now I hadn't given much thought to just how poor some of them really were. I was just glad we weren't as poor as they were. Daddy said we should be thankful for that. And I tried to be.

The Nazarenes had got themselves a new preacher during the summer, a Reverend Calvin Simpson. Reverend and Mrs. Simpson and their six children moved into the Nazarene parsonage right next to the church. Jim Bob Tomlin said they came from somewhere down around Ringwood. The Tomlins were Nazarenes so Jim Bob probably knew what he was talking about. "He's been preachin in a little Nazarene Church that went outta bidness cause mosta the members taken off fer California an Washnton an Or'gon to git work in tha fruit orchards out thattaway," Jim Bob said. The more Jim Bob and the Tweedy boys told me about the Simpson bunch, the more I wondered if they might have been asked to leave the church down by Ringwood because their kids were so ornery. Junie Clifford said the story about their congregation all moving out west was nothing more than a made up story to make the Simpsons look better to the folks who went to the Round Grove Nazarene Church.

Four of the Simpson kids showed up at Round Grove the day school started: two boys and two girls. Thin and tall for a fourteen-year-old, Emmett was the oldest and in the seventh grade. Lillian was twelve, Luther ten, and their little sister, Rose Ann, was seven. It was easy to see the Simpsons were poor. Their clothes were worn out and they didn't have paper tablets or pencils or ink pens or books when they came to school on the first day, like everybody else did. They didn't bring their dinners either. Instead, they all rushed home to eat when we got out at twelve o'clock. It wasn't far if they cut across Alice Mills' flower and vegetable garden. From the first day it was plain to see that Emmett didn't like Round Grove. And even though the Simpson family had been moved in for more than a month, he hadn't made any friends among the Round Grove kids, even those who attended the Nazarene church. I often heard him cussing and talking dirty on the schoolgrounds and from the very first day of school he talked back to Miss Ford right in the schoolroom. From the way Emmett acted I thought he should be in a reform school somewhere instead of at Round Grove.

Nobody liked Emmett. "He ain't nothin but a piss ass!" Jim Bob Tomlin said disgustedly. Like Jim Bob, Marion Hood said Emmett was "a nasty son-of-a-bitch an no good fer nothin!" Stories started going around that he might be wanted by the law somewhere. Several kids said they thought they had seen his picture on wanted posters in the Aline Post Office. Eddie Talmage said he heard that the Simpsons had left their old neighborhood because Major County wanted Emmett for something. He said the sheriff had told the preacher that if he didn't get Emmett under control or out of the county he would arrest him and put him in jail and throw the key away. We thought and talked a lot about Emmett Simpson.

"I've seen him goosin other kids," I told Marion Hood one day, "boys and girls both. I don't think Miss Ford knows he's doin it. I'll bet kids are afraid to tell on him for fear he'll beat up on em."

"He acts just like he's tryin to get hisself expelled," Marion said. "I wish the son-of-a-bitch would go back where he come from."

Emmett often picked on other kids, especially little ones, during recess. Once he came back from dinner earlier than usual and headed straight for the merry-go-round where several little kids were sitting, talking and laughing while they ate their dinner. Before they realized what was happening, it was too late to run. Without a word, Emmett grabbed hold of the merry-go-round and, pulling as hard as he could, he started it turning. As it went around faster and faster, dinner pails flew off into the dirt while the little kids held on for dear life. Faster and faster went the merry-go-round as the terrified children cried and screamed. Hearing the commotion, two eighth grade boys ran over from the baseball diamond, grabbed hold of the merry-go-round, and brought it to a stop, while Emmett leaned against a blackjack tree and laughed and laughed. Miss Ford stepped out onto the rear step of the schoolhouse and stood there. Some of the little kids were so dizzy they couldn't walk or stand up straight. Frankie Hood and Paul Tomlin helped them find their dinner pails. Miss Ford watched in frozen dismay, one hand over her open mouth.

But Miss Ford didn't say anything or do anything to Emmett. School went on that afternoon as if nothing had happened during the dinner hour, but the little kids were still shaken up and scared to death of Emmett Simpson; it showed in their faces.

Another time, on the basketball court, Emmett grabbed Maybelle Finney's arm with both hands and twisted it hard, like when you wring water out of a wet towel. He must have hurt her pretty bad because she screamed, started to cry, and begged Emmett to let her go. Several kids were standing around and saw what happened but nobody said anything to Emmett or tried to stop him, probably for fear he would hurt them, too.

I wasn't exactly afraid of Emmett. I never ran from him but I was careful not to get in his way. I figured Emmett didn't pick on me because my good friend, Leonard Tweedy, was just as big as he was and probably a lot tougher. And Leonard never took anything off Emmett.

Along about this time, Emmett discovered Twila Bailey, who was his age but in the eighth grade. From the way he talked around us boys, he meant to get Twila off into the bushes and get between her legs. One day Emmett walked with us—the Bailey girls, Maybelle Finney, Donnie Banks, and me—all the way to where the Baileys always climbed the barbed wire fence and cut across the plowed field to their house. I didn't see him lay a hand on Twila but he kept talking dirty and making signs to her with a big peter he had whittled from a cottonwood root. Maybelle, Donnie, and I were walking a little ways behind them and could see the Bailey girls were trying to ignore him as they approached their barbed wire fence. We all were embarrassed at what was happening and I hoped Twila and Gladys would tell their folks when they got home. Emmett stood and watched Twila and Gladys climb the fence and run off across the plowed field. Without a word, the three of us walked on by Emmett down the road and in a little ways looked back to see him heading south in the direction of the Nazarene parsonage.

One day around the middle of October we were having a baseball game during the noon hour and the whole school, including Miss Ford, was gathered down at the diamond, either to play or to watch from the sidelines. Miss Ford stood behind the catcher, playing umpire. Emmett Simpson had gone home for dinner at twelve, but had come back to the school twenty minutes later and insisted on playing third base even though Evelyn Campbell was already at third. From the pitcher's box, I could hear him muttering, griping, and calling people insulting names. Miss Ford called him down when she heard him swearing at Dwight Hood, who was standing at home plate with the bat in his hands, waiting for me to throw the ball. Although I was standing in the center of the diamond I saw and heard what happened next. "Emmett," Miss Ford said evenly, "if I ever again hear you using language like that on the schoolgrounds I'll send a note home to your father."

Emmett just stood where he was for a minute, then turned slowly and made a show of spitting on the ground. Through narrowed eyes he glared his hardest at her, looking wild and vicious, not saying a word. All eyes turned from Emmett to Miss Ford but no one spoke. The air was electric. I didn't know what to think or do but I was afraid something terrible could happen; I was sure Emmett was mad enough and mean enough to do almost anything. With his feet firmly planted, he stood there between third and home bases and glared at Miss Ford, as though he were daring her to do something. Neither of them moved; neither spoke. Miss Ford's face had turned red and her arms were folded across her chest. Finally she said, "You can either behave yourself or you'll have to go home until you can learn to behave." She was determined to remain in charge of the situation; she meant business.

I had never heard her talk that way and anyone could see that she was very angry. Emmett answered by suddenly jumping forward and jerking the baseball bat out of Dwight Hood's hands. Swinging it from side to side in a half circle, he moved threateningly toward Miss Ford, who took a step backward, her face now almost white. Just then Leonard Tweedy tackled Emmett from behind, knocked him off balance, yanked the bat from his hands, and wrestled him to the ground, forcing his face into the sand. Flat in the dirt and weeds, Emmett couldn't move. "Now git home, you rotten son-of-a-bitch, git home right now or by God I'll beat tha livin hell outta you right here in fronta everbody!" Leonard was growling, seeming not to care that Miss Ford might hear his rough language. "You try any more of that stuff around here again an by God you'll answer ta me!" With that he got off Emmett's back and stood aside, breathing hard, face sweaty, eyes blazing, fists clenched, waiting to see what Emmett would do.

Getting slowly to his feet, Emmett tried to brush the dust and sandburs off his black corduroy pants. He glared at Leonard, then at Miss Ford, his eyes burning with rage and humiliation. Then, head held high, he stomped off toward the Nazarene parsonage. He never looked back.

The next morning the Bailey girls told me that after school Miss Ford had met with their daddy who was president of the Round Grove School Board. Miss Ford and the girls told him about the trouble Emmett had been causing at

languages, and ate different foods. Although our entire school library didn't quite fill one narrow cupboard, I was able to find books that helped me understand my own part of the world and learn about the Indians who lived in Oklahoma before white people moved in. I had been surprised to learn how many different kinds of people lived in our state. There were several different Indian tribes as well as people who had come to Oklahoma from all over the world.

At Mr. Ewing's urging I had begun reading books on travel; I especially enjoyed the adventures of Richard Halliburton. I couldn't wait to grow up and go to Yucatan and see the Maya's sacred well at Chichen Itza where the Indians sacrificed pretty young maidens to their bird god that looked like a parrot and had a long tail and an unpronounceable name. There wasn't a book or story on American Indians in our school library that I didn't read, either while Mr. Ewing was our teacher or the following year. Miss Ford loaned me books about the Pueblo Indians of Arizona and New Mexico and one about Indians who lived in the southwestern United States in prehistoric times. She even borrowed books for me from the county library in Cherokee, without asking me if I wanted to read them. She knew how interested I was in those subjects.

My spirits soared when, right after Thanksgiving, Mother and Daddy told me we would be taking a trip to Arizona in December and would not come back until after the first of the year. They said Uncle Clyde and Aunt Mildred had invited us down to Phoenix for Christmas and New Year's and asked us to bring Grandma Dollie with us. From listening to Mother and Daddy making plans, I learned that Uncle Clyde had applied for a disability pension, on account of his being a veteran and getting sick with asthma while he was stationed in Siberia with the army during the World War. Uncle Clyde said it would be mighty helpful if Daddy would come to Arizona and explain to the government people what bad shape he had been in when he came home from his service in the army in 1919.

Uncle Clyde wrote that the trip to Phoenix was right at a thousand miles. He said we could drive it in about four days, including time for meals, gas, and rest stops, if we averaged thirty-five miles per hour. He suggested places to camp overnight and to buy the cheapest gas and oil, and recommended which highways to take. He sent road maps on which he had marked the roads in pencil and noted that Texaco filling stations always had the cleanest rest rooms.

One day during the first week of December, Mother drove down to the school at four o'clock to have a talk with Miss Ford. She told her about our planned trip to Arizona and asked if it would be all right to take me out of school for a couple of weeks. Miss Ford said she thought it would be wonderful for me to go on the trip and that we needn't worry much about my schoolwork. "Besides," she said, "the kids will be on vacation most of the time you'll be gone." All I needed to do, she said, was to take my arithmetic book and pencil and paper so I wouldn't get behind in that subject. She told Mother that because I was a good student I would probably get more out of the trip than I would out of being in school anyhow. She told me later that I was very lucky because most kids never got to do what I was going to do.

One night after supper we sat around the dining room table studying the road maps Uncle Clyde had sent, and saw just where we were going and how we were going to get there. We talked about how far we would plan to drive each day and where we could stop for the night, and located on the maps several interesting places we could see along the way. Because Grandma Dollie collected pretty rocks and samples of sand from all over the world, she told Daddy she wanted to visit the Painted Desert and Petrified Forest in Northern Arizona. She had made a bunch of little cloth bags to put the new rock and sand samples in.

To save on lodging costs, Daddy put together a two-wheeled trailer with a box on it that had just enough room inside for a double-bed mattress. He then built a frame shaped like a log cabin and bolted it to the trailer. Over the top he stretched heavy waterproof canvas so the whole thing looked like a neat little tent with wheels under it. He and Mother would sleep in the trailer, he said, and after he took the seats out when we stopped for the day, Grandma Dollie and I would sleep inside the car.

I didn't look forward to sleeping with Grandma Dollie next to me but I figured some of the time I could sleep on the ground out in the wide open spaces, under the stars, close to a big campfire, just like cowboys did. In preparation for the trip, I found a couple of forked blackjack sticks and one that was fairly straight that could be used to hold a pot over the fire like cowboys did in the westerns I had seen at the picture show.

The exciting adventure of my upcoming trip to Arizona was the talk of the school; I was the envy of all my friends. Nancy Rose Fleming was my best girl and I thought she would be happy for me, but she could hardly stand it that I was taking a big trip, longer than any she had ever taken, when she wasn't going anywhere. She was the only one in the whole school who had ever traveled more than a hundred miles from home.

I practically walked on air during the days we were getting ready for the trip and didn't cause anybody any trouble. The trip was on my mind all the time. I guess that was why I forgot about an important upcoming event. As a sixth grader I was now a regular member of the basketball team. Around the end of the second week in December we were scheduled to play in a tournament being held in the Helena High School gym and I completely forgot to tell Mother and Daddy that I needed a new pair of tennis shoes and wouldn't get to play if I didn't have them. Miss Ford offered to help. She said she would be glad to bring out a pair in my size from Bullard's store in Aline, if Daddy would give me the money to pay for them at school.

But there was something else I needed this year that I hadn't needed before. And I had to have it before I could get suited up in my uniform. I was too embarrassed to ask Miss Ford to buy it for me and kept putting off mentioning it to my folks for fear Daddy would laugh and tease me about it. Finally, in desperation, a couple of days before we were to play Dacoma in the tournament, I blurted it right out to Mother. "Mother, I need a jockey strap if I'm gonna play in the game Friday night." My face was probably red as I put the big Sears Roebuck catalog down on the dining room table where she was sitting, sewing a button on one of Daddy's work shirts.

"What's a jockey strap, son?" she asked.

"It's a thing kinda like a cross between a belt an a pair of shorts that boys wear under their basketball pants to keep their privates from showin. Here's what it looks like." I opened the catalog to a page I had marked, and pointed to a picture of the only jockey strap I had found in the catalog.

"Why, this says it's an athletic supporter. Is that what you're calling a 'jockey strap'?"

"Yes, ma'am, it's the same thing, but everybody calls it a 'jockey strap.'"

"Oh, I see. But I don't know where we can get you one. We haven't time to order one from the catalog. Where did the other boys get theirs?"

"Well, Eddie Talmage said his mother got his outta the catalog. But maybe we can get one at Goodno's or Bullard's or maybe the drug store.

"Well," she sighed, "I wish you had told me a long time ago that you needed one of these things. I'll call over to Aline and see if anybody over there has one that will fit you." She talked to all three stores in Aline but not one had a jockey strap any-where near my size. Feeling defeated, I watched her hang up the telephone receiver.

"I just forgot to say anything about it earlier. I guess my

mind was so much on the trip that I never got around to thinkin about it."

Mother looked at me; a small knowing smile crossed her face. "I'll tell you what; maybe I can make you something that will work until we can order the real thing out of the catalog."

"That'll be okay," I said, greatly relieved, sure she would make something that looked like the picture I had shown her.

I didn't think any more about my jockey strap problem until the day of the game. That morning Mother showed me what she had made on her sewing machine, holding it out to me, smiling. What she held in her hands looked nothing like the picture. Instead, it looked just like the girls' cotton panties I had carefully studied in the Sears Roebuck catalog; it even had a narrow band of elastic around the waist and leg holes. The thought of having to wear such a thing raised goose bumps on my arms and legs and a knot tightened in the pit of my stomach. "This doesn't look anything like a jockey strap," I stammered, not wanting to hurt her feelings, not wanting her to think I was complaining. But I was so embarrassed I thought I could die.

"Well, son, I'm sorry you don't approve of what I made. I did the best I could," she added gently. Clearly, her feelings were hurt because I wasn't satisfied with the homemade jockey strap. Then she seemed to sense the real embarrassment I was feeling because I didn't want to hurt her feelings. "If you're afraid the other boys will make fun of you, you can wear your uniform under your regular clothes," she suggested, "and no one will be able to see you're not wearin a real athletic supporter. Nobody will know if you don't tell them."

"Well," I gulped, "it's fer darn sure I ain't tellin anybody!"

Mother had a perfect solution to my problem except for one thing: Miss Ford had all the basketball uniforms with her, along with our school basketball, and I couldn't get suited up until just before the game. And I'd have to take off my regular clothes and suit up in front of all the other boys when I got to Helena. I still had a problem.

Like the rest of the team that evening, I had to walk down the edge of the court to the far end where my uniform shorts and shirt were handed to me by Miss Ford just outside the boys' dressing room. If she noticed my nervousness, she didn't show it. I made myself walk slowly to the dressing room, desperately hoping to avoid anybody seeing me in my homemade jockey strap. I pretended to be in no hurry to get dressed, while everyone around me quickly got out of their clothes and suited up. I took a long time taking off my coat and untying my shoes. I was very lucky that night. Nobody asked me why I was the last boy on the Round Grove team to get out onto the court to warm up. I didn't even notice that Mr. Ewing was there, watching us play, until the second half. After we lost the game, when everybody hurried back to the dressing room to change back into their school clothes, I simply put on my overalls right over my uniform as Mother had suggested. Nobody noticed. Never in my life had I felt so relieved.

In a way I was glad we lost the game to Dacoma that night. It meant that our season was over, and I wouldn't have to worry about getting a real jockey strap for a long time. The next morning I sneaked out the back door of the house, the homemade jockey strap tightly wadded into a ball in my hand, headed for the toilet, stepped inside, and dropped it into the hole.

I had to admit to myself that I couldn't blame anyone else for my trouble, let alone Mother, who had done all she could to help me out when I really needed it. I finally thanked her for coming to my rescue and told her it was all my own fault. From the little smile that crossed her face and from the sparkle in her eyes, I could tell she was pleased that I was big enough to accept the blame. I think she also understood all about my embarrassment. Mother never mentioned it again, and I don't think she even ever told Daddy.

About a week before we were to leave for Phoenix I got a letter from Aunt Mildred. Mother handed it to me the minute I got home from school. It was a real letter, just for me, although she had written across the front of the envelope, right under my name, "Care of Frank Wilson." She had addressed the envelope with a soft-leaded pencil and somebody had smudged the envelope. But I didn't care. It was my letter and I got to open it. According to the postmark it took five days for it to get from Phoenix, Arizona, to our mailbox. I was so excited I tore it open and read it before I even took off my coat.

> Dear Rex,
> How are you? We are just fine.
> We are looking forward to seeing you and
> our folks when you get here.
> Your mother wrote us saying how
> excited you are about your trip to Arizona
> and when you will be getting here. There
> are many things to see around here, like
> the giant saguaro growing in the desert
> just a little ways from where we live,
> and lots and lots of orange and grapefruit
> and palm trees. Some of the palms have
> dates on them but they are not good to eat.
> Your mother said you want to get to
> know some Mexican kids while you are out
> here. Well, one of our neighbors who lives
> pretty close is a Mexican. His wife is also
> Mexican. Their name is Gallegos and he
> and his wife have a boy who is ten, just
> like you are, and a girl who will soon be
> nine years old. I told them all about you
> and they are anxious to meet you and
> get to know you. They said they hoped
> you will want to play with the Gallegos
> kids. The boy's name is Benito and they

call the girl Anita. They both talk Mexican
around their place. I'm sure you're going
to like them both.
We hope you and your folks and
Grandma Dollie have a safe trip to
Phoenix. Have lots of fun!

Love,
Your Aunt Mildred

P.S. Your Uncle Clyde says hello.

I showed the letter first to Mother and later to Daddy. To me it was pretty special, the first real letter with a stamp on it that I had ever gotten through the mail. At supper we talked about Aunt Mildred's letter. "I didn't think you would mind if I mentioned to your Aunt Mildred that you wanted to get to know some Mexican children while you're in Phoenix," Mother said.

"I'm glad you told her. Now I know where they live. I almost feel like I know them already. Do you think maybe they'll teach me to talk Mexican?"

"Well, if they're Mexican I imagine they will be able to teach you a little Spanish. But it's Spanish they speak, not Mexican. There's a difference."

"I thought Mexican people spoke Mexican."

"No," Mother said patiently, "they speak Spanish, and I'm pretty sure the Gallegos family will also speak English, or your Aunt Mildred wouldn't be friends with them."

"I don't care if they speak English or just Spanish," I said firmly. "I think I'm gonna like them and I hope they like me."

When Grandma Dollie said one day that she wanted me to help her look for new and different whiskey bottles on our trip, bottles with nice labels still on them, I was pretty sure she was having fun with me. I had never heard of anybody picking up bottles from out of the ditches where people had thrown them. But I couldn't always tell when Grandma

Dollie was teasing. She had fooled me many times before. Sometimes she would look me straight in the eye and, with a perfectly straight face and without batting her piercing blue eyes, tell me something she didn't mean at all.

Grandma Dollie also told me that while we were in the desert we would need to watch out for Gila Monsters. "What's a Gila Monster, Gramma?" She said they looked something like big brown lizards and are kind of hard to see in the desert. She said they were poisonous, like rattlesnakes and copperheads, and if one got hold of you there was no way in the world you could make him turn loose until he was good and ready or until the sun went down. She said people could die from being bitten by Gila Monsters. I thought for a moment as she sat there watching me.

"You ever seen a Gila Monster, Gramma?"

"Well, I ain't actually seen one, except in books, but I reckon I'd recognize one if I saw it up close."

"I'd get a big rock and smash his head if a Gila Monster tried to bite me," I told her. "I ain't afraid of lizards."

"They's another critter that lives out there in the desert that's even sneakier an more dangerous than Gila Monsters."

"What is it, Gramma?"

"You ever hear of scorpions?"

"I ain't sure. Seems like I read about them someplace. Ain't they kinda like spiders?"

"Well, they's poison, I know that, but if yer thinkin they's like black widda spiders, they ain't. But they's poison as they can be an some people have died from bein stung by scorpions."

"Whatta they look like, Gramma?"

"Well, a scorpion's got little claws kinda like a crawdad has, an a tail with a stinger on the end of it that curls up over his back like the tails of some kinds of dogs. You know what I mean?"

"Yes ma'am, I guess I'd know a funny lookin critter like

that if I ever saw one. Wait, I remember now, I read about scorpions in one of my Big Little Books, the one about Chester Gump in the City of Gold. Chester an his dog kept fightin off bunches of scorpions that were guardin the entrance to the city that was made outta gold."

"One thing you gotta remember, you gotta be real careful about shakin out yer shoes before you put em on in the mornin an be sure one of em don't get into bed with ya. They like to be where people are."

"Don't worry Gramma, I'll be real careful while we're out in Arizona."

No matter how you looked at it, Grandma Dollie was different from anybody else's grandma. She was one of a kind, gruff but gentle, bossy as everything but really nice when you got over being afraid of her. She had been a pretty, red-haired young woman of eighteen when she married Grandpa Pete. She was still pretty in the picture Mother and Daddy had hanging in their bedroom, the one taken of Grandma Dollie and Grandpa Pete with their two girls and three boys in 1906 when Daddy was five years old. Even at sixty-two, Grandma still had the freckles she had as a girl, scattered across her hands and face. During the warm months Grandma Dollie kept herself well covered while outdoors in the sunshine because, like Daddy, she was light complected and sunburned easily.

Grandma Dollie's round face looked pretty ordinary to me except that it always seemed to be puffed up or swollen. I figured it was because she wasn't young any more and that was what happened to peoples' faces when they got old. I couldn't think of any other reason why the bridge of her gold-framed glasses seemed to disappear at the top of her nose where it went from one lens to the other. I marveled at the little pink channel across her freckled nose each time she took her glasses off to clean them. She must have been aware of my fascination but she never said anything about it and neither did I. Her hands, too, seemed puffy and her narrow gold wedding ring, like the bridge of her glasses, had worked itself so deeply into her flesh that I could hardly see it. Her short thick hair was nearly white but there were still streaks of red in it when the light was just right. But most of the time I couldn't see her hair because she almost always wore a faded lavender felt hat that covered almost all of her head. She wore it both inside and outside the house, though she had never wore a hat at the orphans' home. ✦

Chapter 24 ⎯⎯⎯⎯⎯⎯⎯⎯⎯⎯⎯⎯⎯⎯⎯⎯⎯⎯ ❦

It was below freezing at seven o'clock in the morning the day we loaded up and got started off for Arizona. There was frost on everything. Our Model A windows were almost white from the thick frost that had formed during the night and it was a lot of work for Daddy to scrape it off so we could see out. Almost everything we were taking had been loaded the night before and soon we were ready to roll.

Uncle Hubert had come down from Jet the night before to stay at our place and take care of the hogs and chickens and feed and milk the cows. He was going to batch at our place so we didn't have to worry about everything freezing inside the house during the two weeks or so we would be gone. I was cold in the car as we drove down to Grandpa Pete's place.

Grandma Dollie was ready to go when we got to her house. From the looks of things she had been up and around for several hours before we drove in a little before eight that morning. Right away I saw that Grandma Dollie had a different hat on. It was coal black with a wide black band. I figured she probably couldn't see the little bits of white lint and the two or three long white hairs on the brim. Grandpa Pete probably couldn't see them either. Mother never mentioned little things

like that to Grandma Dollie because Grandma would sometimes growl at her the way she growled at me. Unlike the
winter hats Mother and most other women her age wore
when they got dressed up for church or something special,
Grandma Dollie's hat had no netting, ribbon, or any kind of
decoration on it, although, judging from the tiny holes near
the front, some kind of pin or brooch had once been attached.
This hat was pulled down so far on her head that only her
long earlobes were exposed to the crisp air that morning. I
sometimes thought maybe Grandma Dollie took pride in the
way she looked and went out of her way not to look like other
women. One of the things I liked about her was that she did-
n't care what anybody said or thought. Maybe she knew
about the lint and hair after all and just didn't think it was
important to pick them off.

Her battered old black suitcase sat near the kitchen door
so it could be loaded into the trailer first. There were also
several paper and cloth sacks filled, I guessed, with something to eat on the way, and some interesting pasteboard
boxes she had tied together with pieces of cotton string.
Grandma told Daddy the boxes were to go in the back seat. A
heavy handmade wool comforter was folded over her suitcase.

As Daddy and Grandpa Pete loaded her things into the
car and trailer, Grandma Dollie started to put on a long,
black wool coat, one I hadn't seen before. I figured maybe the
coat, like her black hat, was one she wore only on special
occasions, and there weren't many of those. I didn't think it
was a new coat because I could tell from the way it smelled
that it had been in mothballs for quite a while.

I thought Grandma Dollie would be in a good mood that
morning what with our leaving on a big trip to see her oldest
son and a lot of exciting things along the way. But she was as
grumpy as ever when Mother tried to help her put on her
heavy coat. Instead of thanking Mother, Grandma growled

that she was an adult and didn't need anybody to help her put her clothes on. Mother's face turned pink and she mumbled something I couldn't make out as she stepped back to give Grandma Dollie plenty of room to struggle the coat on over her thick gray sweater.

I was glad when we finally said goodbye to Grandpa Pete at the kitchen door. Mother offered to let Grandma sit in the front seat beside Daddy but she refused. She said she never sat in the front seat anymore, not since the time she had been in a car that turned over on the way to Cherokee and she came close to breaking her neck when she was thrown out. She reckoned she was safer in the back seat because there wasn't a door that might fly open if there was an accident. Mother knew why Grandma Dollie didn't like to ride in front, but because she wanted to be nice, she always offered to let her sit up beside Daddy.

It took almost as long to get Grandma Dollie settled into the back seat with me as it did to load all her stuff in the trailer, store the food in the grub box bolted onto the back of the car where the spare tire was supposed to go, and fill the water cans.

I had no idea what Grandma Dollie had added to the grub box but I knew it would be good. I hoped she had brought along some of her homemade bread and cookies. Then I remembered her mentioning that she was going to bake a fresh ham for the trip and bring a bottle of Heinz chili sauce to spread on the ham sandwiches she would make along the way.

When Grandma Dollie finally got comfortable in the back seat, she unfolded her heavy wool comforter and tucked it first around my lap and legs and then around hers to keep us warm. I didn't like it too much being tightly packed into the car like that but I was glad to be under the comforter with Grandma Dollie when we learned that the little manifold heater Daddy had recently put on the car didn't put out much heat; it barely warmed Mother's feet and didn't carry into the back at all. Grandma Dollie and I blew steam from our mouths and noses for what seemed like hours that morning.

We didn't stop anywhere but at filling stations until we got to Clinton, Oklahoma, a little before noon. It had warmed a bit and we were fairly comfortable in the car but Grandma and I were still under the comforter. We had finally stopped blowing steam every time we opened our mouths but it was still plenty cold outside the car. We decided to eat in the car instead of trying to find a place to picnic. On a side street, Daddy found a place to park, killed the engine, and stepped out to stretch his muscles. Grandma Dollie opened one of the pasteboard boxes she had packed between us on the back seat and lifted out all kinds of good things to eat. Mother got out paper plates from under the front seat and opened a quart fruit jar she had filled with fresh water. Daddy climbed back into the driver's seat.

"I forgot to put in the bread," Grandma Dollie announced loudly. "I don't know what in the world I was thinkin of; I put it right out there on the kitchen table so it'd be all ready to go."

"That's all right," Daddy said, "I saw a store down the street a little ways from where we turned the corner back there. I'll run back an buy a loaf or two while you ladies're getting everthing else ready fer dinner. Can ya think of anything else I need to get?"

"You might pick up a head of lettuce if you can find a good one," Mother suggested.

"Okay, I'll be back in a few minutes," Daddy said, opening the car door and stepping onto the ground. He took off at a trot.

In minutes Daddy was back with the bread and lettuce. The bread wasn't sliced but Grandma Dollie cut it with the butcher knife she had brought to use with the fresh ham roast. We all ate very well.

When we got back out onto the road again, Grandma

Dollie said we probably wouldn't find any good whiskey bottles until we got across the Oklahoma State Line and into the Texas Panhandle.

"How come, Gramma?" I asked.

"Well, Oklahoma's a dry state so it's against the law to have any whiskey. It ain't likely there's gonna be any bottles that's fit to pick up till we cross the line to Texas. Texas ain't dry."

During the afternoon we stopped in Elk City, Oklahoma. Grandma Dollie and I sat in the car while Mother and Daddy went shopping. Before long they were back with a two-burner Coleman gas camp stove. Wasting no time, Daddy packed it in the trailer and we got back on the highway. It was close to sundown by the time we crossed over into Texas and we all began to look for a place to camp for the night.

As we drove on and on, things seemed to get more and more tense inside the car. I knew Daddy was trying to find the place Uncle Clyde had suggested we spend the first night. Grandma was getting restless and so was Mother; I figured it was because they had been riding all day long and they were hungry and tired. I was sure neither was looking forward to fixing supper in the dark. Finally, becoming anxious, seeing no lights on the horizon, and with only a vague idea of how far we were from a town, Daddy pulled off the highway into a wide and shallow borrow ditch. He maneuvered the car and trailer onto a level place in the middle of the ditch and stopped. There was no place to unload the car and trailer or to build a fire and cook our supper so in the last twilight we had the same thing for supper we had had for dinner: fresh ham roast sandwiches with lettuce and Heinz chili sauce, apples, sugar cookies, and cold water. Grandma Dollie grumbled because she couldn't fix coffee to drink with her supper but she didn't blame anybody.

The Texas Panhandle was just as cold as Oklahoma and Grandma Dollie and I slept in our clothes so we could keep

warm inside the car. As she tried to get comfortable, Grandma
said that sleeping in the car with me wasn't her idea of a good
way to spend the night but she was thankful, at least, that I
wasn't a bedwetter. Several times before we finally went to
sleep I heard cars speeding by, their tires making a shrill
whining noise on the cement highway.

From the way Mother and Daddy were talking the next
morning, Daddy was going to follow Uncle Clyde's instructions more closely. Mother had one of the road maps open on
her lap all day long so she could tell within a few miles where
we were at any time. Two things kept me busy our second day
on the road: doing my schoolwork and helping Grandma
Dollie look for nice whiskey bottles. She could see the ditch on
her side pretty well from where she sat on the right side
behind Mother. Her eyes were so sharp she could sometimes
tell the condition of a label before she asked Daddy to pull
over and stop.

We were driving straight west on U.S. 66 all the way to
Flagstaff, Arizona, where, Mother said, we would turn south
toward Phoenix. I had never in my life seen so much traffic,
not even when we drove the forty miles into Enid, and I could
see from their license tags that most cars headed west were
from Arkansas, Texas, and Oklahoma. Starting the first afternoon I kept a list of the different license plates I saw on cars
headed west as part of a report Miss Ford had asked me to do.
I arranged them in alphabetical order in my spiral notebook,
and all day long counted the numbers of cars and trucks I saw
from each state. For a while I considered making a list of the
new cars I saw, especially the Fords, Chevrolets, and
Plymouths because I could recognize the differences among
the 1935, 1936, and the brand-new 1937 models. But I decided not to when I realized that most people heading west
weren't driving new or late-model cars. Instead, most were
traveling in cars as old or older than our 1928 Model A.

Each day we passed a dozen or more old cars which were

slowly moving along at no more than about twenty-five or thirty miles per hour, some followed by clouds of black or white smoke. Daddy said when he saw smoke like that he could be pretty sure the car was burning a lot of oil. He said that meant the engine was in bad shape. I looked through Grandma Dollie's window when we went around the old cars and each of them seemed to have a whole family inside. Many cars had mattresses and bedsprings tied on top and sometimes there were beds and chairs and tables and other pieces of furniture tied down on top of the mattresses. Even tin suitcases and pasteboard boxes were tied on top or on the running boards and back ends, all held in place by ropes or baling wire wound around the outside door handles. Some were pulling two-wheeled trailers crammed full of furniture. At least half of these and a few homemade pickups—made by sawing off the back half of a regular car and building a kind of flat bed onto the chassis to make a small truck—had Oklahoma license tags. Most of the others were from Arkansas. As we drove through the Texas Panhandle I noticed I was now also seeing Texas cars with families who were headed west, their household stuff piled on top, just like the Oklahoma and Arkansas cars, as though the people were taking with them everything they owned. I made notes for the report I was writing for Miss Ford. When we got to New Mexico the same thing happened again. I started to see loaded-down old cars with New Mexico license tags. I made notes about that, too.

Shortly after we crossed the New Mexico border on the second day of our trip, we saw, far up ahead, an old black car, with a mattress and other household stuff on top, that was pulled off onto the gravel shoulder of the highway. As we came closer we could see several people standing around, looking bewildered. Daddy said he was sure they were having car trouble. He said they wouldn't have stopped just to admire the scenery or pick up whiskey bottles. Daddy slowed down, pulled up on the shoulder behind them, and stopped. It turned out the people were a man, his wife who was holding a baby over her shoulder, and their three little boys. The boys were all younger than I. Daddy opened his door and stepped out into the cold north wind.

"Ya havin car trouble?" Daddy asked. The man looked like a farmer just in from the field, wearing an old felt hat and a denim jumper over his blue overalls. He reminded me a lot of Mr. Ferguson, the man I met in the Blue Bird Café up at Cherokee.

"Yeah, fraid we got some real trouble," the man said, wiping his runny nose with the back of his hand. "Ya ain't got a jack I could borry have ya?" He pointed to the right rear wheel of his car. "I reckon that wheel probly broke on me when I hit a hole in tha road back there a little ways. I'll have to put the spare on."

Mother didn't say I couldn't, so I climbed out of our car to stretch my legs and look around. I was eager to explore the ditch, to find a good whiskey bottle or maybe a piece of petrified wood. But these folks looked like poor people in a lot of trouble and I quickly decided I was more interested in them and their overloaded old car. I walked slowly around their Dodge Brothers car, and looked at all the household stuff they had managed to tie on it. When I got around to where Daddy was standing with the man I saw that they had a real serious problem. The right rear wheel had come apart and let the car fall on its axle. Like a wagon we had, the wheel had wooden spokes, and it looked like two of them were broken, letting the rim and tire slip off. It looked to me like the wheel was shot and probably couldn't be fixed.

"I got a jack in my car," Daddy offered. "I'll get it out while yer getting yer spare ready to put on."

The little boys had been following me as I circled their car and watched the men. "Where'd you folks come from?" I asked the oldest boy who was about my age.

"We're from over by Vici, Oklahoma," he answered, "ya

know where that's at?"

"Yeah, an uncle of mine used to live out that way but he moved to Arizona," I told him.

"Ya'll from Oklahoma?" He seemed surprised. From the way he said "ya'll" I wondered if he had once lived in Texas.

"Yeah, we're from out east of Aline," I said. "That's about forty miles this side of Enid."

"Oh," he said, "where ya'll headed?"

"Phoenix, Arizona. Where you headed?"

"We're goin to California, I reckon, least that's what Daddy said. We got kinfolk out there an we're gonna live out there. My daddy's sposed to have a job waitin for him out there someplace."

I looked over at their beat-up old four-door sedan again and wondered how they could possibly get it all the way to California before it fell to pieces. They had packed it plumb full with all kinds of stuff: clothes, bedding, and other things no family would want to leave behind. Somewhere in there those boys found a place to ride. Rusty tin suitcases were tied with baling wire onto the running boards on the left side of the car so you could only get in and out on the right side. They were partly held in place by a scissors-like baggage-holding thing that probably had been on the car when it came from the factory.

While Daddy was helping the man change the wheel, I talked with the kids and showed them my Melvin Purvis official G-man ring with the secret compartment. They were dumbfounded when I showed them how the ring could be expanded or made smaller to fit any size finger. All the while the boys' mother walked up and down the shoulder of the highway, calming her crying baby. Mother and Grandma Dollie stayed in our car. Daddy and the man visited like old friends as they jacked up the back end of the old Dodge car to replace the broken wheel. "I see you folks're from Oklahoma, too," the man said as he rolled the spare wheel around to the rear of his car. "Where 'bouts in Oklahoma do ya live?"

"We got a place four miles out east of Aline," Daddy answered. "Ya know where that's at?"

"Heck yes," the man said, grinning, "I got a brother-in-law lives over in that general neck of tha woods, over close to Waynoka. I went over there to his place one time to pick up an old sow. He does some farmin back there. Oh, I forgot to tell ya my name, I'm Cecil Thomas."

"I'm Frank Wilson and this here's my boy, Rex. That's my wife an mother back there in my car." From where he crouched near the rear axle of his car, Mr. Thomas looked up and smiled at me.

"Howdy," he said, "how old are ya, son?"

"I'm ten," I answered.

"So's my oldest boy, but he ain't quite as big as you are." I had been thinking that his boy was younger because he was smaller than I was. My folks were always telling me if I didn't eat more I'd never get as big as I was supposed to be for my age. Maybe the oldest Thomas boy didn't eat much either. "I'm mighty glad you folks come along when ya did." Mr. Thomas grinned at Daddy and me. "We hadn't been stopped more than about five minutes when ya come along. I hoped somebody with a jack would stop because if I wadn't able to get that wheel fixed I reckoned we might just hafta stay here." He chuckled, then coughed hard. He got to his feet and stepped over toward the barbed wire fence and spat where it wouldn't be stepped in.

Struggling and grunting, the two men got the broken wheel off and the spare on. As they worked I studied Mr. Thomas closely. He seemed cheerful and laughed a little now and then between coughing spells. I wondered what he thought was funny. It looked to me like he didn't have anything to laugh about. He and his family had had to give up their farm in Oklahoma, his boys were cold and hungry, he had an awful cough, and he was missing some of his teeth.

From the little I saw of his wife and tiny baby, these folks looked as hard up as anybody I had ever seen and they reminded me a lot of Donnie Banks and his family. I couldn't help noticing that his overalls were worn and patched. And even though they looked fairly clean, they hadn't been ironed like Daddy's and mine always were. I would have bet money he hadn't had a shave in two or three days and he needed a haircut pretty bad. Mr. Thomas was so skinny he looked like he hadn't had a good meal in a month of Sundays. Then I heard the Thomas boys talking to Mother. She had rolled down her window and was speaking to the ten-year-old whose name was Willard.

"You boys look like maybe you could use a cookie," she said. "Are you hungry?"

The two younger boys hung their heads as though they were shy or were trying to hide behind their big brother. Even though Willard might have been a little scared of Mother, he looked right up at her and said flat out, "Yes ma'am, we shore could use a cookie or two right about now!"

"Well," Mother said, smiling, "let's see what we've got in here." By now all three boys had moved closer and were watching her, eyes wide, mouths open in anticipation of something good to eat. From beneath her seat Mother pulled out a paper sack with several big sugar cookies in it. Left over from dinner and supper the day before, they were the last of a big batch Grandma had baked before we left home. Grandma Dollie made the best cookies in Alfalfa County.

The Thomas boys sat on the running board and wolfed down their cookies; even the youngest, who was no more than four, ate his as though he hadn't eaten all day. Mother gave each of the boys a second cookie and when they had finished eating she offered them little yellow apples from Grandma Dollie's orchard. Even though they were scrawny and wrinkled, they were Grimes Golden apples, sweet and full of good flavor. From the grins on their faces I could see the kids were tickled to get these handouts. "Handouts" was Mother's word for food she gave away.

While Daddy and Mr. Thomas were mounting the spare, letting it down on the ground and getting our jack out from under the rear axle of his car, Mr. Thomas told Daddy he had a brother-in-law who left Oklahoma for Fresno, California, a little over a year before to work for a big fruit grower and packer. Mr. Thomas had gotten a letter from him a few weeks ago, saying he could help him get good paying work picking fruit if he could get out there before the first of the year. Mr. Thomas had been sharecropping for three years out in western Oklahoma where things kept going from bad to worse; the wind was blowing away all the good farmland, and the family wasn't making enough to live on. He told Daddy they were sick and tired of living on relief commodities from the state. His boys hadn't had any new clothes for a coon's age and if it hadn't been for the people in the Methodist Church they went to, he didn't know how they would have made it. He said things looked real bad around Vici because of all the drought and dust storms. "I just cain't see no future in the farmin bidness," he said. "I've plumb give up on it. So me an the wife an the kids jus pulled up stakes an taken off fer California. It cain't be no worse out there."

They had had a public sale one Saturday right after Thanksgiving Day and sold everything they couldn't carry on their car, and were on their way, hoping they would get to Fresno before the end of December. He said they had prayed a lot about it. I wondered if they would ever make it to the West Coast in their worn-out old car, even if God did help them. We talked a lot about the Thomases after we left them that afternoon and I figured Mother would pray for them. She would know how. ✦

Chapter 25

Our second night on the road we spent somewhere in New Mexico on what was probably a cattle or sheep ranch. My main job that evening was to gather enough dead wood to get a small campfire started to help keep us warm. It was almost dark but I found an armful of dead limbs and carried them back to our camp. Daddy said the wood was probably mesquite. Grandma said it might be pinyon or juniper. This was my first chance to use the forked sticks I had brought along. I picked out a fairly level spot about fifteen feet from the car and trailer and used a rock to hammer the forked sticks into the ground. Trying to think the way a cowboy would, I laid pieces of the dead wood between the forked sticks. After placing my straight piece of blackjack wood in the forked sticks, I slipped onto the blackjack the two-quart syrup can I planned to heat water in and filled it about half full. Grandma Dollie said I had a good idea, because we could use some water to wash our hands and faces before supper. I was proud of the way the whole thing looked, exactly like pictures I had seen in adventure books, or like what I had seen cowboys use in western picture shows.

I took a sheet of tablet paper from the back seat of the car, twisted it, and, using a kitchen match to light it, I started my fire. Because the wood was dried out, it started right away. Hot flames quickly leaped up and, to my dismay, my forked sticks became part of the fire. In moments my whole creation collapsed, letting the bucket fall. The spilled water almost put out the fire. Well, I figured, my idea wasn't so good after all and I said to Daddy, "It's lucky we stopped back there an bought that camp stove to cook on." Nobody scolded me for wasting the water.

While Mother and Grandma Dollie fixed supper, Daddy got everything ready for us to get to bed early. The thick vegetable soup Grandma served was some she had canned from her big garden during the summer and fall and it was the best I ever had. It was thick with a lot of tomatoes, corn, slices of okra, and small chunks of potatoes. Mother never made vegetable soup that tasted as good, partly because she always put beef in hers and I didn't like the way it made the soup taste. Grandma Dollie never put meat of any kind in her soup when she canned it and she hadn't put in any of the beef she had brought along to eat on the trip. Sometimes I wondered if she was thinking of me because she knew I liked vegetable soup with no meat in it. We had soda crackers with the soup and even had dessert, which I never expected. As we were eating the last of the soup, Grandma Dollie surprised us with a mincemeat pie she had brought along in one of her pasteboard boxes. Grandma also made a small pot of coffee so she and Mother could have some with their pie. Daddy didn't drink coffee and neither did I.

It took more than four days for us to drive to Phoenix. By the time we arrived there, late in the afternoon of the 22nd of December, our little trailer was so full of whiskey bottles, sacks of sand, dead cactus, pieces of petrified wood, and pretty rocks Grandma had collected that there wasn't enough room for much of anything else.

Benito and Anita Gallegos were waiting patiently on the

front porch of Uncle Clyde's house when I woke up the next morning, and they were eager to invite me over to their house to spend the day. They weren't at all shy and not as dark-skinned as I had expected them to be. Except for their straight, coal-black hair, black eyes, and brown skin, they looked pretty much like the kids back in Oklahoma. I figured that when you live in Arizona where there is a lot of sun-shine, you are supposed to look brown. It didn't take long to get acquainted and we talked until Aunt Mildred called me in to breakfast. She had donuts and orange juice and I didn't want to miss out on my share. Benito and Anita promised to wait outside until I had finished eating. "Give these dough-nuts to Benito and Anita," Aunt Mildred said to me when I was ready to leave the table. "Tell them they're from me."

Mrs. Gallegos asked me to have "lonche" with them. She said she had spoken to Mother and it would be all right. Mrs. Gallegos called it "lonche" but I knew what she meant. "'Almuerzo' is the real way to say 'lunch' in Spanish but around here we just say 'lonche,'" she explained. "I hope you like it."

I thought it was wonderful. We sometimes had chili for supper during the winter at our house and I was familiar with hot and spicy food. The Gallegos family seemed sur-prised when I ate everything Mrs. Gallegos had put on my plate, the same things she gave Benito and Anita, including pinto beans with little pieces of green chili she had cooked in a cast-iron pot that looked like one I had seen Grandma Dollie use. She didn't serve bread or soda crackers but gave each of us a round, white, thin pancake about the size of a plate. "I've never had one of these before," I said.

"We call these 'tortillas,'" Mrs. Gallegos explained. "They're really just flour and water and a little lard. I cook em right on top of the stove." As I watched, she tore her tor-tilla in half, spread it with butter, rolled it up, and ate it. Mr. Gallegos rolled his tortilla and used it to push beans and chili onto his spoon. After a second helping of beans he cleaned his plate with what was left of his second tortilla. I was delighted with the tortilla and asked for a second one. It was a great "lonche."

Grandma Dollie wasted no time taking over Aunt Mildred's kitchen. Like in her own house, she was in complete charge even though she was where Aunt Mildred and Uncle Clyde lived. While she worked, Mother and Aunt Mildred tried to stay out of Grandma's way and didn't seem to mind letting her tell them what and what not to do. About all I saw Aunt Mildred do was mix up a batch of oleomargarine. She called it "oleo," something I had never heard of. Mother said it was a substitute for butter that was made from some kind of vegetable. Fascinated, I watched Aunt Mildred remove the chunk of greasy stuff from a waxed cardboard box and take off the thin waxed-paper wrapping. It looked exactly like the compound or shortening that Mother bought in Aline and used for frying instead of lard. Aunt Mildred dropped the white chunk into a mixing bowl, then sprinkled some orange-colored powder on it that came in a small paper envelope with the "oleo." She mixed and mixed with a wooden spoon and gradually the white chunk turned yellow so the whole thing looked almost like the butter we churned from cream in Oklahoma. It didn't taste as good, though.

One morning Uncle Clyde, Daddy, and I went in our car to a place called "the Farmer's Market." "They got every kinda vegetable an fruit you ever thought of an some ya didn't," Uncle Clyde said. He's right about that, I thought, as the three of us walked from one end of the market to the other. I never knew there were such places in the world and I told myself I must remember to tell Eddie Talmage about it. We left with a gunny sack half full of lettuce that Uncle Clyde bought from a kid who was wearing an old cap that had "PAY-AN-TAKE-IT" printed on the front in yellow letters. "Lettuce is cheap cause what the farmers sell here ain't good enough to ship up north an back east; they say that if they don't sell it here they just throw it away," Uncle Clyde explained.

"I like lettuce," Daddy said, "but it always makes me sleepy." We ate lettuce twice a day all that week and it was the first time I had ever had all I wanted.

Almost before I knew it, we had to pack up and head back to Oklahoma. Christmas had come and gone. Santa Claus hadn't left anything for me but Daddy gave me a red plastic pipe with a wooden stem made so I could blow three soap bubbles at the same time. It came with a little bottle of soapy stuff to make bubbles with. The label said it was made in Japan. Mother gave me a kaleidoscope, the first one I had ever seen. There was no present from Grandma Dollie and nothing from Uncle Clyde and Aunt Mildred. So there wasn't much for me under the little pinyon tree in Aunt Mildred's front room when I awoke on Christmas morning. Strangely, I wasn't disappointed. In fact, I was surprised and happy to get anything at all. Truly, the trip was Christmas present enough.

A day or two before we planned to leave Phoenix, Grandma Dollie's youngest sister, Great Aunt Sue, and Great Uncle Harvey drove up in their big black Oldsmobile with Aunt Edith. The three of them had spent Christmas in Mexico and had come through Phoenix on their way back to where they lived in Montana but Aunt Edith would be riding back to Grandma Dollie's with us.

I had to give up my place by the window in the back seat of the car and now had to sit between Aunt Edith and Grandma Dollie. We were jammed in so tight I could hardly move. I was glad to be going home. I missed my friends at Round Grove School and was eager to see them again and tell them about my trip.

We took a different route back to Oklahoma. Grandma Dollie wanted to see Colossal Cave in Southern Arizona and stop in Juarez, Mexico. She had visited Juarez a year before but hoped to find more things the Mexicans made from a black stone called "onyx." She said she couldn't get onyx in the United States. Grandma Dollie's collections were wrapped in old newspapers and packed inside the trailer along with all of Aunt Edith's things. It made sense to me that we weren't going to camp out on the way home.

Nobody mentioned any other side trips and I was thrilled when we stopped at Casa Grande Ruins National Monument around the middle of the morning. Mother showed me on the map where we were between Phoenix and Tucson and told me this was a special surprise, just for me. She explained that the Casa Grande Ruins was an archeological site, an ancient village where Indians had lived in prehistoric times. I asked her if she knew where the Indians were now. She said there would be someone at the monument who could answer my questions. Daddy parked the car and we followed little brown signs along a short trail to the museum, a building that looked ancient, like the big ruins nearby. It reminded me of pictures in the book on Pueblo Indians that Miss Ford had loaned me.

A friendly man in a dark green uniform seemed to be waiting for us just inside the museum. He suggested we take time to get a good look at the exhibits before he took us on a tour of the ruins. He said that would give us a better understanding of what we would be seeing. Unlike most adults I knew, he didn't seem annoyed by my many questions.

We were the only tourists in the museum and it was very quiet except for the squeak in one of my shoes and the whispering sounds Mother made as she read the exhibit signs and labels to Daddy. I stayed ahead of the others so I could read the labels for myself. They explained how Hohokam Indians happened to be there in the first place, how they lived, and how they built their houses almost six hundred years ago. Spanish explorers who came to Southern Arizona in the sixteenth century called the largest ruin "Casa Grande" because those words mean "big house" in their language, even though the Indians probably called it something else.

With a model and some drawings, one exhibit explained how the Indians managed to get water out of the Gila River to irrigate their crops while they lived at Casa Grande. According to the label, archeologists had found evidence of miles and miles of irrigation canals. I also learned that the Indians had been very good engineers.

There were many glass cases full of pottery of all kinds that the Indians had made, some for cooking, some for storing corn and other seeds, and some for storing water. One label said the beautifully painted pots were probably intended for something other than cooking or storage, but the archeologists weren't sure. The pots may have been used in a religious ceremony of some kind. Archeologists found some of the big, plain pots buried in graves and some, with corn in them, had been discovered beneath the floors of the adobe houses. One exhibit was an Indian skeleton that had been put back together the way the archeologists had found it buried under a dirt floor. Painted pots of several shapes and sizes had been placed around the skull and around the feet of the Indian who had been buried. According to the exhibit label there may have been food in the pots when they were placed inside the grave so the dead Indian would have something to eat while on his way to where he was going.

From what I learned in the museum, it seemed the Indian women at Casa Grande made lots of pottery but broke most of it. When a pot was broken and couldn't be fixed, they threw it outside their houses the same way some people back in Oklahoma threw junk out their back doors. At Casa Grande, so much broken pottery had been thrown away that it was piled up something like the leaves that collected in our yard every fall. I was very impressed by the Indian pots and thought to myself how nice it would be to have one for my own, to keep in my room to look at or to take to school and show to Miss Ford and all my friends. I decided if I saw a little pot just lying around while I was taking the tour through the ruins, I would ask the man in uniform if I could take it home with me.

The man in uniform was with a Park Service ranger. It said so on the badge he wore on the pocket of his jacket. In a brown hat with a wide, flat brim, he was waiting for us beside the door when we finished looking at the museum exhibits. He said his name was Earl Jackson, that he was a National Park Service ranger, and that he would be happy to take us on a tour of the ruins. If we would just follow him, he said, he would tell us about them and try to answer our questions.

As we started our tour with the main ruins, I looked up at the huge roof, which was like a giant umbrella held up by four huge steel pipes. It was about twice as high as our windmill. The ruin it covered was at least two stories high, but the ceilings were not as high as in our two-story house back home. The ranger said one reason the house had low ceilings was because the Indians who built it were all much shorter. But because the roof and some other parts of the building were missing, I couldn't be sure the Indians hadn't built it three stories high. The ancient building called "Casa Grande" had been built out of river cobbles and a lot of dried mud. The ranger said rain had dissolved the mud and after the Indians left Casa Grande there was nobody to take care of the pueblo. "It wasn't long," he said, "before it began to come apart. We're lucky to have anything more than a pile of rubble." He said the umbrella-like thing had been built to keep rain from washing any more of it away, which was what I had already figured out.

"But it don't rain much in this neck of the woods, does it?" Daddy asked. "You sure couldn't grow any wheat around here."

"Well, no, it doesn't rain much here," the ranger said, "but a little rain each year can melt a lot of dried mud in six hundred years."

I was fascinated by everything the ranger said. He made it all so clear and interesting. He said the Indians who lived in Casa Grande were farmers who grew their crops along the Gila River. "Right over there," he said, and pointed. He said the river had a lot of water in it several times a year in prehistoric times and the Indians knew the exact time each year to plant their crops and when they were ready to harvest. He said they irrigated the same way people did today who grew oranges and vegetables in the desert country around Phoenix. Pointing to two holes high up in the walls of the largest part of the ruins, he said the Indians looked at them every day.

"Why'd they do that?" I asked. He told us that when the sun shone through both holes and ended up in a bright round spot on another wall, the Indians knew it was the spring equinox and time to plant their corn. Then he explained what "spring equinox" meant. Those Indians were very smart, even if they didn't go to school, I thought, to know something like that. I asked Mr. Jackson why the Indians left Casa Grande. He said a long drought set in and the whole country dried up and they couldn't get enough water out of the Gila River to grow enough food to live on. "Couldn't they eat wild animals and birds?" I asked.

"No," he said, "the Hohokam didn't hunt very much." He said the Indians were mainly farmers and didn't eat much meat. He told us the Indians finally got tired of starving and just up and left one day. I thought of the Thomas family back on the highway. Mr. Jackson promised to give me some pamphlets to read and take back to my school. He laughed when he told my folks he had never seen a boy come through the monument who was so interested in Indians and prehistory. He told Mother maybe I would grow up to be an archeologist.

As we headed back to our car, I saw a small piece of brown pottery lying beside the trail close to where we had parked. Lagging behind, I stepped gently on the potsherd and carefully dragged it beneath my shoe through the sand to the car.

Then I picked it up and slipped it into my overalls pocket. Although dragging it across the ground had worn off some of the paint, I was glad to have a little souvenir of Casa Grande to show people when I got back home. I didn't tell Mother and Daddy what I had done.

By the middle of that afternoon I knew for sure my folks had made the right decision about not camping out on the way back to Oklahoma, because, all of a sudden, we ran into heavy snow. We were a long way from Benson, which was between Tucson and the New Mexico State Line. Daddy couldn't even be sure where the highway was, there was so much blowing snow.

Daddy slowed down until he could see the road better and we drove on through falling snow almost all the way to Willcox where we found a tourist camp that had a vacant cabin. Everything was covered by at least a foot of snow. By now the snow had stopped coming down and there were only a few clouds left in the sky, and we could see that the moon was almost full. The mountains were white with snow and very pretty, especially where the moon was shining on them. The man at the filling station told us the road east was clear. And as he was filling our car with gas I heard him telling Daddy that snow in southern Arizona was most unusual.

"In fact," he said, "it ain't snowed nothin like this in the thirty years I've been in this part of the country." I had never before seen so much snowfall all at one time. Although I thought it was wonderful, Daddy didn't like snow. He was more interested in getting an early start in the morning.

Around three o'clock the next day we left our car and trailer parked on a side street in El Paso, Texas, and walked across the bridge over the Rio Grande toward Ciudad Juarez, Mexico. I couldn't wait to spit into the river even though Grandma Dollie had warned me—very seriously—that if I did I would never tell the truth again. My mouth was full of saved-up spit by the time I got to the middle of the bridge.

Taking aim, I let go of the mouthful of spit and watched until it went splat into the slow-moving stream of water directly below. I made certain Grandma Dollie saw me do it. "Ya oughtened to of done that," she seemed to scold. "Now you'll never tell the truth again." I grinned at her and when she grinned back at me I knew for sure the whole business about spitting in the river was nothing but a joke and I could tell she was enjoying it as much as I was. She probably knew all along that I didn't believe her.

Juarez was unlike any place I had ever imagined. The air was dirty, the people looked odd, and even the stores had a strange foreign look and smell. And except for us and the other tourists, no one was speaking English. We all bought souvenirs of Mexico. Mother had given me a half-dollar to spend for anything I wanted. "Anything but food," she cautioned. "Don't eat anything!" She warned me to keep my fingers away from my eyes and not to put anything into my mouth unless she said it was all right.

I found a silver ring just my size with a little piece of green stone in it and gave the shopkeeper my half-dollar. Without a word she dropped the ring into a little paper sack and handed it to me along with several Mexican coins. We spent about two hours in Juarez going from one store to another, seeing the same kinds of things in every store, hoping Grandma Dollie would find some polished onyx she liked enough to spend her money for. Finally, after she settled on a few pieces, we walked back over the long international bridge to El Paso. About halfway across, I leaned over the railing once again and let go of a mouthful of spit into the Rio Grande. This time I didn't wait for it to land but hurried to catch up with the others. Later, as we were once again on the road home, Grandma Dollie remembered that she had been mistaken about the river I wasn't supposed to spit into. It was the Gila River, in Arizona, she said, not the Rio Grande. She looked at me and smiled so wide her eyes closed, and I smiled back at her. "Did ya spit in the Gila River?" she asked, solemnly, knowing very well I hadn't.

It was late when we stopped at a tourist court in Van Horn, Texas, the second night out of Phoenix. Like the night before, it was too dark to see anything much when we parked and got out of the car. I grumbled to Grandma Dollie about it. "Yer not missin anything," she grumbled back. "I been here before an there ain't nothin to see but desert." A strong cold wind was blowing from the north and the air was dusty and gritty even inside our cabin. I could feel the grit on the linoleum floor beneath my shoes.

There was no heat in the only cabin that was vacant. The old man at the desk told Daddy he wouldn't be able to get the heat on until the next day. "But," he drawled, "I'll let ya stay for half price if you can get by on a little less heat." He handed Daddy several extra blankets. Lighting both burners of the small gas stove in the kitchenette in one corner of our cabin, Mother took enough chill out of the room for us to be fairly comfortable. Mother and Grandma heated some soup and we wore our coats while we ate supper in the room. After turning off the stove we went to bed. But it was so cold Daddy had to unpack some of the blankets and quilts from our trailer. There were two double beds. Grandma and Aunt Edith slept in one bed, Mother and Daddy took the other, and Mother fixed a pallet for me on the floor.

Two more days on the road and we were home, having driven in snow again most of the last day. I was glad Uncle Hubert had milked and fed the cows while we were away. But I was really glad there was so much snow on the ground, about six inches, the most I had ever seen in Alfalfa County. It meant I could use the sled Mother and Daddy had given me for Christmas the year before. ✦

Chapter 26 ————————————————————————— ⋙

On account of our not getting home until Thursday night, I missed four days of school and didn't go back to Round Grove until Friday morning. Because I had all my books, home-work, road maps, postcards, and other souvenirs to carry, Mother took me to school in the car. She let me put my sled in the back seat. She said it would be all right if I took it to school just so long as I brought it home that afternoon and didn't piddle around on the way so I would be late getting my evening chores done.

When it came time for the sixth grade to recite that morning, Miss Ford asked me to tell the whole school about my trip, what I had seen, what I had done, something about new people I had met, and what it looked like out there in Arizona. At recess Eddie Talmage wanted to be the first to slide down our little hill, the one between the schoolhouse and the basketball court, on my fancy sled. Even Miss Ford took her turn and seemed to enjoy herself. She said she had never been on a sled like that and I believed her. One time she managed to turn the sled over, rolling down the hill and getting covered with snow while all the kids laughed. She was laughing when she got up off the snow so I figured she was having a good time. Jim Bob Tomlin took a couple of slides. "Yer folks must be awful rich to be able to give you a sled like this," he said.

Using the rope tied to the front to pull, I let the Bailey girls, Donnie Banks, and Maybelle Finney put their books and lunch pails on the sled with mine so they wouldn't have to carry their stuff all the way home. We had barely started down the road before Gladys Bailey told me Miss Ford had announced in school Monday morning that during the holiday vacation she had become engaged and was going to be married right after school got out in April. Gladys said Miss Ford probably wouldn't be back next fall because she and her husband were going to live in Cherokee where he had a good job with the railroad and she would probably get a job teaching up there somewhere. Gladys knew a lot about our teacher because Miss Ford had spent a night with the Baileys early in the week to talk to Roger Bailey about her plans because he was the president of the Round Grove school board.

I was sorry to hear that Miss Ford would be leaving because I liked her a whole lot. But I reckoned she would be happy for one thing at least: she wouldn't have to put up with Emmett Simpson if he came back to school in September.

After school I told Mother that Miss Ford wouldn't be my teacher next year.

"Well," she said, "just try not to brood about it. I imagine your new teacher will be just as nice as Miss Ford is."

By the end of the week I had more important things to think about.

Sometimes if Eddie Talmage got something before I did, I couldn't stand it until I had it, too. Like a fountain pen or yo-yo or a bicycle. Especially a bicycle. His folks bought him a blue-and-white one for his eleventh birthday in February. The only other boy at Round Grove who had a bike was Junie Clifford but his was old-fashioned, was painted black, and had skinny high-pressure tires. Eddie and I thought that kind of bicycle was not only ugly and stupid to ride on the sandy roads, but, because Junie's had a little wire basket attached to the handlebars, it looked sissy. Eddie's looked like a real boy's bicycle. His folks bought it in Enid and it had balloon tires. It was used but it looked almost new and they had found it in a pawnshop.

All that spring I tried to convince Mother and Daddy that if I got a bicycle with balloon tires I would be able to ride on top of the loose sand in the road instead of through it. "If Eddie Talmage can ride on top of the sand I can, too," I argued. I needed to explain things like that, I figured, because they were old-fashioned and probably didn't know that nowadays bikes came with balloon tires. Mainly, I didn't want them to haul off and buy me a bike with high-pressure tires because they didn't know any better. To Eddie and me, having a bike with high-pressure tires would have been even worse than having overalls with only one back pocket. Cheap and dumb-looking.

Toward the end of the school year I finally got a bike of my own, but only after I had saved ten dollars. Most of the money came from selling Ed, the calf Daddy had given me to raise.

Mother and Daddy bought the bike in Enid one week day, one of the times I got to stay at Grandma Dollie's house after school. When my folks came back from Enid just before dark that evening they had a full-sized boy's bike in the back seat of the car. Daddy was able to load it by taking off the front wheel and loosening the chrome handlebars so they could be turned.

It was a well-used Hawthorne that had come originally from Montgomery Ward but it was in good shape and worth my ten dollars. They said they had found it in Lytle's Pawn Shop on the south side of the square. It was painted black with white trim, and the only rust I could see was where the paint had been scratched or chipped. Because its chrome wheels didn't wobble when they turned, I knew the bike had been taken care of by the former owner. I was disappointed there wasn't any light on the front fender like Eddie's bike had, but the Hawthorne did have a streamlined metal tank with a door on the right side that opened and closed tight. There was enough room in it for a screwdriver and a tire repair kit, basic things I needed to have with me in case I had a flat tire on the road. Both fenders needed a little tightening. The stand that was supposed to be on the back fender was missing so I had to lay the bike on its side or lean it up against something when I wasn't riding it. I didn't worry about the missing stand; I was sure I could save the money to order one out of the catalog.

Although I now had a bike, I didn't know how to ride it. If I had been thinking ahead I would have learned to ride Eddie's bike before I got one of my own. Daddy and Uncle Hubert said they would help me learn to ride. The corral seemed like the best place to start. My idea was to ride at the upper end where there wasn't so much fresh cow manure. I wanted to stay away from the water tank and the barn because it was lower there and usually ankle deep in squishy, green manure during the winter and spring. Our single row corn binder and the salt block were both sitting at the south end of the corral right about where it would have been best for me to ride and I was a little bit afraid I might run into them. But Daddy said he would help me steer around them.

For my first run Daddy held onto one side while Uncle Hubert held onto the other until it was time to shove me forward. Warning me to keep pedaling, they gave me a strong push down the gentle slope. I rolled right by the salt block and the corn binder, got by the cement water tank and the wooden windmill beside it, and managed to avoid several piles of manure. But I finally fell over pretty much in the middle of where I didn't want to be, where the cows liked best to stand around before milking time. It was disgusting and embarrassing to land in the cow manure. Daddy couldn't stop laughing and kept wiping tears from his eyes with the back of his hand. He and Uncle Hubert both thought it was very funny. Mother had me take off my clothes so she could wash them. Later I used a scrub brush and a bucket of water and cleaned the green mess off my shoes and bicycle.

"Well," Daddy said one Saturday morning, "I reckon if you ain't gonna be ridin ole Charger to school next fall you ain't gonna be needin them cowboy boots you been wantin fer so long. Don't that sound about right?"

Daddy surprised me. I had just about decided he and Mother had forgotten about my wanting to grow up to be a cowboy, which had been why I needed the boots. I had been trying for a long time to teach my feet not to run my heels over to the inside. And I had been doing pretty well; in fact, I was already wearing my heels down like I was supposed to. "I'm just kiddin ya son. We've noticed you been doin real good learnin to walk right. So maybe it'd be all right if ya had some cowboy boots." He was smiling. Mother, too, was smiling. And so was I. "How'd that be?" he asked.

"Yessirree Bob!" I blurted, using an expression I had been hearing Daddy use ever since I came to live with them.

"That'd be just fine!"

Another surprise was that they were planning a trip to Enid later in the morning. Daddy had been thinking for some time about buying a hammermill so he could grind cattle feed and he had finally decided it was time to make a deal with the Minneapolis-Moline people. "While we're down there we kin scout around an see if somebody's got a pair of boots that'll fit ya," he said.

Daddy felt good about the deal he made on the hammermill and was in a good mood as we drove up the hill to the downtown square, parked near Coldiron's store, and went inside. Mr. Coldiron sold clothes as well as boots and shoes. He had everything you could think of except for really dressy things. "We're not tryin to compete with Herzberg's," our clerk told us, and chuckled. "What can I show you?"

"This here's yer customer," Daddy said. "He's a cowboy but he don't look like one cause he ain't got no cowboy boots. Whatcha got that'll help him look tha part?"

Mother explained to the man the trouble I had been having with running my heels over to the inside. "We think he's got some more growin to do before he gets into boots with high heels. Do you have something with lower heels?"

"Yes ma'am, I think I've got a boot that oughta be just the ticket for this cowboy." He measured my right foot. "Well, ma'am, we might wanta fit him a little big so's his feet can grow a little, don't you think?" Mother nodded. The man left and promptly returned with a big cardboard box. Inside was a beautiful pair of boots. I was dazzled by the handsomeness of their fancy stitching. "Well, whatta you think?" the clerk asked me.

"They'll be just fine," I said. "I wanted higher heels, but these will do just fine!" The boots came with spurs with black rubber rowels. I couldn't have been happier. I thanked Mother and Daddy all the way home. More than ever I was glad I was their boy.

"Don't you want to say goodbye to Miss Ford?" Mother asked on the last day of school as she was helping load my books and things into the car. "It may be a long time before you see her again. You do like her, don't you?" She's right, I thought. I should go up to Miss Ford and say something nice and congratulate her on getting married soon. And if the other kids are saying goodbye to her, I guess nobody will make fun of me if I say it, too.

The basket dinner was over, most of the cakes and pies had been eaten, nothing but the necks were left of the fried chicken on several plates, paper plates had been sailed around the schoolyard and across the road into the hedgeapple trees, the annual baseball game was over, and people were leaving for home. I found Miss Ford inside the schoolhouse, standing at the front of the room where she stood most of the time she was teaching. She was surrounded by girls she had taught at Round Grove, girls who almost worshipped her. Most were crying or had been crying, from the looks of their red eyes. Gladys Bailey had hold of Miss Ford's hand and never took her eyes from her face. With tears flowing down both cheeks, she stood there for the longest time, not saying a word. Gladys is really going to miss Miss Ford, I thought. And so will I. If I can get her to look at me I'll just say goodbye and good luck, then walk away before I start to cry myself. I was the only boy in the room. I wondered if any of the other boys had said goodbye to her. I tried not to look at the girls hanging around Miss Ford and it didn't look to me like they even noticed me standing there, waiting to say something. They're trying to keep her all to themselves, I thought. Going to the desk I had used all year, I sat down. If I don't get to speak to her pretty soon, I thought, Mother's liable to come in and tell me we have to get on home before I have a chance to tell Miss Ford anything. I put an elbow on my desk, leaned my head in my hand, and waited. All year I hadn't gotten even one whipping from Miss Ford. In fact, I didn't think she had whipped anybody. The only one who should have been whipped was Emmett Simpson and he was expelled, which was better than his getting whipped because he wasn't allowed to come back.

Maybe it was because I was getting bigger that I didn't get into as many fistfights in sixth grade. Or maybe it was because I had learned not to fly off the handle if somebody teased me at school. I decided it was a little of both. If anybody, all year, had said even the slightest thing about my being adopted or suggested I go back to the orphans' home, I had completely forgotten about it. I felt awfully good about that. It had been a long time since anybody had accused me of having a chip on my shoulder.

Miss Ford had given me good grades all year, even for

conduct, and I continued to get a nickel from Daddy every time I brought home a report card with at least a ninety written in the deportment column. And she had written "recommended for promotion to seventh grade" on my report card. So far as I knew everybody in school got promoted to the next higher grade. Eddie Talmage showed me his card, proud that he was moving up to sixth grade. "Sixth grade ain't too hard," I told him.

I don't know how long I slouched on my desk daydreaming, waiting to say goodbye to Miss Ford. I wasn't watching her or the girls who were huddled around her but suddenly it became quiet. I looked up and the girls were gone. "Were you waiting to see me, Rex?" Miss Ford asked, smiling.

"Yes, ma'am," I replied, "I was waitin to say goodbye to you. And I wanted to tell you that I'm glad you're gettin married. But mainly I wanted to say that I wish you were comin back next year."

"Well, I sort of wish I was, too," she said, "but my husband-to-be has a good job in Cherokee and we'll be living up there. They've hired me to teach in the grade school starting next fall so I won't be coming back to Round Grove."

"Well," I mumbled, feeling my eyes starting to get damp, "good luck."

"And my very best wishes to you, too," she said with a little bit of a smile. "You were a good student and I enjoyed teaching you."

"Goodbye, Miss Ford, see you later."

"Goodbye Rex. Thank you for helping make it the best year I've ever had."

That was all I could take. "Bye," I said hastily, awkwardly, and almost fell in my rush to get to the front door. I always hated to say goodbye to somebody I especially liked, and I had to get out of there before I started crying like a girl. ✦

Chapter 27 ———————————————————— ✦

A half mile south and three quarters of a mile west of our place there was a two-story stuccoed house about the size of ours. It had a half basement, which was why a big family could live comfortably there. So it was different from most houses, even ours, because almost nobody in our part of the country had a basement. Everybody, it seemed, had a cellar instead, although Daddy called ours a "cave," for storing canned and fresh fruit and vegetables, especially potatoes and onions, so they wouldn't freeze during the winter. Daddy said we didn't store turnips in the cave because, as he put it, "they git to stinkin so bad you can't stand to go down there." His solution was to bury our turnips in a hole in the ground right south of our house near the clothesline. He marked the place with a wooden stake.

The stuccoed house over west of us had a long driveway lined on one side with runty little apple trees and on the other by hackberries. Early in June, a large family, new to the neighborhood, moved in. Their name was "Cooke" and one of the boys, George, was about my age. My folks and I got to know them right away because they had no more than moved in when Mr. Cooke—his first name was "Ollie"—

came over to our place to borrow something.

Mr. Cooke liked to talk, even about private kinds of things that Daddy said weren't anybody else's business and we didn't talk about to people outside our family. But Mr. Cooke told us right off that Mrs. Cooke had been married before. To a soldier, he said, who had been in the army during the World War, who had been killed overseas in one of the big battles over there. Because of that, Mrs. Cooke got a check in the mail from the government once a month. They pretty much lived off that government check, he said.

We liked the Cookes and Mother and Daddy did their best to make them feel welcome in our community. Mother invited them to come to our church and Daddy loaned things to Mr. Cooke and let him bring grain over to grind in our hammermill. Before the end of the summer he had borrowed our blacksmith shop, well-drilling tools, .22 Special Winchester pump gun, shorthorn bull, and ice cream freezer. And because Mother planted too much garden every year, during July and August she gave Thelma Cooke lots of snap beans, beets, onions, turnips, and potatoes from our garden and even gave her several dozen quart jars to can them in. About once a week the Cookes drove over and went home with a bushel or so of tomatoes and cucumbers.

After my folks learned that the Cookes liked to play pitch, they would sometimes come over and play cards with Mother and Daddy until after midnight. So the kids they brought along had to bed down wherever Mother could find room for them.

George Cooke and I became good friends. He would let me ride their Shetland ponies and sometimes we would take off on Saturday mornings and ride for miles when the weather was nice. George didn't have a bicycle but he made up for it by having the ponies and the saddles that were made for them. "Besides," he said, "ya kin go a lot further on a horse than ya kin on a bike an with a lot less work. Cowboys don't ride bicycles anyhow. Come to think of it, a guy'd look purty silly wearin cowboy boots an ridin a bike down the road."

Riding the neat little pony was different from riding big old Charger. It was good to use a saddle that wasn't too big and it was fun to put my feet in the stirrups for a change. George and I had a great time riding those ponies and we talked about everything. Like school. George wanted to know all about Round Grove. He was interested in basketball and hoped to be on the team. I told him I wasn't sure who was going to be our teacher when school started in September, because Tam Ford who taught last year got married and wasn't coming back. Whoever it turns out to be, I said, the teacher will be new to both of us. George said he hoped we would have a good basketball team.

We talked a lot about what we wanted to be when we grew up and I was glad he wanted to be a cowboy, too. He showed up in Aline one Saturday afternoon in a brand-new pair of cowboy boots, exactly like mine. To show everybody that he had some new boots, George had stuffed his overall legs down inside them to reveal the little flowers and stars that were stitched on the fancy tops.

One day, not long after harvest, Grandpa Williams came driving into our place in his old Black Willis Knight. From where I was chopping weeds in the back yard I could hear that ugly old car grinding up our driveway in low gear. What's he doing here? I wondered. Why does he always come alone? Maybe Grandma Williams stays at home because she's too high-toned to visit us out in the country. But in trying to understand why she never came with Grandpa, I had to remember that she had a nice brick house in Jet with electricity and fans to keep her cool in the summertime and we didn't have either one. And, too, I didn't imagine she would enjoy riding with Grandpa all over the country to look at farms for sale on hot, dusty summer days.

I was never happy to see Grandpa Williams but Mother

and Daddy always seemed glad to have him come and eat dinner with us. When he came I was careful to use the table manners Mother had taken pains to teach me, like how to hold my knife and fork and to ask to be excused when I had finished eating.

When I was little I thought it strange that Grandpa Williams always seemed to show up at noon when Daddy came in for dinner. When I got older, I figured it out: he wasn't just coming to see us because we were family; it was because he spent a lot of time looking for land he could buy at rock-bottom prices and when it came dinner time he knew he could eat at our house for nothing.

Grandpa Williams came into the house wearing what looked like the same old black wool suit and white shirt he always wore. Mother scurried around to set another place at the table while Daddy got washed up. When it was time to eat, Grandpa started to sit down at the table but then straightened up, took off his coat, and dropped it across the foot of the day bed that I slept on. I was glad he hadn't put his sweaty coat on my pillow. I tried not to stare while noticing that he had sweated through his shirt, especially under his arms and in the back clear down to the top of his pants. When he finally sat down, ready to eat, Grandpa's huge belly kept him from getting close to the table.

As usual, Mother asked him to return thanks. And this time as always, he prayed on and on, and I couldn't help thinking how inferior I had once felt because I was not related by blood to Grandpa T.T. and his family. I no longer thought much about it. In fact, only Uncle Hubert still reminded me once in a while that I was not one of them. And when he mentioned it I wondered why he kept bringing it up when I had done my best to show him I didn't really care a hoot that I wasn't a Williams. So as I sat there watching Grandpa Williams huff and puff, his Santa Claus belly heaving up and down as he worked himself into a fresh sweat during his prayer, a lot of things went through my mind. Mother would have been horrified by what I was thinking instead of listening to Grandpa's blessing.

His prayers always sounded the same. Starting out loud like he was talking business with God, right there at the table, he would go on and on and on. It wasn't until the last few minutes of the prayer that he finally got around to asking God to bless the food "to the nourishment of our bodies and ourselves to thy service and in the end own us as Thine, Amen." I listened closely for the "Amen" part because by the time Grandpa got to it he was so out of breath and whispering so softly I wasn't sure I heard it.

I never outgrew thinking that he finally ended his very long blessings because, like a top, he had simply run down.

The evangelists who occasionally ate at our house usually said very short blessings, which was good. Most of them bowed their heads so low they didn't spray little dabs of spit all over their side of the table the way Grandpa Williams always did.

Naturally, I never let on to anybody what I thought as I sat opposite Grandpa at the dining room table. I wondered why he goes on and on and on in his prayers; wouldn't a short blessing do just as well? Does God like long prayers more than short ones? Why is his belly so big? Does he care that I'm the only one of his grandsons who doesn't look just like him? Does he even like me? Why is it that he never bothers to say anything much to me? He's not as much fun as Grandpa Pete. Why is it he never gives me Christmas presents or remembers my birthday? Maybe I can get by without having to eat something he has sprayed spit on. I hope Mother doesn't set the pie on his side of the table.

I watched Grandpa Williams pile his plate completely full and marveled as he heaped food onto his knife and shoved it into his gaping mouth. Mother once said he ate like that because he grew up in Missouri where people used their table knives that way instead of a fork the way we did. Grandpa really did pretty well keeping green peas on his knife blade, considering how far it was from the plate to his mouth. Mother said I was never to eat that way.

"What brings you down this way, Papa?" Mother asked.

"Well," he said, "I got wind of a quarter section that might be goin on the market; it's the old Beckett place about a half mile south of the Brethren Church." He said a bank up at Alva already owned the place because of all the money owing on it and was fixing to foreclose on the mortgage. "There ain't no way in the world the Beckett boy can hold onto that place," he declared. Grandpa asked Daddy what he knew about the property.

"Well, the place has been let run down," Daddy said, "but they's a good barn an the house ain't in too bad a shape. There's a purty good windmill an a good well that's still pumpin a nice stream of good drinkin water."

"How much of the land's in cultivation?"

"Well, I can't say fer certain, but I'd guess they's around a hundred acres put mainly to wheat an sowed feed. The rest's in pasture. They's lotsa trees on the pasture land, mainly blackjacks."

"That land's mighty sandy, ain't it?"

"It's sandy, all right, but it ain't nowhere near as sandy as this place is. An Alvin Beckett coulda probably got some good wheat crops off of that place if he'd spent more time at it. He don't seem to put much effort into farmin."

"How much you figure the place is worth?"

"I ain't got the least idea but it's a full 160 acres an I figure a man that's willin to work hard could make a fair livin off of it."

Grandpa Williams didn't buy the Beckett place. Mother said she didn't think he would, because by the time he heard it was up for sale, the bank over at Alva probably owned it anyway. And as everybody knows, it's harder to deal with a bank than it is with a farmer. And besides, she said, he never bought land unless he could get it at a bargain. Mother told me he was a financial genius.

By now I had known Eddie Talmage for a long time. Even though we didn't agree on everything, we were still the best of friends. One of the things we didn't agree on was what we wanted to be when we grew up. Ever since we started school together, I thought he wanted to be a cowboy, same as me. But by the spring of 1937, I finally realized he had changed his mind; he didn't want to be a cowboy after all. One day we were talking about it and he said, "I reckon I'll just be a farmer when I get big an git outta school." I didn't believe him; at least, I didn't want to believe him. Maybe he had never known a real cowboy like I had, so he didn't realize being a cowboy would be a lot better way to live. Farming meant getting up early every morning to milk the cows and then milking them again in the evening while wading around ankle deep in cow manure. It meant never being able to go away anywhere because you had to feed and milk the cows every single day. If Eddie had known Chet Bias, a real cowboy who traveled all over the country performing in rodeos riding broncs and bulls, who wore real Levi's and cowboy boots that were made special for him in San Antonio, he would have wanted to be as much like him as I did.

Chet was only about seventeen or eighteen when he worked for us during harvest and was the first man I ever saw up close who was wearing real Levi's and a wide, hand-tooled belt that looked like it came from Texas. His black hat was the same kind I had seen the cowboys wear in rodeos down at Cleo. One day when I was helping him fix fences, I asked him about the clothes he wore. He said, "I gotta tell ya, Mustang"—'Mustang' was what he used to call me—"no real Texas cowboy'd be caught dead in any other kinda pants but them made by the Levi Strauss Company out in San Francisco, California." He said real cowboys never wore overalls like all the farmers in our part of the country did. I believed every word he said.

"Mother," I asked one day during harvest when we were alone, "can I get some Levi's? Like Chet wears?"

"Don't say 'can I,' say 'may I.' Well, do you remember we bought you some everyday belt pants one time but you couldn't keep your shirt tail inside?"

"Yes, but they wadn't Levi's. They wadn't real cowboy pants," I argued, "an that was when I was a lot littler than I am now."

"You don't really want to wear pants like that do you? I don't think any of the other Round Grove boys wear pants like that. Besides, you would always have to be pulling them up on your hips and tucking in your shirt tail the way you do with your Sunday pants."

"Well, Chet says cowboys don't wear overalls. How can I be a cowboy if I don't look like one?"

"I don't think you need to worry too much about that at your age. Even Chet didn't start being a cowboy until he was older than you are."

"Well," I said, not yet ready to give up, "can I, may I, get some Levi's if I promise to keep my shirt tail in?"

Mother sighed, gave me a little smile, and said, "Let me think about it. And I'll talk to your daddy first time I get the chance." I figured that was probably the end of that. Mother would mean to say something to Daddy, but likely not until after harvest when things slowed down a little and by that time she probably would have forgotten all about it.

That August we took George Cooke with us to all three days of the big annual rodeo down at Cleo Springs. Going to that rodeo with George along was almost as much fun as Christmas and the Fourth of July put together. "Gosh," he kept saying, "I never spected anything like this." By the end of the third day George was talking in an exaggerated drawl like somebody from Texas. He even started using new words that he heard from the bronc rider who got thrown off right in front of the grandstand and who got into a big, loud argument with one of the clowns. Everybody in the stands could hear them yelling at one another but I couldn't be sure if they were mad or if they were just putting on a show for the crowd. The cowboy had this thick drawl. He kept saying "yawl" this and "yawl" that. No doubt about it, I thought, he's a real Texan.

"You think they're fixin to get into a fight?" I asked Daddy, who was sitting beside me.

"I don't think so, son," he said, smiling. "I reckon they's just foolin around. They may look like they's tryin to hit one another but I spect they's just clowin around." He grinned at me when he said "clownin around." And Daddy was right about the whole thing being just a put-on act for the grandstand. As soon as the loudspeaker announcer started talking about the next bronc rider who was mounted and ready to leave the chute, giving us his name and home town, the one who got thrown off his horse and the clown shook hands in front of the grandstand, bowed to the applauding crowd, bowed to each other, and walked off together toward the judges' stand.

The Cleo Springs rodeo ended on Sunday afternoon and we didn't go home until the whole thing was over. According to what people said as we left, some of the cowboys went straight to the hospital in Fairview. Those who could still walk limped off and drove away, pulling horse trailers behind their pickups. Just north of the rodeo arena a big corral with a high fence was crowded with bulls and broncs and calves that had been ridden or roped in the rodeo that day. Daddy said they were kept in the corral until the owners could load them into trucks and haul them off to another rodeo somewhere else. "I don't reckon them livestock belongs to anybody around here," he said. ✦

Chapter 28

On the way home, George and I decided to put on a rodeo of our own. We decided families and friends could watch without having to pay, but other people would have to pay a quarter apiece, and we decided that ten o'clock the next morning would be a good time to get together and work it all out.

First, we took inventory. George's daddy had ten or eleven heifer calves that he planned to fatten during the winter and sell for a good price in the spring when they would be around a year old. If we used the Cookes' calves we could hold our rodeo in their nice big corral. It was a good strong corral with an almost-new barbed wire fence and it wasn't as full of cow manure as our corral was. Daddy helped me make a surcingle that looked pretty much like the ones the bull riders down at Cleo used. He cut the rope plenty long so there was enough to go around the calf's belly and run up through the loop at one end, with plenty left for me to double it over and get a good grip with my left hand. From watching closely at the rodeo, I knew that a bull rider held on to the surcingle with his left hand and waved his hat to the crowd with the right.

"A cowboy can't hold tha surcingle with both his hands, no matter how hard the bull is buckin an tryin to throw him off.

It just ain't somethin a real cowboy'd do," Daddy said. I already knew that.

Daddy also found an old sheep bell hanging on a nail down at the barn and strung it on the rope so it could hang under the calf's belly and go "clang, clang" when the calf bucked or jumped around. Although it was smaller, it was the same kind of bell the bull riders down at Cleo used on their surcingles. Daddy said every rider had his own surcingle and never had to borrow somebody else's.

George and I couldn't think of anything else we needed in the way of equipment. George's daddy, Ollie Cooke, said he would help round up the calves and said he would keep them in the barn until we were ready to ride. "Then you kin ride them calves or all of them, you kin take yer choices," he said. George and I told everybody we saw to be at the Cooke corral at two o'clock the next Sunday afternoon, the day before Labor Day, two days before school got started.

Mother and I went to Sunday school and church during the morning of the big day while Daddy took his usual Sunday morning nap. Mother said I would have to let my dinner settle for at least a half hour before George and I could start our rodeo.

I still didn't have a pair of Levi's so I could look and feel like a real cowboy, but Mother saw to it that I had the next best thing, a new pair of Big Mac overalls to wear. Daddy had to help me get my chaps on over my new overalls before we left home. It was a struggle because he had had them made for me when I was eight years old and a good bit smaller, back when he wanted me to look like a cowboy when I got up on the stage and sang cowboy songs during the PTA meetings. My chaps had been made from the hide of a whiteface calf we had butchered. Daddy had paid a man to tan the hide and make the chaps with the calf's red hair on the outside.

But I was bigger now, and taller, and because the chaps had been hanging on a nail in one of the upstairs rooms at our house for several years, and because the man hadn't done a very good job tanning the hide, they were pretty stiff. And what with their being too small, they were hard to get into. But Daddy was able to tie the long leather thongs that held the chaps around my waist and legs. With my cowboy boots on, with a Mexican straw hat on my head, and with my surcingle already loaded in the back seat of the car, I was ready by one-thirty. I grinned when I told my folks that it was time for us to hit the trail.

Daddy and Mother wanted to see George and me ride and so did Grandpa Pete. We drove down to his place, he climbed into the back seat with me, and we headed on over to the Cookes'. On the way, I told Grandpa Pete all about the rodeo George and I were going to put on. I was mighty proud that he wanted to come along, even though Grandma Dollie complained about his going and grumbled about not wanting to have anything to do with any rodeo when there was work to be done. I was glad when he took his old brown-and-black pipe out of the bib pocket of his overalls, packed it full of Golden Grain tobacco, struck a kitchen match on the sole of his work-shoe, and lit up. His smoke filled the back of the car and it smelled good. Grandpa Pete made things smell good wherever he went because he was always smoking that pipe. "How old are them calves you kids is gonna be ridin today?" he asked as we drove north by the Finneys' house.

"I don't know Grampa," I said, "but they're big enough to ride, I reckon. They're probably the same calves we were ridin just before harvest."

"Ain't you afraid of bein throwed off?"

"Naw, I don't think those calves are big enough to throw us off. Besides, we know how to ride anyhow. All ya gotta do is hold onto the surcingle real tight and not let go till the calf gets tired and settles down."

"Anybody besides you an the Cooke boy gonna be ridin in this here rodeo?"

"No, it's just George and me; we didn't ask anybody else."

"What about yer pal Eddie Talmage?" Daddy asked from the front seat.

"Eddie ain't interested in cowboyin. He said he didn't want anything to do with bein a cowboy anymore."

Because we were a little late getting to the Cooke place, Mrs. Cooke and the kids had already walked out to the corral, each carrying a kitchen chair or stool to sit on, but there was nothing to shade them from the hot sun or to keep off the gnats and flies that lived around the corral and in the ragweeds and cheat grass. There were eight of the Cookes and four of us Wilsons at the rodeo. None of our other friends came.

Daddy, Mother, and Grandpa Pete walked over through the ragweeds and dry cheat grass and joined the Cookes on the west side, outside the corral, so they wouldn't scare the calves or get in their way and maybe get hurt. Besides, from over there they could see better because they wouldn't be facing directly into the sun during the rodeo. A pretty nice crowd, I thought, and eager to watch our every move, ready to be thrilled by our bravery. I figured George was the only one of the Cookes who had ever been to a rodeo. I was pretty sure he had told them all about how it worked so they wouldn't be asking dumb questions or trying to tell us how to ride.

George was up at the barn. He had found some boards and had fixed up the barn kind of like they had the chutes arranged down at Cleo. I told him he had done a good job. Mr. Cooke was out in the barn, helping George get everything ready. "Howdy, Rex," he said, glancing at my chaps with a wide grin on his face.

"Howdy, Mr. Cooke," I answered, and grinned back. I really felt good.

"You an George shore do look like a coupla cowboys but are ya sure ya wanta ride them calves? They're purty big, bigger than they was when you boys was a ridin em about the time we was movin in down here."

"I don't figger they're too big for us," I said confidently. "If George's big enough to ride em, I'm big enough, too!"

I wondered if Mr. Cooke was hinting that maybe George and I didn't know what we were doing. But I wasn't even a little afraid to ride, and I was sure George wasn't either. I was determined to ride like a real rodeo cowboy. After all, I had seen lots of rodeos and knew how it was done. All I had to do was hang on to the surcingle, sit up straight, and keep my knees tight against the calf's ribs. I'd never been thrown off a calf and I didn't figure on this being the first time, especially in front of all these people. I kept thinking how nice it would be if Chet Bias was still working for us, so he could be there watching, too.

George and I didn't take into account several important things that every rodeo cowboy has to keep in mind every time he climbs up on top of an untamed Brahma bull. As he's sitting there waiting for the chute to fly open he's thinking to himself: If I get thrown off or have to jump off before I'm supposed to, how will I land? Will there be grass or loose dirt or sawdust or something soft to land on? If I get thrown off should I try to roll out of the way of the bull's hooves? How can I land so I won't break an arm? Or a leg? Or my head? Or get badly bruised or cut up?

As George's guest and good buddy, I got to ride first. It was then I noticed that the calf I was to ride had grown a lot since I had ridden her back in June. But I reckoned she was, after all, just a calf and not nearly as big, or as mean, or as dangerous as a full-grown milk cow or the Brahma bulls the cowboys down at Cleo rode.

Approaching the heifer slowly and carefully so as not to scare her and the other calves inside the barn, we led and pushed her into a corner and George slipped a loop of rope over her head. She's as tame as a pet dog, I thought.

With the rope snug around the heifer's neck, George pulled and I pushed her to the narrow chute where the gate at the back of the barn opened into the corral. George held onto the rope with one hand and grabbed hold of the gate with the other, ready to throw it open as soon as I was mounted and ready to go. My signal was to holler "let er go!" when I wanted him to open the gate, like we had heard the cowboys down at Cleo yell.

The heifer acted about half-asleep, calm, kind of lazy, like maybe she was tired. She stood there and chewed her cud and occasionally swung her tail to knock the flies off her back. She didn't seem nervous, hardly moving a muscle as I put the surcingle around her, a little behind her shoulders, pulled the free end through the loop, checked to see that the bell was at the bottom, and cinched it up good and snug. With George holding the rope on her neck and with the heifer pushed up close to the gate, I climbed on, pulling the loose end of the surcingle even tighter and getting a firm hold of it with my left hand. She didn't move anything but her tail while all this was taking place and I began to think I might look like some kind of sissy if the calf just walked lazily out of the barn with me kicking on her ribs, trying to get her to do something. George kept his eyes on me and the calf, with one of his hands holding the rope and the other on the gate to the corral, all ready for me to give the go-ahead. "Let her go!" I yelled.

To my great surprise, the heifer took off like a shot, heading for the far end of the corral, dragging the rope around her neck. She seemed to be doing everything she could to throw me off her back as I struggled to keep my balance, to stay on top, holding as tight as I could to the surcingle with my left hand, trying to remember to keep my knees tight against her ribs, forgetting to wave my straw hat to the cheering little crowd. I didn't even realize that my hat had flown off right outside the starting gate.

"Kick her in the ribs, make her buck!" That was Daddy.

"Ride em, cowboy!" That was Mother.

"Watch out for the barbwire fence!" That was Mr. Cooke.

I began to think it was time to dismount, like the riders

down at Cleo Springs usually did when the whistle blew. Many of them landed on their feet, but others landed on their sides and some landed on their shoulders and rolled over to come up on their feet. The cowboys who did that always got a big hand from the grandstand. The rodeo cowboys always tried to stay on until the whistle blew and I didn't hear any whistle. George and I had forgotten about a timer who would blow a whistle after about a minute's ride. The fact was, I was having such a hard time staying on the heifer that I probably wouldn't have heard a whistle even if somebody had blown one. I kept looking for a soft place to land in case I lost my balance and didn't end up on my feet. What I saw, as the heifer ran back and forth and around in tight circles and every which way around the lower end of the corral, was bare, hard ground that had once been muddy but was now bone-dry, with a pocked surface made by cattle walking around in the mud before it got all dried out in the sun and wind. The ground looked hard as a rock and I knew I was going to have some bruises if I had to land on it, especially if I landed on something besides my feet.

I figured I'd better get off the first chance I got, but before I could let go of my grip on the surcingle, the heifer quickly reversed directions and ran straight for the barbed wire fence at the far end of the corral, then turned suddenly and ran along close to the fence. Luckily for me, my heavy, stiff chaps kept me from being cut by the sharp barbs, but the heifer still made sure my right leg would be bruised from hitting the fence posts as we went by. I couldn't get my leg out of the way as the calf forced me against the fence posts time after time.

By now it was clear the heifer could hold out longer than I could and I let go of my grip on the surcingle, trying to swing my right leg across her back and jump off all at the same time. It didn't work. Rather than land on my feet, I landed in a heap. As I hit the rough, hard ground, I tried to roll over to get out of the heifer's way and to lessen the impact, but that only partly worked. She didn't step on me or run over me, but I wouldn't have felt more beat-up if she had. Instead, she just trotted off a little ways, the surcingle still dragging the sheep bell beneath her belly, George's rope still looped around her neck, then stopped still, turned around, and looked at me. I could barely hear the little crowd yelling encouragement from where they stood leaning on the other side of the barbed wire fence.

I got slowly to my feet, feeling unsteady and dazed. Nothing was broken but I was sweaty and dirty all over and everything hurt. I waved to the cheering crowd like rodeo cowboys are supposed to do but I didn't feel like a hero and didn't think I had made a really good ride, mainly because the calf was still bucking when I decided to dismount. One sleeve of my blue workshirt was ripped open about halfway down, and I could see that some skin had been scraped off my elbow and it was bleeding. My knees hurt, especially the right one where the heifer had run me into several fence posts, and my rear end felt like I had been kicked by a horse. What looked like handfuls of red hair had been torn off the right leg of my chaps and were hanging on sections of the barbed wire fence. I figured I was mighty lucky to be wearing the chaps. I picked up my surcingle—the heifer had finally managed to get loose from it—and hobbled over toward the "grandstand." I faked a grin to show everybody how tough I was and that I wasn't hurt. I had had enough riding for one day but I didn't want anybody to guess how I felt. I decided it would be better to get back up to the barn to help George get ready for his first ride. I looked up and saw him standing by the gate, grinning. "Good ride, Rex!" he said by way of congratulation, but I could tell he was glad I was the one to ride that heifer and not him. "Now it's my turn," he said bravely.

We cornered another heifer, one that looked like a twin sister of the one I had just ridden, and George took his turn at being a rodeo cowboy. I didn't think he rode any better than I did, but he landed on his feet when he jumped off and didn't hurt himself. He picked up his surcingle and walked back to the barn, sort of bowlegged, like the real cowboys did. Everybody clapped, yelled, and whistled, and George grinned broadly. It was plain to see that he was proud of himself.

Having been careful to pick out smaller calves, we each rode two more. That was enough for one day, we figured. "We gave them everything they paid for," I muttered to George. I didn't know how he was feeling, but I reckoned I had had enough rodeoing to last me the rest of my life. I was bruised from head to foot, and my scratches and scrapes burned from the salty, dirty sweat that was all over them. My clothes were torn and filthy and big hunks of red hair were missing from my chaps. I smelled like the barnyard from the brown dirt and fresh cow manure smeared here and there on my shirt and overalls because I hadn't been able to miss it when I had gotten thrown off the second and third calves. I was so sore I could hardly walk and I had trouble focusing my eyes, and my head was throbbing so badly I thought it would explode. I told George I'd had enough; no more rodeoing for me, I said. I even gave him my surcingle. "In case you ever need an extra," I said. I didn't need any reminders of that Sunday afternoon's disaster.

Finally, as we were taking Grandpa Pete back to his house, somebody got around to saying something about the show George and I had put on. "You and George rode pretty well, but I'm sorry you got so bruised and scuffed up," Mother said.

"I'm proud of ya son. You didn't cry none even though ya got hurt some. That there ground's kinda hard, ain't it?" Daddy said.

"Yeah," I said, "it was harder than I thought it was gonna be."

"Next time," Daddy said, "you might wanta pick out some calves that's littler."

"There ain't gonna be a next time," I muttered.✦

Chapter 29 ━━━━━━━━━━━━━━━━━━━━━━━━━ ⚜

My new teacher, Wilson Maddox, was one of a family of Maddoxes from out west of Aline and had taught in a grade school out there somewhere. Maybe Boiling Springs. I had never seen him before and knew nothing about him except that he was replacing Tam Ford. I guess it was normal to figure I wouldn't like him as well as I did Miss Ford.

"I don't know him," Mother said.

"I don't either," Daddy said. Mother vaguely remembered seeing an article in the *Chronoscope* about a Wilson Maddox getting married one time. She remembered because not many people in Alfalfa County used a last name for a first name.

"Does he live in Aline?" I asked.

"I don't even know that," Mother answered.

When I got home the first day of school Mother asked me what I thought of my new teacher. "Well, he's different, I'll say that," I said.

"You think you'll like him?"

"Well, I'll try but I don't think he's gonna be anything like Miss Ford was."

"I'm really sorry she couldn't be your teacher again this

year," she said. "I know how much all you kids thought of her,"

"But what's Mr. Maddox like?" she asked. I was beginning to wonder if Mother was testing me.

For as long as I had been with them, Mother and Daddy had told me over and over that if I couldn't say something nice about somebody, not to say anything at all, especially if it was about something they couldn't help. So I didn't want Mother to think I was being unfair to Mr. Maddox. But we were alone—Daddy was working in the south field—and from the way Mother talked and acted and looked at me I believed she really wanted to hear my first impression of my seventh grade teacher.

"He's a little taller than you are, but not much," I said, "and he's got brown hair that he combs straight back and he's got brown eyes. I guess he's about the same size Uncle Clyde is. He wears gold rimless glasses."

"Like the ones I wear?"

"Yes, ma'am, they look almost just like yours. And one of his legs is shorter than the other, kinda like old man DePew's leg. So one of his shoes has a real thick sole on it. An he uses a cane most of the time."

"Well, he can't help that. He probably broke his leg and it didn't heal right, or he might have had infantile paralysis when he was a boy and didn't completely get over it."

"I could tell from standin up close to him that he smokes because I saw a package of Camels in his shirt pocket an I could smell it on his breath. And I noticed that the fingers of his left hand were yellow, like maybe he's a heavy smoker."

What I didn't tell Mother was something that had happened that morning. In front of the whole school, Mr. Maddox had suddenly called my name so loud everybody heard him and looked right at me.

"Rex Wilson, this is a schoolroom, not a place to be makin love to your girlfriend." He said it with a kind of growl as though he expected all the kids to laugh. "No talking while

I'm talking!" he added loudly. Maybe I deserved to be humiliated. I was in the wrong. I had been whispering to Nancy Rose
Fleming when I should have been paying attention to what he
was saying to the whole school. But I thought he had made an
underhanded wisecrack and I didn't like it. I ducked my head
in embarrassment and, like all the other kids, sat there and
listened to the rest of what he had to say.

Instead of telling Mother about what had happened that
morning, I said, "One of the worst things, it ain't bad enough
that we got a new teacher who ain't nearly as nice as Miss
Ford, that danged Emmett Simpson has come back to school!"

"Don't say 'ain't,' son."

At the close of that first day, Mr. Maddox had asked
George along with Annie and Don Cooke to stay for a few minutes after school, and the next morning during recess George
told me why. He said that Mr. Maddox had made a really good
deal with them. Mr. Maddox would give the three of them a
ride to school and back every day in his car, saving them a
two-and-a-half-mile walk each way, if they would be ready to
leave in the morning when he drove by their place around a
quarter after seven o'clock. George said his part of the deal
was to carry in a bucket of coal and start a fire in the heating
stove on cold mornings and to sweep the schoolhouse floor
every day after school when all the kids had gone home. In
return for the ride to and from school, Annie and Don agreed
to empty the large wastebasket from beside Mr. Maddox's
desk, clean the blackboard erasers, and make sure there was
an adequate supply of toilet paper in the toilets. When George
said that, I thought, hey, that's just one more good thing Miss
Ford got done while she was our teacher; she was able to talk
the school board out of enough money to keep the school sup-
plied with regular toilet paper so we wouldn't have to use old
mail order catalogs.

I tried my best not to get crosswise again with Mr.
Maddox and I tried to like him. If he told me to do something,

I did it. I did my best as a forward on the basketball team. I did my homework and tried never to give him any trouble. He just didn't seem to like me. I don't think he liked any of us.

It wasn't that Mr. Maddox didn't know how to teach. He had been to college and had taught for several years, but he just seemed to plod along through every recitation, whether it was arithmetic or history or geography. Unlike Mr. Ewing and Miss Ford, he didn't seem interested in making learning fun for any of us. He was often short with anybody who had mispronounced a word or who had been afraid to answer a direct question. He would make sarcastic remarks about Jim Bob Tomlin's little brother Henry, who couldn't seem to understand that ancient Pueblo Indians would pull their ladders inside their houses to protect themselves from enemies, not enemas. We all knew Henry had trouble pronouncing some words. But Mr. Maddox seemed to think that Henry was making a joke when he said "enemas" and he kept him in during recess one day. After Miss Ford, and her creative ways, it just wasn't much fun being at Round Grove School any more.

The days dragged. I began to think Mr. Maddox was crotchety with the whole world. He seemed touchy when asked questions during PTA meetings, and some days at school he didn't even try to be pleasant or say anything positive. Maybe his leg hurt. Maybe he really didn't want to be teaching at Round Grove.

Mother and Daddy seldom asked me any more how I was liking school, what I was learning, or how I liked Mr. Maddox. They didn't seem as concerned as they were when I had been little about what was happening with me at Round Grove. Perhaps I should have talked more about school when we were together at the supper table but, in general, those were times they did the talking and I kept quiet. Anyway, the newness of Mr. Maddox had worn off and I doubted they would still be interested in knowing what I thought of my seventh grade teacher and how I was getting along with him.

Another reason I didn't discuss school with my folks was that I could expect them to take up for the teacher. In the past I often had been scolded for finding fault when, in their view, there was none. I would be accused of whining or told that I wasn't being fair. Rather than risk that, I said nothing.

But in thinking of Mr. Maddox, I did try to be fair. Daddy always stressed fairness at all times and with all people, although I believed he had often punished me unfairly. But in being fair with other people I tried to be like him. Maybe Mr. Maddox had a right to be down in the mouth sometimes, to seem unhappy to be teaching at Round Grove, to be impatient with us. He surely knew he had followed a teacher who had been very popular with the students and admired by their parents. He couldn't expect to be liked that well, and his crippled leg may have pained him and he may have been frustrated at its limiting his ability to move or walk or get into or out of a chair. He sometimes tried to run when he was teaching us a basketball play but anyone could see it was difficult for him because he sort of dragged his bad leg. I couldn't blame him for not making any jokes about his physical condition; in fact, he seemed sensitive about it and never mentioned it. I came to accept Mr. Maddox for what he was. Then an unexpected thing happened that impressed me deeply.

It was early December. Our class had been talking about Christmas and how kids think about Christmas, about giving and receiving gifts. It was snowing that day, and it was too cold and nasty to be outside, and Mr. Maddox joined Eddie Talmage and me as we sat on a corner of our little stage having our dinner. The schoolroom wasn't crowded, because many of the older kids had gone down to the barn to have their dinner. "May I join you fellas?" he asked. Mainly to be polite, I asked him if he and Mrs. Maddox would be spending Christmas with his folks and he said that yes, they would be. Then he went on to say some very nice things about his parents and told us of some of the Christmases he had enjoyed as a boy. We had never heard him talk this freely before, like we were real friends. Then he said that one Christmas, especially, was different from all the others because he had given his parents a gift they could not possibly have afforded, a brand-new car. He grinned and added, "As an additional surprise, I made up a great big red bow and hung it on the driver's door." Eddie and I were impressed.

"Boy howdy!" Eddie said. "Didn't that cost a lot of money?"

"Well, yes. As a matter of fact it did," Mr. Maddox replied. "But I was teaching by then and I had been secretly saving up for several years."

"Didn't they already have a car?" I asked.

"Yes, they had a car but it was about worn out and was in the shop most of the time. Not only was it terribly inconvenient for them, it cost them money they couldn't spare. I was the only one of their children who had a steady job. I was glad I was able to buy them the car and I would do it again." We talked more about the kind of car it was—a Ford—where he bought it, and how delighted his parents had been that Christmas Day.

By sharing that Christmas story he had shown me that people weren't always what they seemed. When he had first started to teach us, we had all thought he was gruff and uncaring. And he really wasn't like that at all.

One Tuesday morning, sometime in the spring, Mr. Maddox announced there was going to be a poultry competition over at Oak Grove School, three miles west of Round Grove, on Friday. He said the show was being held by the County Agent and the rules were simple: you could enter one hen and one rooster so long as they were pure-blooded instead of just being chickens. He said a first, second, and third prize would be awarded for each breed of chicken entered in the contest, and that first prize was worth a dollar, the second place winner would get seventy-five cents, and third prize was worth fifty cents. The County Agent would judge the chickens in the morning and would present the ribbons and prize money after dinner. Everybody would get something, if only a certificate just for bringing chickens, no matter if they weren't fat, or outstanding examples of their breeds.

Most of us were familiar with the poultry competitions at the county fairs but had never before heard of doing it at schools out in the country. It would be easy and fun to take part in. We all talked about the poultry competition—which soon became "the chicken show"—during morning recess. Most of us figured it was a good way to make some money. After all, everybody raised chickens.

Each spring Mother and Daddy bought a bunch of leghorn chicks that were guaranteed purebred. Charlie Summers ordered our chicks, and kept them in the back of his feed-and-seed store where he fed and watered them until we came and got them. A lot of people around Aline did the same thing we did. Some folks I knew had chickens that were part this and part that, so mixed up you couldn't recognize any particular breed by looking at them. But Mother always ordered pure-bred white leghorns. She said she liked them because they laid average-sized white eggs, and never got too big and lazy like Grandma Dollie's Jersey White Giants did.

Mr. Maddox reminded us Thursday afternoon to be sure to have our chickens over at Oak Grove School by ten o'clock Friday morning or we would be too late to enter the competition. He also said the Oak Grove PTA would have a hot dog and pop stand set up at the school so we wouldn't have to carry our dinner along with our chickens over to Oak Grove. And he made it plain that if we didn't have chickens to show, we could either stay home or come to watch the competition if we wanted to. And he said that because the poultry show was a special event for the kids from Round Grove and Oak Grove, nobody would have to do any schoolwork on Friday. That evening after supper and after the chickens had long gone to roost, I went down to our henhouse and caught the best-looking, healthiest, cleanest, fattest hen and rooster I could get my hands on. I carried them over to the small granaries in the barn where we kept feed for the cows. I put them in the one we often used for storing seed wheat and made sure the door was tightly closed.

After breakfast on Friday morning I hurried down to the barn where I had put the hen and rooster the evening before. From the look and feel of their crops they had spent part of the night gorging themselves on the grains of wheat caught in the cracks of the old wooden floor of the granary. They were easy to catch again and put into the two good gunnysacks that didn't have holes in them. Using binder twine I tied the open ends of the sacks, carried them over to our Model A, and laid them on the floor between the front and back seats.

Mother and I started off for Oak Grove School in plenty of time to go by the Talmage's house to pick up Eddie and his two chickens and get registered before ten o'clock. Mr. Haskell, the County Agent, had set up a long row of wire chicken cages, stacked three high, on the south side of the schoolhouse just below the windows. The first thing Eddie and I did was get in line to register our chickens. When we finally reached Mr. Haskell, he gave us numbers to tie on the cages where we put our chickens. By this time the cages were almost all in use. According to the labels on the cages there were several breeds represented, and I was acquainted with most of them. I was pleased to see my mother and several other mothers laughing and talking as they enjoyed themselves looking over all the chickens. When she was sure Eddie and I were all checked in, Mother told us that Mrs. Talmage would come for us at two o'clock after the contest was over. Before driving away, Mother handed me two dimes to buy my dinner. With that much money I could buy a bottle of pop, two hot dogs, and a candy bar.

The schoolground quickly became crowded. Kids swarmed

all over the merry-go-round and were hanging around the swings and teeter-totters, waiting their turns. Everybody seemed to be having a good time. Eddie and I walked around, trying to think of something to do until dinnertime. Several of the girls were skipping rope with a piece of old cotton clothesline; others were playing jacks. Some had brought dolls. Many of the boys were on their knees, playing mumblety-peggy with jack knives, others were spiking tops, and the two teachers stood on the top step of the schoolhouse keeping an eye on everything. Around behind the school one group of eight boys was squatting in a large circle, playing marbles. Playing for keeps. Neither Eddie nor I had brought anything to play with, so we just stood out of the way and watched them. I didn't want to get into the marble game. Playing for keeps was something I never did. Daddy had told me I was never to get into a marble game where they played for keeps because that was a kind of gambling. Besides, he said, the big boys were usually the best and most experienced marble players and they would win all my marbles in no time at all. "You wouldn't stand a chance in a marble game with a bunch of bigger boys," he warned. Eddie said he didn't play for keeps, either, because his daddy had told him the same thing.

On the shady side, the other side of the building, the chickens were now in the slow process of being judged. But Eddie and I were more interested in watching skilled marble shooters. Each player, squatting on the ground, kept his eyes on the several dozen marbles of all colors clustered somewhere near the center of a circle the boys had scratched in the soft dirt. Four of the boys were from Round Grove: Mike and Leonard Tweedy as well as Marion Hood and Emmett Simpson. I had hoped Emmett wouldn't come to the chicken show but there he was down on the ground with the other big boys. I was sure he came just to cause trouble. Mr. Maddox should have told him to stay home.

I hated Emmett Simpson and I never stopped hoping he

would be sent off to reform school. Being expelled for a year hadn't changed him one bit, but Mr. Maddox was able to handle him in the classroom and kept an eye on him on the schoolyard. As I looked over the group I noticed that one of the players was a full-grown man. He was squatting beside Marion in the circle directly opposite Emmett, taking part in the game, a shooter in his hand. It was Vernon Stallings. I knew who he was because I had seen him many times in Aline. He lived with his wife and two little girls just up the road north of Oak Grove School. Eddie and I looked at one another and frowned; it was pretty silly for someone Mr. Stallings' age to be down there on the ground acting like a kid. The Round Grove boys looked up at us and Leonard smiled, but no one invited us to join their game. After a few minutes Eddie and I started to walk away, hoping to find something more interesting to do until dinnertime.

We weren't even to the corner of the schoolhouse when we heard a commotion behind us, with yelling and swearing and boys scrambling to get out of the way of Mr. Stallings and Emmett Simpson. Both had jumped to their feet right on top of the marbles in the middle of the ring and were facing one another like two angry roosters, glaring, breathing hard. For a moment they just stood there looking at one another, each wordlessly daring the other to make a move. Then they were toe to toe, trading shoves. The next thing I knew, Emmett took a wide swing at Mr. Stallings' head, but Mr. Stallings grabbed his arm and wrestled him to the ground. Over and over they rolled on the damp sand, each trying to get the better of the other. Before long Emmett gained the upper hand. On his knees, astride Mr. Stallings, pinning him flat on the ground by his shoulders, Emmett growled, "Ya had enough?"

"Yeah," Mr. Stallings grunted, "nough."

"Well, I'm gonna let ya go this time but don't ya never go callin me a cheater again or tha next time I won't be so easy on ya!" He said it loud enough that everyone standing on that side of the schoolhouse could hear him clearly. Then, giving Mr. Stallings' shoulders another shove into the dirt for good measure, Emmett got to his feet and started brushing the dirt off his corduroy pants. Without pausing to pick up his hat lying partly mashed into the ground, Mr. Stallings took off at a run toward the road, then he turned right and kept running north toward his house. Eddie and I watched until he disappeared behind the tall weeds that were growing along the road near the fence row.

Except for all the excitement over the fight, the chicken show didn't amount to a whole lot, but I doubt that many went home disappointed, not even Jim Bob Tomlin, who got a certificate for his mixed-breed chickens.

Eddie Talmage was happy because he got a first for his Rhode Island Red rooster and a red ribbon for his hen. Eddie was too big to complain because he didn't get two blue ribbons, although I heard Nancy Rose Fleming carrying on because the bantam rooster she had borrowed from her grandma just for the show didn't even place. Compared with the other leghorns at the show, mine had looked like winners to me. And they did to the County Agent, too, because both the rooster and hen got blue ribbons and I got two dollars. I figured my chickens looked so good because they had spent the night before filling up on wheat, so they felt heavy and fat to Mr. Haskell when he judged them.

Marion Hood told Eddie and me at school the next Monday that there should never have been a fight over the marble game Friday morning. "There wouldn'ta been no fight if ole Emmett hadn't been lookin fer trouble as usual. Ya know how he is. But then ole Vernon Stallings oughtn't of been in that there marble game in tha first place, especially since he didn't even know how ta shoot a marble. He flat out accused ole Emmett of crowfudgin which, ya know, ain't legal. An ole Emmett probably was cheatin, it'a been just like him ta cheat if he thought he could get away with it. An then they got into it." I told Daddy about the marble game fight and he just shook his head in disbelief.

Something was troubling Leonard Tweedy. It was written all over his face when Mother and Daddy and I got to Round Grove just after eleven o'clock Friday morning, the last day of school. Mother needed to arrive early to help the PTA women set up for the basket dinner at noon. Daddy usually helped by laying the long wide boards across some of the desktops to set the food on and anything else the women needed him to do. My only job was to clean out my desk and carry all my things out to the car so they wouldn't be left at school all summer.

Leonard was just sort of hanging around as though he had nothing to do. From the way he looked and spoke as I helped Mother carry in her fried chicken and potato salad, I wondered if he had been waiting for me. I didn't see him when I walked back out the front door, but when I started off in the direction of the baseball diamond I noticed him sitting quietly by himself on the little cement bench that was built into the southeast corner of the schoolhouse. "How ya doin, Buddy?" I smiled. Leonard was one of my favorite people at Round Grove and I was especially proud that we were friends.

"Not so good, Peewee," he answered glumly. I had never seen him look so discouraged, so defeated, not even when we had lost a basketball game. This was a special day, the last day of school; we had all been looking forward to it and it was a time to be happy about everything.

"What's the matter?" I asked.

"Well, I got me a big problem an I ain't sure how I'm gonna handle it. Maybe you kin tell me what I ought do." I had never heard Leonard ask advice of anyone before. He was the one always ready to give advice, and he was asking me?

"What's it all about?"

"That son-of-a-bitch didn't pass me outta tha eighth

grade. He wrote a bunch of stuff on my report card that said I failed ta make a passin grade in readin an history an in rithmetic; he even failed me in agriculture an I figgered I'd git a good grade in that. He recommended that I take eighth grade all over agin next year. Tha son-of-a-bitch!"

"Good gosh!" I said in disbelief. "I didn't have the least idea you wouldn't pass. I figured you'd be goin to high school up at Helena next year an playin basketball for Glen Ewing."

"Well, that's kinda what I figgered on doin if I couldn't git me a good job someplace, but I reckon I ain't gonna be doin that after all."

"Then you're gonna be back here next year?"

"Yeah, I ain't got no choice. My mother's gonna make me take tha eighth grade agin. They don't seem to be no way I'm gonna go to high school next fall."

"Well, to tell you the truth, I'm glad you'll be comin back. That way you can still play basketball for us an we'll be in the eighth grade together."

"Well, they's one other thing we kin both be glad about," Leonard answered. I nodded, for I guessed what he was about to say. "That ole bastard ain't comin back as tha teacher. We'll be gittin somebody else. An that ain't gonna hurt none." I hadn't said anything much about it but I, too, hadn't been sorry when Mr. Maddox had told us on Thursday that he wouldn't be coming back to Round Grove next year. Wasting no time, he handed out our report cards and sent us home early "Since we're gonna be in tha same grade, maybe you kin help me study so's I'll be sure an pass next year," Leonard said, looking me right in the eye. I could tell he was dead serious. "Ya know, I've told ya before that I've got tha brawn but you've got tha brain."

"You betcher life, old buddy," I said. And I meant it. "I'll help any way I can." With that, Leonard's mood noticeably improved. He let out a long sigh. He sat up straighter, smacked the palms of his hands down sharply on his knees, and stood up. My big loyal friend, Leonard, who had looked out for me so many times back when I was little. Now it would be my turn to help him. It was a good feeling. He grinned at me.

"C'mon, Peewee, less git that baseball diamond ready to play on. I got a feelin we're gonna skunk them ole guys today!" ❧

Chapter 30 ⸺⸺⸺⸺⸺⸺⸺⸺⸺⸺⸺⸺⸺⸺⸺≪

Mrs. Helen Bross, our new teacher in the fall of 1938, drove out from Aline every day, right past the Cooke's place on the way to Round Grove School. The three Cooke kids stood down at the end of their driveway where she would pick them up, same as Mr. Maddox had done. What made it even better for the Cooke kids was Mrs. Bross had a brand-new Ford V-8 for them to ride in. The best I could do was ride my bike as far as Grandpa Pete's house, where I leaned it against one of their big shade trees and walked the rest of the way to school. Daddy said I didn't have any business taking that bike onto the school grounds, but he never seemed to mind that sometimes after school I would go to Grandpa Pete's, get my bike, and ride up and down the road for a few minutes with Eddie Talmage. The main thing was I had to be home by five. Daddy got me an Ingersoll pocket watch like his so I wouldn't have any excuse for being late.

I was surprised when not one of the Simpson kids showed up for school the first day. "The son-of-a-bitches moved out to California," Leonard Tweedy said when I asked what had happened to them. "It's a wonder somebody didn't up an shoot that God damned Emmett Simpson!"

I was thinking that very same thing, only I left God's name out of it, and I didn't say anything to Leonard, just nodded my head in agreement. But if Leonard had said the Simpsons had gone to live in McAlester because Emmett was in the State Penitentiary over there, I would not have been surprised. I never knew the name of the preacher who replaced Reverend Simpson at the Nazarene church and I didn't give a hoot. The main thing was he and his wife didn't have any kids to send to Round Grove and that was all I wanted to know.

Mrs. Bross was proving to be a good teacher. It was my last year in grade school and everything seemed to be going well. Schoolwork was easy, I never had to take home any homework, and I even had time to daydream and goof off. Our basketball team was shaping up; we even got a new basketball to start the season. I had met Mrs. Bross' pretty daughter Patsy and promptly forgot all the girlfriends I had ever had. I made sure George Cooke knew I didn't think of Nancy Rose Fleming as my girl any more. At first he thought I had done him a great favor, but he soon got over that. For one thing, he found out Nancy Rose was bossy and possessive and thought she owned him. She would pout or get mad if he didn't do everything she wanted. One time, after she had been all over him about something, I told him she was henpecking him like my Aunt Hazel was always henpecking my Uncle Earl.

"No," he said, "it ain't nothin like that." But I reckoned being henpecked was being henpecked even if he did have some other name for it. Because George was my good friend I put on a little laugh about it so he wouldn't take it personally. For a long time I had thought of Nancy Rose as my girl and I knew her pretty well.

Although everything was going well at school, it disturbed me when I began hearing stories about people coming home from town to find that someone had been there and had taken something. If I heard Daddy say it once, I heard him say it a dozen times, that folks in our part of the country were honest, hard-working, God-fearing, dependable people who respected their neighbors. That included their neighbors' property, which meant you left it alone. "When you walk off an leave somethin, it's gonna be there when ya git back," he said.

I doubt that anybody in our neck of the woods ever locked their houses at night or when they were away from home. We never locked ours, and besides, there wasn't a door in the whole place that had a lock that worked, even if we had had keys. Mother and Daddy never talked about needing to lock the house, the car, the barn, the chicken house, the milk-house, or the fifty-five-gallon oil drums that Daddy kept coal oil and gasoline in. People just didn't take things that didn't belong to them and they didn't borrow anything without asking first; they wouldn't even think of it. So it didn't make any sense to lock things up. Besides, Daddy said, if one of the neighbors came by when you were gone and saw that everything was locked up, he might get the idea you didn't trust other people. Daddy and Mother would have been insulted if anybody had suggested one of our neighbors might come by while we were away and take something that belonged to us.

Generally speaking, if people didn't live in our neighborhood they didn't have any business being there. About the only time a stranger showed up was when he was lost or was trying to sell something, like magazine subscriptions. We didn't think of the McNess and Watkins Products salesmen as strangers. They came by about every six months and were expected.

One of the best things about the people out where we lived was if a man gave his word you could expect him to honor it and if he made a bet with you and lost, he would pay up. Daddy taught me from the time I was little to be trustworthy and he set a good example. He told me I should always give the other man the benefit of the doubt.

I knew, even if my folks didn't, that there were some dishonest people in the world, even in our part of Alfalfa County, who stole things from people when they weren't looking. Every so often I heard in school about some kid supposedly running off from the orphans' home up at Helena and stealing things. Nobody ever seemed to know exactly who the kid was or what he stole, but people believed if an orphan kid ran off from the home he was sure to steal something from somebody.

"What can you expect from those orphan kids?" people would ask, getting nods of agreement every time. When I heard that kind of talk it made me angry. Except for taking the piece of Indian pottery that time in Arizona, I had never stolen anything from anybody, because my folks taught me how wrong it was to steal. Another reason I didn't steal was because I didn't want people talking about me the way they did about kids from the orphans' home. Besides, if I took something that belonged to somebody else, my folks were bound to find out and Daddy would whip the tar out of me.

Even though nobody wanted to talk about it, there was some stealing going on in our neighborhood, and it wasn't any runaway kid from the Helena orphans' home who was responsible. I'm not sure anybody ever stole from us, but our gasoline barrel sat right out in plain sight of the road between the house and the barn and all somebody would have had to do would be to wait until nobody was home, then just drive up and help himself. If he didn't take more than a few gallons Daddy would never know it had happened. Some of the boys at school said people were losing chickens and eggs because there was always somebody who would buy them. A thief could steal a few chickens or carry off some of your eggs, take them into the next county, and sell them to someone who didn't know they were stolen. Bobby Edwards said his folks had three bushel baskets of new potatoes on their back porch and one day they came back from town to find that somebody had taken all but one bushel. Someone had flat out stolen most of their potato crop.

"Does it seem to you like maybe we're missing some laying hens?" Mother asked Daddy one morning at breakfast.

"I ain't counted lately but I ain't carried off a dead hen since last winter. So if they's some missin it ain't because they's just up an died."

"I haven't counted lately, either. But for some reason I'm not getting as many eggs as I did last spring. Of course, hens don't lay as well in warm weather, but I don't think the weather's the reason we're not getting the eggs we used to get," Mother said.

"It kinda sticks in my mind that we had around sixty layin hens the last time we counted."

"I believe I wrote it down on the calendar. I'll look." Mother got up from the table and took two steps to the drug store calendar hanging on the wall by the door to the kitchen, by the bridle rein that hadn't been used for quite a while but was still hanging there as a reminder.

"Here it is. Yes. We had sixty-two hens and two roosters. At least that's how many we had on the third of March when we brought home the hundred chicks from Charlie Summers and put them in the brooder house."

After breakfast the three of us walked down to the henhouse to get another count of how many laying hens and roosters we had. Daddy started clucking with his tongue and scattering handfuls of corn in the henhouse pen and when they saw he had something for them to eat, all the chickens came running. The remaining almost-grown pullets in the next pen over, the ones we hadn't killed and eaten yet, became interested in what was going on in the hen yard. They watched the laying hens gather inside the pen, scratching and pecking at the kernels of corn. Mother quickly closed the gate so they couldn't get back out. Then, as Daddy caught the hens one at a time with a long piece of number nine wire that had a hook on the end, Mother put them inside the henhouse. I kept track of how many we had on a piece of tablet paper.

"How many we got?" Daddy asked when the last chicken had been put inside the henhouse.

"I counted two roosters and forty-eight hens," I reported. "We're missing fourteen hens the way I figure it."

"Good grief," Mother sighed, "I'm afraid either something's carrying them off or somebody's come by and helped himself."

"I hate ta think there's chicken stealin goin on but I'm afraid maybe that's what happened," Daddy said. "They ain't much we kin do about it now. Probably some kids took em to get a little spendin money."

"Probably," Mother said.

"Probably," I said. "You gonna call the sheriff, Daddy?"

"I don't think it'd do any good. I ain't got tha least notion who it mighta been or when they was takin em. Ain't nothin I could tell the sheriff that'd help him find out who done it." To prove his point Daddy and I looked all around the henhouse but didn't see any strange car tire tracks, footprints, or other clues as to what or who might have stolen the hens. "No sir, they ain't anything we kin do about it," Daddy said. "I guess we oughta be thankful they only took a few hens an not somethin that's worth a lotta money."

We had almost forgotten about the missing chickens when an extraordinary thing happened in early October at Round Grove. It was a Friday and unusually hot. The schoolhouse windows and the front and back doors were wide open. A car drove up close to the front of the school; I heard the engine cut off, then a door being opened and slammed shut. Without even knocking, a tall, slim man strode right through the cloakroom into the schoolroom, like Gary Cooper playing the part of a town marshal walking into a Dodge City saloon, each heel of his cowboy boots hitting the greasy wooden floor with a firm thud. He didn't wait at the back of the room for Mrs. Bross to notice him; he just walked right in without saying a word. Maybe Mrs. Bross was expecting him. She looked up and nodded a greeting as he came up to the front of the room where she was standing near the stove, writing test questions on the blackboard for the sixth grade arithmetic class. Although I had never seen the man up close, I knew he was the county sheriff. Even though he took his hat off in the schoolroom, I recognized him from his campaign posters.

His face was lined and deeply tanned below where his hat came on his forehead. He ought to be wearing a six-shooter on his hip, I thought, but he wasn't and if he had a gun on him somewhere else I couldn't see it. I figured he probably had shotguns, rifles, and several pistols in his car so they would be handy if he needed them. Maybe he had a little gun strapped to one of his legs out of sight of everybody or a holster in the top of one of his boots. I hoped he would stay until after recess, so I could talk to him, get a close look at his boots, and maybe get a look inside his car. I glanced around the room; nobody looked back because everybody's eyes were on the sheriff. I looked over my shoulder at George Cooke in the row next to mine. His eyes were about as big as saucers and he looked scared. His Adam's apple kept bobbing up and down. It looked to me like he was trying his best to keep from choking on something.

Tom Grady was the sheriff's name. He was over six feet tall and had a fresh haircut, and his neck, the part between his ears and the top of his white shirt collar, had a lot of long wrinkles in it like my Grandpa Pete's had. Because his hair was only a little gray, I was pretty sure he was older than Daddy was but not nearly as old as Grandpa Pete. And like Roy Rogers and Hopalong Cassidy, there wasn't an ounce of fat on him. I always thought sheriffs in Oklahoma dressed like cowboys, but he didn't look like the ones I had imagined, except for his boots and the broad-brimmed hat he held in one hand. His cowboy boots were well-shined, from what I could see of them below the cuffs of his black wool pants. I would have bet he didn't order them out of the Sears Roebuck catalog. I wondered if he had bought them from the Hyer Company up at Olathe, Kansas, where they made the best boots. Mr. Grady was dressed pretty much like men I had seen working in banks or at the big stores in Enid with a white shirt and dark blue silk tie. His unbuttoned coat and vest matched his black wool pants and his gold sheriff's badge was pinned to the lower pocket on the left side of his vest. There was something written on the badge but I wasn't close enough to read the words. A brass watch fob was hanging out of his bottom vest pocket on the right side and I knew he had a watch in there.

Mr. Grady didn't look mean, but he did look very stern. He didn't crack even a little smile as he moved over to where Mrs. Bross was standing. Although he spoke softly to Mrs. Bross, he had a deep voice and it carried clearly all the way back to where I was sitting in one of the newer desks given to the seventh and eighth graders.

"Good mornin, ma'am," he said, "how are you this mornin? I'm Tom Grady, Alfalfa County Sheriff." The sheriff held out his big, brown hand with gray hairs all over the back of it, and shook Mrs. Bross' small white hand. Without waiting for her to answer, he continued, "Mrs. Bross, would you please step outside with me for a minute?"

"Surely," she answered, gesturing toward the front door in the southeast corner of the room near the last window.

Mrs. Bross followed the sheriff as he walked back out the way he had just come in, between the rows of desks, not looking at anybody. He passed near enough to where I sat that I could have reached out and touched him. He was so close I could smell tobacco on his clothes and could see that the first two fingers of his left hand were yellow like he was used to holding a burning cigarette in that hand like Uncle Hubert did. I decided that Mr. Grady probably smoked a lot of cigarettes. Everybody watched the sheriff and Mrs. Bross as they left the schoolroom but nobody moved their feet and nobody spoke. As soon as Mrs. Bross closed the front door the kids all started looking around at one another. We all were wondering what was going on outside. We could hear the low rumble of the sheriff's voice through the open windows, but couldn't make out what he was saying.

After two or three minutes they came back inside, Mrs. Bross leading the sheriff up to the front of the room. Even though the room was quiet, Mrs. Bross called for attention, and introduced our visitor as Mr. Tom Grady, the Alfalfa County sheriff. "Students," she said in a lower, firmer voice than usual, one I hadn't heard before, "please pay close attention to what Mr. Grady has to say; it's important that you all listen closely."

Every eye was on the sheriff as we all sat quietly. I didn't know about everybody else, but I was so excited I could hardly breathe. Leonard Tweedy seemed to be coughing a lot, George Cooke kept clearing his throat, and Mrs. Bross stood over by her desk, looking serious. "I'm tryin to clear up a little mystery in the neighborhood," Sheriff Grady said, "an I figured maybe one of you might help me get to the bottom of it. But before I get into that. . ." He paused and took something out of his vest pocket that looked like gold; it was about the size of a half-dollar. "I want to show you something that might belong to one of you," he said. He held up the round thing in his left hand high enough that everybody could see it. "I need to find the owner of this pin so's I can give it back." From over by the blackboards, Mike Tweedy almost jumped out of his seat he was so excited. Raising his hand, he sputtered, "That there's my pin! Where'd ya find it?"

Mr. Grady didn't answer but looked at Mike and asked softly, "What's your name, son?"

"Mike Tweedy. An I lost that there pin some place. It's mine an I kin prove it!"

"Mike," the sheriff asked kindly, "you got any brothers and sisters here at Round Grove?"

"Yeah," Mike answered eagerly, pointing toward the back of the room as he swung around in his seat, "that there's my brother Leonard, on over yonder's Marvin, he's my brother, too." Mike turned back around at his desk, facing the sheriff again. "Them's my sisters Lucille and Jewell, right in frontta you, right where yer standin." The big grin on his face showed how pleased he was with himself.

I wondered why the sheriff was asking Mike questions about his family. Why, I wondered, didn't he just take Mike's word for it and give him back his gold pin? You would have thought from the way Mike was acting that the sheriff had taken a liking to him. I looked back at Mr. Grady and saw a little smile on his face—the kind I had seen on Mother's face when she had beaten me at checkers—and it looked to me like he was satisfied, like a mystery was finally solved. But he didn't give Mike his pin or ask him to prove that it really belonged to him. Instead, he just stood there looking right at Mike, the little smile still on his face, turning the pin over a couple of times in his hand before putting it back into his vest pocket.

"Now folks, what I'd like to do," the sheriff said, "is to have Mike an his two brothers keep their seats while the rest of you go ahead an take your recess. That all right with you, Mrs. Bross?"

"Surely," she replied, by now looking much relieved. "Students," she announced, "you may go to recess now, but let's show Mr. Grady how orderly we can clear the classroom."

Just before I got to the door I looked back at the Tweedy boys who, by now, were sitting close together, near the front of the room, talking to Mr. Grady, who had sat down on

Dwight Hood's desk. Something's going on here, I thought; the sheriff wouldn't drive all the way down here from Cherokee just to give Mike Tweedy his fancy gold pin. As soon as I got outside, I cornered George. He looked flat scared half to death. "How come you're acting so nervous?" I asked.

"Well," George confided, under his breath, "if you wadn't one of my best friends, I wouldn't tell you what I think's goin on." He jerked his head in the direction of the coalhouse where we could talk in private, just the two of us. ✦

Chapter 31 ——————————————— ≪

Without a word, George and I walked slowly around the back of the school, to the shady rear of the coalhouse, out of sight of the other kids. George seemed eager to talk.

"Now don't go tellin this around tha school, but I think them Tweedy boys been goin round stealin stuff from people. An I bet that there pin Mike lost has got somethin to do with it. I reckon a lotta people know I been ridin horses on weekends with them boys. Well, not with Leonard but with Mike an Marvin, an I shore would hate for tha sheriff to think that just because I been runnin around with them guys that I'm mixed up with stealin from anybody."

"What makes you think they've been stealin?" I asked, surprised by what he had just said.

"I can't tell you that now," he answered nervously, "but I'm tellin ya the God's truth, I ain't never stole nothin from nobody!"

"Well," I offered, wondering what in the world had been going on, "even though Leonard's a good friend of mine, what he does outside of school is none of my business. But I sure wouldn't want the sheriff to think just because we're friends that I do the same things he does."

"I don't know if Leonard's got anything to do with what Mike an Marvin's been up to. He's been runnin around with some ole boy from over by Ringwood. Just cause he's fifteen years old, Leonard thinks he's a man an he don't like to fool around with younger kids like Marvin an Mike."

"If I were in your place I'd just forget about those guys. And if they're in trouble with the law, that's their problem, not yours."

"Well, Rex, I shore do appreciate yer sayin that. You made me feel a whole lot better."

Right then Mrs. Bross rang the school bell, calling us all back in from recess. As George and I walked back to the front of the schoolhouse we watched the sheriff's V-8 back out into the middle of the road, then head south, with Mike and Marvin Tweedy in the back seat. The sheriff, I figured, is headed straight for the Tweedy's place. If Mike and Marvin are in trouble with the law, Mr. Grady is taking them home so he can have a talk with Mrs. Tweedy. Leonard and his two little sisters stood down at the end of the cement walk, watching the sheriff's black Ford as it disappeared down the road in a cloud of dust. "I bet he's makin fifty miles an hour," George said.

After dinner the following Sunday, I asked my folks if I could ride my bike over to the Cookes' place. They said it would be all right if I got home before time to start the chores. There was a lot of loose sand in the road so it took me about thirty minutes to ride over there. I found George between the road and his house picking up windfalls that had dropped off the scrawny little apple trees growing along the driveway. He seemed glad to see me and didn't even wait for me to ask about the Tweedy boys.

"How bout les go ridin on tha ponies," he suggested, looking at me, plainly still worried. "I'll tell tha folks what we're gonna be doin. That way we kin talk better."

As soon as we were riding side by side down the road a

ways, George started telling me all about it. It was plain to see from the way he was acting that he just wanted to get the whole thing off his chest. I figured the best thing I could do was just keep my mouth shut and listen to what he had to say.

First George explained how he started hanging out with Mike and Marvin Tweedy. They had saddle horses, too, and the three of them had taken to riding around in the country almost every Saturday and Sunday. Nothing unusual about that. George cleared his throat and sighed. I looked over at him. "How come you took up with those guys?" I asked.

"Hell, Rex," George said bitterly, "they taken up with me!" He explained that he had been invited to ride over to visit the Tweedy boys one Saturday afternoon in early September, right after school got started, and they had been riding on weekends ever since.

"Yeah," I said, "I've seen your tracks. I can always tell on Monday morning when somebody's been ridin down the road over the weekend from the hoof prints and manure in the middle of the road. Of course, sometimes the wind blows so hard it erases all the hoof prints but it never blows away all the manure that wadn't there on Friday when I rode my bike home from school. I can even tell how many horses came by and, depending on the freshness of the manure, whether they were on the road on Saturday or Sunday, or on both days. It's easy to tell which direction they had been going and whenever I see one set of hoof prints that are a lot smaller than the others, I'm pretty sure you were one of the riders because, so far as I know, you're the only kid in our part of the country who rides a Shetland pony." I grinned at him.

"That's purty smart of you, Rex," George replied, not smiling back, "an that's part of what's got me so worried. I'm wonderin how many other people notice hoof prints in tha road." He went right on talking. "Saturday before last tha folks went up to Cherokee cause they heard the Safeway store was having a big sale on bananas. They took tha little kids with em but left Darla and Beverly home to take care of things while they was gone. Well, you wouldn't know it but them girls are all tha time naggin me when Mother ain't there to keep em under control. So I went an saddled up old Daisy an rode east over by yer church an turned south. I run into the Tweedy boys near Talmage's place. I asked them where they was headed an Mike said they was just out havin a good time." George stopped talking for a minute, looked over at me, cleared his throat, and continued. "It was a mighty nice day to be ridin, there wadn't hardly no wind, an tha three of us started up the road goin north." Of course I knew the road he was talking about, and knew everybody who lived up and down it from our church to the Tweedy's place almost three miles south. George continued to talk, not looking at me or anything else in particular, just sort of gazing off into space.

"We passed a place where an old lady was out in her garden close to tha road. It looked to me like she was diggin sweet taters. Mike hollered to her, 'Howdy, Mrs. Grimes!' and Marvin an me did tha same an waved. She waved but didn't say nothin. Bout a quarter mile on up the road we come to a place where a house was settin on a little rise quite a ways back on tha west side of the road. We could see everthing—tha toilet, tha chicken houses, tha barn—all right out there in plain sight of the road. They wadn't no trees around tha house like they is around most houses."

"Sounds like ole man DePew's place," I said. "Was there a big tall windmill over on the north side of the barn?" George nodded. "That's where Junie Clifford lives with his mother and sister and grandpa." George looked over at me again, his face sick with worry.

"I was really surprised when Mike loped off down that long driveway just like he lived there. Marvin followed right behind, so I reined ole Daisy over an went ridin in after em. I wondered why tha hell they was a goin up to that house when anybody could see they wadn't nobody home. Hell, Rex, I didn't even know whose house it was," George said. "I was beginin to git a little scared; I figgered we didn't have no bidness ridin up in the yard if they wadn't nobody home. But I figgered Mike and Marvin knew the people that lived there.

"Nothin around the place was movin cept a bunch of white chickens out by the barn. I couldn't see no car an tha door to tha house was shut up tight. Bein it was Saturday, I just figgered them folks had gone to town to do their tradin. A scraggly ole dog was layin in a big hole right by tha front porch. But he just stayed there pantin an pawin the flies an gnats away from his eyes. He didn't even bark. I figgered maybe he was acquainted with Marvin an Mike. Then them boys got off their horses an tied em to the windmill next to the water tank. I watched as them horses filled up with water. An I just stayed right there on ole Daisy, at the end of the driveway, getting scareder by the minute. But them boys was as cool as cucumbers. They went over toward the house, stopped fer a minute to listen carefully an take a good look up an down the road. Everthing was quiet; the only noise was them chickens cacklin an them horses swallowin that water. Then Mike he walks real fast over to the house, pulls open tha fly screen, an knocks hard on the front door, while Marvin goes around to the back. That ole dog just laid all hunkered down pantin and watchin. Then Mike just flat opened up that there front door an walked right in ta that house as big as ya please! Jesus H. Christ, I thought, I never figgered he'd go an do a thing like that!" I didn't know what to say.

"I wanted outta there before somebody come home an caught us. Hell, Rex, I didn't even know whose house it was," George said again. He took a deep breath and went on.

"Right away Mike he come back outta the front door an called to Marvin to come round to the front of the house. I figgered ole Mike taken somethin outta that house but I could see he didn't have nothin in his hands. By then I was wishin

like everthing I would of stayed home with Darla an Beverly.
I wadn't about to take no part in what them boys was up to.
Well, then Mike come over to where I was settin on Daisy an
he says, 'Les go have a look in that there henhouse. Come on
Cooke, don't just set there doin nothin, come on!' By damn,
Rex, I shoulda up an left right then but I figgered if I did
them boys would think I was a runnin off to tell on em. So I
just stayed right there on ole Daisy an told Mike I would keep
a lookout fer anybody that might be comin down the road.

"Well, them boys hurried over to that there henhouse an
went right in like it belonged to em. Then I heard a lot of
squawkin like hens bein scared off their nests. They wadn't
in there but a minute or two when they come runnin out with
tha hens squawkin an scatterin, leavin dust an white feathers everwhere. Mike was carryin an old chicken feed sack
with somethin inside it.

"'Les get tha hell outta here!' Mike yelled, like maybe he
was mad at me fer not goin in tha henhouse, or maybe,"
George said thoughtfully, "Mike was a little scared, too. By
now I was more than just scared, I was mad as hell! I kicked
ole Daisy in the ribs an the three of us took off down the driveway toward the road, turned right by the mailbox an headed south at a full gallop. We didn't slow down till we was a
quarter mile south of the Grimes' place. I was so damn mad
I looked right at Mike an I yelled, 'Don't ya know they kin put
ya in jail or send ya to tha reform school fer stealin?' But ole
Mike, he just hollered right back at me, 'I ain't worried none!
That ole son-of-a-bitch ain't gonna know who took his
damned ole eggs! Besides, he's got lotsa eggs, he ain't never
gonna miss a few of em.' An then I yelled, 'Them folks are
gonna be mad as hell when they find out somebody helped
hisself to their eggs!' Just yellin back at Mike give me the
nerve to go on. I said, 'I didn't know you guys was gonna steal
stuff or I wouldn't of come ridin with ya today!' But Mike, he
had an answer to that, too, an he said, 'Ole man DePew never

said we couldn't take some of his eggs. Besides, he ain't never gonna find out we taken em, is he? Ain't that right, Cooke?' Rex, he just kept getting louder an louder. He was really hollerin at me, 'He ain't gonna find out it was us taken em, is he Cooke? You ain't gonna be chicken shit an tell im, are ya?'

"Well, by then I wadn't mad no more. But I damn shore wadn't over bein scared. So I says to Mike, 'I ain't sayin nothin to nobody, but I'm tellin ya fer a fact, I ain't fixin to go to no jail fer stealin!'" At last George paused for a minute, took a deep breath, and let the air out slowly. "Nobody said nothin after that. I was still scared half outta my mind an was sure that sooner or later Mike an Marvin was gonna get caught stealin an I didn't want no part of nothin like that. So I taken off fer home at a full gallop."

Our ponies had stopped to nibble the tall grass growing along the side of the road. "I'm feelin better now that I told somebody. But I'm still scared that this ain't over. I been havin trouble eatin an sleepin, especially since tha sheriff come ta school an taken the Tweedy boys away. I keep wonderin if they told the sheriff about me bein with them."

"Well, George," I said, "I won't say anything to anybody. One thing for sure, you didn't really do anything wrong, so even if Marvin and Mike say somethin about you being with them over at the DePew place, they know and you know you kept out of it. If the sheriff asks you, just tell him the truth. Tell him what you just told me." I could see the beginnings of relief come into George's face and he smiled a little for the first time that day.

"Thanks for bein my friend, Rex, an fer takin up fer me," he said. "You're the only one I kin talk to about this." And I could see from the look on his face that he meant it.

When we got back to the Cookes' barn I pulled out my dollar Ingersoll and saw it was about time to go home. "Well," I said, "I gotta be gettin home, an you can be sure I won't say anything to my folks about this."

We unsaddled our ponies and put away the riding gear in companionable silence. "I'll see you at school in the morning," I called back over my shoulder as I walked toward where I had left my bike leaning against the near side of the barn.

I wasn't prepared Monday morning to see a completely changed and relaxed George waiting for me at the schoolhouse front door. "Howdy, Rex!" he greeted me happily, "Everthing's okay. I done just what you said I oughta do an everthing's fine."

"What do you mean?" I asked, just as Mrs. Bross stepped outside the door, ringing the school bell to start the day.

"I'll tell you at recess," George said, and we went inside together.

When Mrs. Bross dismissed us for morning recess, George and I sneaked around behind the coalhouse, away from the rest of the kids. "What did you mean, you did just what I said you oughta do?" I asked.

"Well, you remember how yesterday afternoon ya told me to tell the sheriff the truth if he asked me anything. Well, right after you left, in fact, I had just finished lettin the ponies into the corral an was comin outta the barn when I heard a car pullin into our place. The minute I turned to look I recognized the sheriff's V-8 an I nearly peed in my pants I was so scared. Dad had come outta the house down to where the sheriff was gettin outta his car. The sheriff stuck out his hand and said, 'Mr. Cooke?'

"'Why, yeah, yes sir, I'm Ollie Cooke,' Dad said, 'what kin I do fer ya?'

"'Mr. Cooke, I'm Tom Grady, County Sheriff, an I'm lookin for a little help. Figured you might be the one to ask.'

"'Well, sir, I'll shore help ya any way I kin,' Dad answered, with a puzzled look on his face.

"'Well,' Tom Grady says, 'I got a complaint from one of your neighbors that somebody came to his place an took off with several dozen eggs from his henhouse without askin for them or payin for them. It was Saturday a week ago, sometime in the afternoon when he an his family were over in Helena doin their tradin. Looked like maybe it was somebody ridin horses; from the tracks it looked like there were two, maybe three horses. Looks like they just rode in while he and his folks were in town an helped themselves. Took every egg in the hen-house.'

"'Well, I swear, I ain't heard nothin about anything like that,' Dad said, 'but I'll help ya any way I kin.'

"Then, fer the first time the sheriff turned an looked right at me an said to Dad, 'Is this yer boy here?'

"'Yes sir, Sheriff,' Dad answered, 'I got three boys but I doubt any of em knows anything about no eggs bein stolen. This here's George, he's my oldest boy.'

"Then the sheriff looked at me again. 'Come on over here son,' he said. He just stood there an waited till I walked over from the barn. Then he asked, 'How old are you George?'

"I told him I was twelve years old. Rex, I was so scared I couldn't hardly talk. But he kept right on talkin.

"'As I was just tellin yer Dad, I'm tryin to clear up a prob-lem about some eggs bein taken from Mr. DePew's henhouse sometime last Saturday afternoon. If you know anything I'd be much obliged if you'd tell me what you know.'

"'I didn't take no eggs, Sheriff, no sir,' I told him. 'Now son, you don't need to be afraid of me; I didn't figure you took the eggs but I thought you might have an idea who did. Is there anything you can tell me?' I was having trouble gettin the words out but I was tryin to do like ya said I oughta do. Then Dad spoke up.

"'Now son, don't ya be ascared ta tell the absolute truth cause tha sheriff's gonna know if ya story to him.'

"Then the sheriff said, 'Yer dad's right son, an you don't need to worry about tellin on somebody you know has broken the law. It's yer duty as a good citizen to help the law. I've pret-ty much got it figured out anyway. But if you can fill in the blanks in the story, it might help me close this case.'

"I could tell the sheriff knew all about it anyway. But he was bein awful nice to me an, you know, all at once I wadn't afraid no more an it wadn't as if I was gonna be tattlin on the Tweedy boys if Mr. Grady already knew they was tha ones that stole them eggs. Heck, I told him about everthing that happened.

"Well, Dad he just stood there lookin like somebody taken an hit him over the head with a two-by-four, like he couldn't believe what he was hearin. When I got through tellin, the sheriff looked from me to Dad an then back to me.

"'Now let me be sure I've got this straight,' he said. 'Now you, yerself, didn't take anything from Mr. DePew's place? An you never even got off yer horse?'

"'Yes sir,' I said, 'I didn't take nothin an that's the God's truth. I was really scared an I never got off my horse. I was just out ridin with them boys an didn't have no idea what they was gonna do.'

"'Well, son,' Mr. Grady said, 'I'd be mighty careful if I were you about who I run around with from now on. Always obey the law, son. If anything like this ever happens again, you just tell yer dad. He'll know what to do.'

"'Yes sir, I shore will,' I told him. An I gotta tell ya Rex, I was mighty relieved to know the sheriff wadn't holdin me to blame fer anything."

Later on George told me he learned that Mike and Marvin Tweedy had in mind all along to steal eggs from Mr. DePew if he wasn't at home that Saturday afternoon. "Mike said they never woulda did it except they'd been put up to it by Doc Mullins, an ole bachelor that worked in their apple orchard ever fall when they was pickin." Mike also told George that the Tweedy boys liked Doc, that he had been kind of a father to them ever since their own daddy died. It turned out that Doc Mullins had made a deal with the Tweedy boys: they would steal eggs, chickens, wheat, tires, gasoline, or anything else that he, in turn, could trade or sell to keep himself in cigarettes and beer. After Doc sold what the boys had stolen, he would give them candy and cigarettes, a little pocket change, and an occasional bottle of Coca-Cola. They were especially glad to get the Coca-Cola, because their mother thought it was a sinful drink and wouldn't allow it in their house. Mrs. Tweedy never gave the boys any spending money, Mike said, not even during apple harvest when people came from miles around to buy their apples.

"How'd the sheriff figure out who stole the eggs from ole man DePew?" I asked.

"Well, it was mainly cause Mike was careless out in the henhouse that day. You remember that there gold pin the sheriff showed us? Well, somehow or other, Mike managed to lose it in the henhouse that Saturday. An when ole man DePew come home an saw all them tracks, he figgered somebody'd come in there on horseback an stole a bunch of his eggs. So he called up ole Ira States, who's some kinda deputy sheriff or somethin like that."

"I didn't know Ira States was a deputy sheriff."

"Well, I don't even know him, but anyway, Ira States come down to the DePew place an right away saw all them hoof prints, an he could still see Mike an Marvin's footprints between tha windmill an the henhouse. He looked around real good an saw Mike's fancy gold pin just alayin there on the floor of the henhouse. Him an ole man DePew jumped in the car an drove up to Cherokee to see Tom Grady. Then Mr. Grady went around to different people's places an showed em that there fancy pin until some kid who went to Round Grove School recognized it an told the sheriff who it belonged to. That's why the sheriff come to school that day."

"What happened then? What did the sheriff do to Mike and Marvin?" I asked eagerly.

"Well," George said, by now thoroughly enjoying the telling of the story, "the sheriff scolded them boys real good an scared em half to death; but that wadn't the worst part.

When ole Elijah Moore, their older half brother, got wind of what had happened, he whipped them boys to within an inch of their lives. Mike flat couldn't set down on a chair fer two or three days after that. Elijah Moore made them boys walk all the way up to ole man DePew's place an apologize fer what they'd done an Mrs. Tweedy made em take Mr. DePew a half bushel of her biggest Grimes Golden apples to make up fer the eggs they stole. I don't think them boys are gonna be stealin anything else fer a while."

"What about ole Doc Mullins? Didn't the sheriff arrest that son-of-a-bitch for puttin the Tweedy boys up to stealin stuff for him?"

"I ain't heard nothin about that. But I figger Tom Grady'll be keepin his eye on that ole boy from now on." ✦

Chapter 32 ⟵

Mrs. Bross said, "Leonard, you and Rex will need to do a laboratory project for your agriculture course before school's out. And you need to start thinking about what you want to do and how you plan to do it. There are some examples of projects in the back of your agriculture textbook. Now, I want you to come up with a plan on what you are going to do and what supplies and tools you will need to carry it out. Have your plan written out on paper ready to hand in to me next Monday morning. You may sit together while you're working on your plan but be as quiet as you can so you don't disturb the other students." Then she turned to Maybelle Finney, the only other member of our eighth grade class, and asked her to step up to her desk so they could plan her home economics project. I figured it would be sewing, cooking, or something like that.

We sat at Leonard's desk. It was one of the old double ones over by the blackboards in the back corner of the schoolroom. We found several examples of agriculture laboratory projects in an appendix and decided that none of them would work at Round Grove School, that most of them had been designed for city schools. One example was for planting corn and wheat and legumes. But because it was already late March, we both knew it was the wrong time of year to plant crops like that. Even the girls at Round Grove knew you planted cowpeas and corn in the early summer and wheat sometime in September. We decided we would have to plan something more practical. "We could put in a little garden," I suggested, "like some Irish potatoes and peas and onions. We've already planted things like that at home. We always plant our potatoes on St. Patrick's Day."

"Yeah," Leonard agreed, "we could plant them things then set back an watch em grow. How big ya wanta make this here garden?"

"Let's not make it very big, nothin like as big as the one we've got at home. Besides, school's gonna be out before the stuff gets big enough to eat anyhow. Maybe around half a dozen hills of potatoes and about the same number of peas. Maybe ten or twelve onion sets'll be enough. How's that sound to you?"

"We kin do that, I reckon," Leonard said thoughtfully. "Where you wanta put it? It's gotta be someplace outta the way, where little kids won't be walkin all over it."

We picked the southwest corner of the school grounds for our plot next to Elza Mills' barbed wire fence. The fence made a right angle turn there so our garden would already have a fence halfway around it. We even worked out on paper where we wanted to plant the garden and where the different crops would go. We listed everything we needed that we could think of, starting with the tools, onion sets, potatoes, seed peas, and other things we had to have before we could get started. We even wrote out a watering schedule. Then Leonard made a final suggestion. He said I had forgotten to include a gunnysack of dry cow manure.

The following Monday morning Leonard spent quite a while reading over our report that I had carefully written out on ink paper. He was a slow reader and while he was reading I made a fresh copy of the scale drawing that went with our plan. "Yer a better writer an speller than me," he said when he was all finished, "an a better drawer, too."

"As you're always sayin, I'm the brain, you're the brawn," I said with a grin. Leonard grinned in agreement. He knew that if Mrs. Bross gave me a good grade in agriculture he would get a good grade, too. After helping him all year with his lessons, I was pretty sure he would pass eighth grade this time.

We hoped Mrs. Bross would be satisfied with our garden plan and I watched for some expression on her face as she read the report. We wanted her to think that we were very serious about the laboratory project. She studied our drawing, looked up at us, and smiled. We both knew she liked it.

Because Leonard was fifteen and a lot bigger than I was, he did most of the hard work of getting the seed bed ready for planting. Again he reminded me, as he puffed and sweated with the spade, "Yer tha brain, I'm tha brawn."

I liked working with Leonard, especially on our laboratory project, because it was just the two of us. We spent an hour each day, from eleven o'clock until dinnertime, partly outside and party inside the schoolhouse, depending on the weather. Mrs. Bross, it seemed, didn't mind our doing pretty much as we pleased. Because Elza Mills' fence already protected two sides, we tied several strands of binder twine on cottonwood sticks to protect the other two sides of the garden. We knew that anybody could step over the binder twine, but because it was half Leonard's project, we were pretty sure nobody would dare mess with it. After our garden was all planted Leonard decided we needed a place to sit and watch it grow. He liked to work with his hands and I didn't mind watching him as he did most of the digging of a dugout deep and wide enough for us both to sit down in. Using some small limbs that had fallen from the chinaberry trees and some old gunnysacks, we fashioned a roof for the dugout. We talked as we worked together. Along the north side we built a windbreak out of an old car door and some orange crates we found in the coal-house. It was held in place by sturdy cottonwood sticks we col-lected from over by Oliver Wharton's place, right across the road from the schoolhouse, where Harry Vealy used to live.

Some days we spent the whole hour outside, breaking up the soil around our plants and pouring on water from a little syrup bucket, through a tomato can with holes punched in the bottom. Most of the time we just sat in the dugout and talked. Mrs. Bross never knew that Leonard was smoking cigarettes down there in our dugout because she never once came out to check on us. We never ran out of things to talk about and it was a real treat for me. In some ways, Leonard was like a big brother.

"Wouldn't it be nice to give the school a present from our class when we graduate next month?" I suggested to Leonard one day. "Somethin nice so they'd remember us. We could probably get our folks to chip in an pay for it."

"Yeah," Leonard said, "that's a good idea. What'er ya thinkin about, Peewee?"

"I'm thinkin it'd be nice to get the school a radio. Wouldn't that be a good thing to have, to listen to current events an things like that?"

"Yeah, that'd be real nice, but how you gonna be able ta have a radio when ya ain't got no electricity?"

"You don't always need electricity. They could run the radio the same way we run the one at our place, with a regu-lar six-volt car battery. The PTA could buy a battery or the teacher could just drive right up to the schoolhouse and run some wires from the car battery into the schoolhouse, then unhook the wires when she was ready to go home at night."

"Yeah, that'd work okay. I know an ole boy down by Ringwood who would make us a radio for nothin; he makes em outta wood. I seen some of the radios he's made an they're real nice. All we'd hafta do is draw him a little pitcher an he'd do all tha rest."

"You ain't kiddin? You really know somebody who can build a radio from parts? I didn't know you could do that."

"Yeah, this ole boy's built lotsa radios. I seen em an they look like they was made in a factory, like tha ones that's in tha catalog."

"Is that a fact?" I said. I couldn't believe anybody could make a homemade radio that looked as good as the table model Zenith we had at home, the one with the five push buttons on it. I told him to be sure and tell the man that we wanted some push buttons on our radio for the school. Although I was finding it hard to believe that anybody could build a radio from scratch, if Leonard said he knew somebody who could do it, it must have been so.

Sitting in our dugout, rolling and smoking his Bull Durham cigarettes one right after the other, Leonard sooner or later got to talking about his experiences with women. He knew a lot about women, he said, about what women liked, especially what they liked about him, especially what he kept inside his pants. "I'm a stud horse. I'm always up an rarin ta go. An women like that. You kin tell when a woman's hot an ready fer it," he said one day. "You know how ya tell if a woman's hot?" he asked me, a serious look on his face.

"Well, I reckon if you can see her sweatin she's probably hot. Everybody sweats when they get hot."

"That ain't tha kinda hot I'm talkin about," he said, smiling at me like he knew something I didn't. "I mean when she's hot ta trot, when she's wantin ta git laid. Ya know how cows act when they're ready ta git bred? Well, women's like that. I kin always tell when a woman's ready fer it."

"Oh," I said. I knew about cows and how they acted when they were in heat, but I didn't know much about women and didn't know that women acted the same way cows did. In fact, I had never even thought about it.

"Yeah, even Mrs. Bross gits hot once in a while. Ain't ya never noticed how she gits up close ta me, sorta rubs up against me? Like I said, ya kin tell when a woman's ready."

He's lying, just making this up, I thought. I know he's lying. Mrs. Bross wouldn't be rubbin up against him or anybody else! Surely he doesn't expect me to believe all this crap.

"You remember tha time Darla Cooke visited school last fall?" he asked.

"Yeah, I remember. She sat with you in your double desk."

"Yeah, that was tha time. An did ya see how I had my hand on her leg an up her dress most of tha time she was settin with me?" This was no lie; I had watched them at his desk that day and had wondered why she let him do that to her when she was older and bigger than he was.

"Yeah," I said, "I looked over at you once and saw you were holding onto her thigh. She looked kinda embarrassed to me, like she didn't want you to be doin that to her." Leonard just looked at me and grinned.

"She wanted it all right," he said.

One time we got to talking about old times at Round Grove, kids and things we remembered from the time we started to school. Leonard remembered more than I did, because he had already been in school for two years by the time I started in 1932. He had failed eighth grade and what with my skipping second grade we were ready to graduate together even though he was fifteen, nearly full grown, and I was only twelve and small for my age. We were huddled in our dugout, protected from a cold west wind. He was smoking Bull Durham and I was trying to roast some small potatoes I had brought from home over a little fire we had built just outside the dugout entrance. He looked right at me and said, "I kin remember tha first time I saw you, Peewee, when you was comin to school fer tha first time. I guess you was barely six years old. I even remember what you looked like," he said. "I kin see ya in my mind's eye. You looked scared an ya kinda stayed off by yerself, off from the other kids. I didn't know ya an neither did most of tha other kids. Everbody kinda left you alone. Twila Bailey said Frank Wilson had taken ya outta tha orphans' home up to Helena an you was livin with them. She said they'd adopted you an even changed yer name from what it used to be. Funny how I kin remember all that from so long ago. But I kin still remember, maybe its cause I never knew anybody that was adopted before. Hell, I never even knew what the word meant. Funny, ain't it?"

I remembered how scared and alone I had felt that first day. To me there was nothing funny about it. "I remember another time when you got in a fight with Harry Lewis DePew. He was a smart aleck little shit, an bigger than you was, an ya bloodied his nose fer him. He started cryin an run off ta tell Mr. Ewing what you done."

"Yeah, he told Mr. Ewing I started the fight and it was all my fault. But Eddie Talmage and I told him what really happened and Mr. Ewing didn't punish me. He just told me that fist fights never settle anything."

"Was it you started that fight? You remember?"

"Yeah, I remember. Harry Lewis was callin me names because he was jealous that I was a good speller and had been promoted. Then he brought up my bein adopted and havin to have my name changed and that made me really mad. I socked the son-of-a-bitch in the nose and made him cry. And that was the end of the fight. He never even tried to hit me."

"Well, I don't blame you fer what ya done; I'da done tha same thing an probly lots worse if I'da been in your place. Somebody oughta had stomped tha shit outta that little sawed off son-of-a-bitch!"

Maybe, I thought, one of the reasons Leonard always took up for me was because he respected me for having the guts to stand up to a bully who needed to have his nose bloodied. Maybe it wasn't just because we were on the basketball team or that we were in the same grade. Leonard

and I had been good friends every year I'd been at Round
Grove and we had never gotten into a fight. He seemed to
understand me better than most other people, even though I
had to help him with his schoolwork. Daddy always said you
couldn't have too many friends, and he was right.

"Speakin of fights," I said, "I remember the time when
Emmett Simpson was swingin that baseball bat around like
he was gonna hit Miss Ford with it. I remember how you
came up behind him and took that bat right outta his hands
an threw him down on the ground and jumped on top of him.
I was mighty glad you did what you did that day and I'm sure
everybody else was, too."

"Yeah, he made me plenty mad all right," Leonard sort of
growled, "but I'd been lookin fer him ta do somethin like that
an I was ready for him. He had it comin. He'd had it comin
fer a long time. I probably shoulda just beat tha shit outta
him that day instead of lettin him go like I did. But I swear
ta God, Peewee, if he'd a hit Miss Ford, I mighta just killed
tha son-of-a-bitch right then an there. I don't spect anybody
would of blamed me, him threatenin Miss Ford tha way he
was adoin. He deserved to be expelled." Leonard grinned,
spat out the front of the dugout, and rolled another cigarette.

Going home that afternoon I couldn't stop thinking of all
Leonard and I had talked about during our hour each day in
the dugout, and my mind overflowed with memories of my
seven years at Round Grove. So much had happened to me
during those years. I had made more friends than I had made
enemies. I had known disappointments and accomplish-
ments. School would be over in less than a month, I thought.
I would graduate and might never step inside the Round
Grove schoolhouse again. I might never see Emmett Simpson
or Harry Lewis DePew again; I hoped I wouldn't. I might
never even see Leonard or Eddie or George again, even
though we were good friends. Yet I knew things seemed to
turn out that way once you stopped being kids in grade school

together. I wondered whatever happened to Donnie Banks, Sharon DePew, Olive Pritchard, and others I had liked but whose names I couldn't even remember. Thoughts went round and round in my mind as I rode my bike up the road toward home, through the loose sand and blowing dust. And as I lay in bed that night, trying to get to sleep, I kept remembering.

"Graduation exercises are gonna be held in the County Courthouse next Friday afternoon, startin at two o'clock," Mother said to Daddy on Monday morning of the first week after school let out. "There's an article about it in the *Chronoscope.*"

Well, I guess they ain't nothin we hafta do cept go," Daddy said. "They ain't nothin we need ta do ta git ready, is there?"

"I wonder where Leonard is," I said to Maybelle Finney. She was wearing a brand-new red dress. I was wearing my regular Sunday clothes. She was sitting all alone in the balcony of the Alfalfa County Courthouse auditorium, in a section of four seats marked "Reserved for Round Grove, District 99." I looked around the balcony where eighth graders from all over the county were rapidly gathering with their teachers, then I stepped over to the railing and searched the seats on the main floor beneath the balcony. I located my folks but couldn't see Leonard or his mother. "I wonder where Leonard is," I repeated to Maybelle. She shrugged but said nothing. But there was a concerned look on Maybelle's face because she liked Leonard, too.

"I don't know," she finally said, "I just got here a few minutes ago."

"Well," I said, "it's almost time for the program to get started an it'll be a shame if he doesn't show up. Did you come with your folks?"

"No, Daddy couldn't get the car started so Mother an I came with Mrs. Bross. Mrs. Bross left for a minute but said she'd be back before the program got started. Are your folks here?"

"They're sittin downstairs. Looks to me like they've got their seatin arrangements just backwards; the kids ought to be down there and their folks ought to be up here in the balcony."

"Yeah, I think you're right," Maybelle agreed. Just then Mrs. Bross joined us and took the vacant seat between Maybelle and me.

The program got started a little after two o'clock. Miss Neva Wilson, the county school superintendent, stepped up to the front of the stage. I knew who she was; she was the one who talked with Mother and Daddy when Mr. Ewing had me skip the second grade and the one who gave me certificates for winning a first and second place in the Alfalfa County Fine Arts Contest when I was in fourth grade. She asked everyone to stand and led us all in the Pledge of Allegiance. All the kids and teachers in the balcony standing up at the same time made a lot of noise. A preacher from one of the Cherokee churches gave an opening prayer, said "Amen," and told us we could all be seated. There was more noise as we all sat down again. Then Warner Hardesty, County Judge, gave a speech, telling us to be proud of what we had accomplished over the last eight years. He urged us to be good citizens, go on to high school, and set high goals for our futures. Looking uncomfortable in his overstarched shirt and tight, black, double-breasted suit, Judge Hardesty smiled constantly as he spoke That's just not natural, I thought, people don't grin like that when they're being serious. As he spoke he moved his eyes in a sweeping motion from one side of the balcony to the other. Once or twice I was sure he looked straight at me. He looks familiar, I thought. And as he droned on and on about school, America, and how some day one of us might become Governor of Oklahoma, I searched my memory.

Then it came to me, and very clearly. How could I have forgotten? I had seen this man before. I knew who he was. He was the judge Mother and Daddy had talked to when I was adopted, the one who had signed the papers that changed my name. He had grinned the whole time and his grinning had bothered me a lot. I didn't see anything funny about getting adopted. He had been the first one to tell me what a lucky little boy I was to be given such a fine home and to have such fine parents like Mr. and Mrs. Wilson. No, I thought, I will never forget that day and grinning Judge Hardesty. Maybe he recognizes me sitting up here, and that's why he keeps looking up this way.

When Judge Hardesty finally sat down we all clapped politely. Somebody started playing a march on a piano at one side of the stage, away from the temporary steps that were pushed up against both sides of the front. I figured they had been put there so the graduating eighth graders could march onto one side of the stage to get their certificates, then march off using the steps on the other side.

Teachers began lining up their graduates for the walk down from the balcony into the back of the auditorium. The line soon filled the downstairs right-side aisle, all the way to the steps by the stage. The noise of people standing up and walking and forming the line almost drowned out the piano march being played on and on down on the stage below. As each school group reached the bottom of the steps, the teacher would call out the name of the school. The graduating eighth graders then followed their teacher onto the stage where the class was presented to Miss Wilson, who called out the names as she handed across the certificates and shook each graduate's hand. Because the school districts were taken in order, and Round Grove was number ninety-nine, Maybelle Finney and I saw practically everybody get their certificates before it came our turn. When Miss Wilson called out Leonard's name, Mrs. Bross took his certificate for him. Leonard never came.

"Where's Leonard?" I asked Mrs. Bross after the ceremonies were over and we were leaving the courthouse to go home.

"Well," she said, concern showing on her face and in her voice, "I just don't know. Surely Mrs. Tweedy would have called me if she didn't have a way to get to Cherokee. I would have been glad to drop by the Tweedys' house to pick them up." I was really worried now, wondering what had kept Leonard from his graduation. I knew it was important to him. We had talked about it in our dugout.

"What does it feel like to be an eighth-grade graduate?" Mother asked me, just, I figured, to be polite. I don't think she would have been surprised if I hadn't answered. I looked up and could see she was facing straight ahead, looking through the windshield, not at me, as we headed home from Cherokee.

"It feels okay," I answered, hoping she wouldn't say any more about it. And it did feel good. I was glad to be finished with grade school and felt ready to move on to Aline High School in the fall, even though I would be leaving most of my old friends behind. When Mother and Daddy began to talk about how the wheat was looking along both sides of the road, I stopped listening to what they were saying.

It wasn't long before I found out why Leonard Tweedy hadn't been in the courthouse auditorium to collect his graduation certificate. He was in the courthouse all right, but downstairs on the other side of the building, locked up in the county jail, and Sheriff Grady wouldn't let him out, not even for such an important event. Eddie Talmage knew all about it because he had been talking with Mike Tweedy. The next time I saw Eddie in Aline he told me why Leonard hadn't shown up to graduate with Maybelle Finney and me. "The sheriff finally caught up with ole Doc Mullins, an Leonard was with him when it happened. Somehow or other Tom Grady found out whose chickens Doc and Leonard was plannin ta steal an he was waitin fer em when they got there after dark last Wednesday night. They both been in tha county jail since then an ain't goin nowhere till somebody pays em out."

I was totally unprepared for what Eddie had dropped on me and couldn't think of a single thing to say. I could hardly believe the Leonard I knew and liked so much would steal chickens or anything else. Even if Mike and Marvin had stolen eggs from old man DePew, I thought Leonard, my friend who always took up for me, was too good and honorable to sneak around in the dark stealing from people. But I was wrong. Eddie had his facts straight. I had never suspected Leonard even when I knew he sometimes ran around with Doc Mullins. Old Doc must have threatened Leonard or lied to him or else he wouldn't have agreed to steal those chickens. ✦

Chapter 33 ─────────────────────────── ⟪

For eight long years I had been growing up out east of Aline,
becoming part of the Wilson family and the Round Grove community. And still, after all that time, every so often someone,
usually a relative at the annual Williams family reunion,
would remind me that I wasn't really one of them. How long
was it going to take, I wondered, how much more would I have
to prove, until I was just like everybody else? When I was little I had almost believed those who said that all adopted kids
went wrong. And I had worried that no matter how hard I
tried to be like the other kids I would end up in jail or have to
go back to the orphans' home.

And all that time, right there in my own neighborhood,
where I was the only adopted kid, it had been the Tweedy
boys, who lived with their real mother and older half brother,
who had been going bad and getting into trouble with the law.
They were the ones who turned bad and stole from their
neighbors, who maybe even had stolen our hens that time
when we found some of them were missing. Now Leonard was
in jail. "Disgraceful!" Mother had said. "I feel real sorry for
Grace Tweedy."

When, I wondered, were people out where we lived,

including my folks, going to realize that turning bad had nothing to do with being adopted? I kept waiting to hear someone, anyone, say that it wasn't some kid from the orphans' home or some adopted kid who had been caught stealing chickens or breaking into somebody's house, but a boy from right here in our community who went to the Nazarene Church, who lived with his parents until his daddy died and still lived with his widowed mother. What I did hear at church, in town, and from the neighbors was "My, my, ain't it a shame that the Tweedy boy got himself into trouble, causin all this pain for his good, kind, hard-workin mother."

It's downright unfair, I thought, and it made me angry. What made it hardest to take was that there was nobody around that I could talk to about it. Once again, I felt betrayed by someone I had trusted. Leonard had been my older, stronger friend. In my mind I could still hear him say, "I'm tha brawn, yer tha brain," and I could see his wide grin as he looked over at me, and I could hardly stand it. Why did he allow himself to get into this mess? Why would he let himself be taken in by a no-account bum like Doc Mullins? Then it came to me that there was one person I could talk to about what had happened: Mr. Ewing. He would understand why I was particularly troubled.

Back when I was still new at Round Grove, still trying to adjust to my new life, with a new name and a new family, no longer Billy Joe Tolliver, Mr. Ewing had helped me turn my life around and start realizing that adoption had nothing to do with who I really was or what I could make of my life. And it was all because Harry Lewis DePew often tormented me in those days, when he would ask with a snarl, "Yer name's really 'Billy Joe Tolliver,' ain't it?" That seemed so long ago. I hadn't been called 'Billy Joe' since Harry Lewis moved away. I hardly remembered the name. I was Rex Wilson.

But there was this mess Leonard had gotten himself into. And my hurt and anger wouldn't go away, because I needed someone to talk to, man to man. And the only one was Mr. Ewing. I knew he was living in Helena now, but perhaps he came back to his folks' place on weekends. It was my only chance to see him.

One day I rode my bike all the way over to the Ewing place, a mile and a half through loose sand. It was one of the first hot days of spring, a sure sign that summer was coming soon. I was drenched with sweat by the time I had rolled into the Ewing driveway. But Mr. Ewing wasn't there. One of his sisters told me he had been living in Helena for almost a year now, boarding with one of their mother's cousins, and no, he seldom came to the farm on weekends. She offered me a drink of good well water to help me cool off before my long, hot ride back home.

As the days passed, busy with our getting ready for wheat harvest and all the extra work I had to do as a result, I kept hoping my folks would need to make a trip to Helena where maybe I could find Mr. Ewing and talk to him for a little while. But days became weeks, and my anger and bitterness began to fade as talk about Leonard's thievery and what a shame it was died down. People were too busy getting ready for harvest to think of anything else.

I began to accept the truth that people, perhaps even my folks, were never going to realize that being adopted had nothing to do with someone going bad. It wasn't ever going to change. People weren't going to change; they were always going to think adopted people were different. I had been wrong about Leonard. He wasn't adopted, he lived with his real family, he hadn't been given away. What made him go bad?

But I was right about something else. I never saw Harry Lewis DePew, Emmett Simpson, or some of the other Round Grove guys again, just as I had figured. And I never saw Leonard again, never even learned what happened to him after his mother got him out of jail, but I never forgot him, and I never forgot how, in spite of everything, he had been a good friend to me. And I couldn't forget those days we spent down at our little vegetable garden, jammed into our dugout, trying to keep out of the cold wind, Leonard smoking his hand-rolled Bull Durham cigarettes, me trying to roast those little potatoes that never got done enough to eat.

By the end of the summer I was pretty sure I could handle the stigma of being adopted, because I knew that as a thirteen-year-old I made friends easily and people seemed to like me for what I was, the same as everybody else. High school was ahead of me, it would be exciting and different, and I would be going to classes with kids from all over the Aline area. I was pretty sure no one would give a hoot that I was adopted. ❖

Epilogue

The reader is entitled to know what happened to the adopted boy, the subject of this book.

I am one of the fortunate few who got to do what he wanted with his life. From boyhood my dream was to be an archeologist. Taking full advantage of the Federal Government's generous G.I. Bill for veterans of World War II and the Korean conflict, I became an archeologist and enjoyed a fine career with the U.S. Department of the Interior.

Fortunately for me, my adoptive mother believed strongly in education. She studied for two years at the State Teachers College in Alva, Oklahom. She had a serene disposition and found great joy in life. She often sang at her work around the house, adding music to my world. As an avid reader, she knew a great deal about the world outside our community.

On the other hand, my dad had only finished the eighth grade at Round Grove School. He was interested only in farming, and he was very good at it. He didn't seem to care much about things that had little or nothing to do with farming. He didn't swear or gossip, he was honest to a fault. I am indebted to him for teaching me the difference between a "real man" and a "sissy" or somebody who is "less than a man." He taught me the honorable way to fight, and told me I must never cheat, lie, or steal. I have profited from his common wisdom. For example, "Look for something to do, don't wait to be told," and "If you can't talk and work at the same time, don't talk." And much more. Although I was often fearful of him I was very proud of my dad, and thought he was a better man than any other I knew. I've no doubt he was one of the most highly respected men in our entire community. I am grateful to Frank and Erma Wilson for adopting me. Because they did, I was well prepared to face life.

I felt compelled to write this book, not only to relieve my mind of some bitter memories, but also to assure all adopted children that their biological parents did love them, even in the act of giving them away. The separation is never the adopted child's fault. Economic pressures and difficult circumstances play a large part in all adoptions.

An adopted child needs more than anything to be loved, and to belong. It is well and good to tell him, "You are special—we chose you because we wanted you." What he really needs to hear is, "We love you."

An adopted child does not want to hear, "You are a very lucky boy to be chosen by these nice people." He wants no words that set him apart as different, like "chosen" or "special," not quite "family." He hungers for the assurance that he is family. He needs hugs and cuddling to show him that he belongs.

After serving in the South Pacific during World War II, I returned to marry my college sweetheart. Together we reared three fine sons and now have three lovely daughters-in-law and seven grandchildren. We are a close and loving family.

About the Author

Rex L. Wilson is a retired
archeologist with the
National Park Service.

Photo courtesy of Leona Ikenberry.

Book design by Geiger Vallery Stradinger Design Co.
Typefaces: Century Schoolbook and Belwe Light
Printed and bound by Thomson-Shore Inc.

Leo.Meire@Infineon.com